Tweeting Scared

Oxford Studies in Digital Politics

Founder and Series Editor: Andrew Chadwick, Professor of Political Communication and Director of the Online Civic Culture Centre (O3C) in the Department of Communication and Media, Loughborough University

Apostles of Certainty: Data Journalism and the Politics of Doubt
C. W. Anderson

Using Technology, Building Democracy: Digital Campaigning and the Construction of Citizenship
Jessica Baldwin-Philippi

Hacking Hybrid Media: Power and Practice in an Age of Manipulation
Stephen R. Barnard

Expect Us: Online Communities and Political Mobilization
Jessica L. Beyer

Observed Correction: How We Can All Respond to Misinformation on Social Media
Leticia Bode and Emily K. Vraga

If... Then: Algorithmic Power and Politics
Taina Bucher

The Hybrid Media System: Politics and Power
Andrew Chadwick

We Tried to Tell Y'All: Black Twitter and the Rise of Digital Counternarratives
Meredith D. Clark

News and Democratic Citizens in the Mobile Era
Johanna Dunaway and Kathleen Searles

The Fifth Estate: The Power Shift of the Digital Age
William H. Dutton

The Only Constant Is Change: Technology, Political Communication, and Innovation over Time
Ben Epstein

Designing for Democracy: How to Build Community in Digital Environments
Jennifer Forestal

Directed Digital Dissidence in Autocracies: How China Wins Online
Jason Gainous, Rongbin Han, Andrew W. MacDonald, and Kevin M. Wagner

Tweeting to Power: The Social Media Revolution in American Politics
Jason Gainous and Kevin M. Wagner

When the Nerds Go Marching In: How Digital Technology Moved from the Margins to the Mainstream of Political Campaigns
Rachel K. Gibson

The Politics of Platform Regulation: How Governments Shape Online Content Moderation
Robert Gorwa

Trolling Ourselves to Death: Democracy in the Age of Social Media
Jason Hannan

Risk and Hyperconnectivity: Media and Memories of Neoliberalism
Andrew Hoskins and John Tulloch

Democracy's Fourth Wave? Digital Media and the Arab Spring
Philip N. Howard and Muzammil M. Hussain

The Digital Origins of Dictatorship and Democracy: Information Technology and Political Islam
Philip N. Howard

Analytic Activism: Digital Listening and the New Political Strategy
David Karpf

The MoveOn Effect: The Unexpected Transformation of American Political Advocacy
David Karpf

News Nerds: Institutional Change in Journalism
Allie Kosterich

Prototype Politics: Technology-Intensive Campaigning and the Data of Democracy
Daniel Kreiss

Taking Our Country Back: The Crafting of Networked Politics from Howard Dean to Barack Obama
Daniel Kreiss

Media and Protest Logics in the Digital Era: The Umbrella Movement in Hong Kong
Francis L. F. Lee and Joseph M. Chan

Bits and Atoms: Information and Communication Technology in Areas of Limited Statehood
Steven Livingston and Gregor Walter-Drop

Digital Feminist Activism: Girls and Women Fight Back against Rape Culture
Kaitlynn Mendes, Jessica Ringrose, and Jessalynn Keller

Digital Cities: The Internet and the Geography of Opportunity
Karen Mossberger, Caroline J. Tolbert, and William W. Franko

The Power of Platforms: Shaping Media and Society
Rasmus Kleis Nielsen and Sarah Anne Ganter

Revolution Stalled: The Political Limits of the Internet in the Post-Soviet Sphere
Sarah Oates

Disruptive Power: The Crisis of the State in the Digital Age
Taylor Owen

Affective Publics: Sentiment, Technology, and Politics
Zizi Papacharissi

Money Code Space: Hidden Power in Bitcoin, Blockchain, and Decentralisation
Jack Parkin

The Citizen Marketer: Promoting Political Opinion in the Social Media Age
Joel Penney

Tweeting Is Leading: How Senators Communicate and Represent in the Age of Twitter
Annelise Russell

The Ubiquitous Presidency: Presidential Communication and Digital Democracy in Tumultuous Times
Joshua M. Scacco and Kevin Coe

China's Digital Nationalism
Florian Schneider

Networked Collective Actions: The Making of an Impeachment
Hyunjin Seo

Credible Threat: Attacks against Women Online and the Future of Democracy
Sarah Sobieraj

Presidential Campaigning in the Internet Age
Jennifer Stromer-Galley

News on the Internet: Information and Citizenship in the 21st Century
David Tewksbury and Jason Rittenberg

Outside the Bubble: Social Media and Political Participation in Western Democracies
Cristian Vaccari and Augusto Valeriani

The Internet and Political Protest in Autocracies
Nils B. Weidmann and Espen Geelmuyden Rød

The Civic Organization and the Digital Citizen: Communicating Engagement in a Networked Age
Chris Wells

Computational Propaganda: Political Parties, Politicians, and Political Manipulation on Social Media
Samuel Woolley and Philip N. Howard

Networked Publics and Digital Contention: The Politics of Everyday Life in Tunisia
Mohamed Zayani

The Digital Double Bind: Change and Stasis in the Middle East
Mohamed Zayani and Joe F. Khalil

Tweeting Scared

Congress's Crisis of Communication

Annelise Russell

OXFORD
UNIVERSITY PRESS

Oxford University Press is a department of the University of Oxford. It furthers the University's objective of excellence in research, scholarship, and education by publishing worldwide. Oxford is a registered trade mark of Oxford University Press in the UK and in certain other countries.

Published in the United States of America by Oxford University Press
198 Madison Avenue, New York, NY 10016, United States of America.

CIP data is on file at the Library of Congress.

ISBN 9780197808313

ISBN 9780197808306 (hbk.)

DOI: 10.1093/9780197808344.001.0001

Paperback Printed by Integrated Books International, United States of America

The manufacturer's authorized representative in the EU for product safety is Oxford University Press España S.A. of Parque Empresarial San Fernando de Henares, Avenida de Castilla, 2 – 28830 Madrid (www.oup.es/en or product.safety@oup.com). OUP España S.A. also acts as importer into Spain of products made by the manufacturer.

Cheers to the pediatrician, Longworth Dunkin',
and peanut-butter-filled oatmeal.

Contents

Acknowledgments x

1. **Introduction** 1
2. **A Crisis Framework for Congressional Communication** 19
3. **A History of Playing Catch-Up in Congressional Communication** 39
4. **Organizing a Press Office in Congress** 59
5. **Crisis Implications: Asymmetric Resources and Constrained Capacity** 87
6. **Crisis Implications: Partisan Pressures and Political Incentives for Digital** 114
7. **The Future and Implications of a Digital Congress** 134

Appendix 153

Bibliography 159
Index 166

Acknowledgments

So, this book and I have been through a lot together. It's like herpes—doing interviews in Congress is a recurring endeavor. Put more kindly, this behind-the-scenes comms project has been the extra family member who never leaves. I had the great foresight to start this book three weeks before a pandemic, and along it rolled with the highs and lows of the tenure track. Whenever I read these pages (which is as little as possible), I'm reminded of the sheer terror of university IRB, the beauty of a well-crafted interview email, and people who trudged down to the Longworth Dunkin' to make this book possible. The seeds for this project were planted when some goobers at *Congressional Quarterly* decided to let me hang out for six months before grad school, and I've been hanging on to that world one tweet at a time since.

I'm incredibly lucky to have had help, feedback, and support from an awesome community of scholars in political science, communication, and public policy. Huge thanks go out to the Martin School for Public Policy and Administration at the University of Kentucky, the Kluge Center at the Library of Congress, the Center for Effective Lawmaking, and the Dirksen Congressional Center for providing the support for these pages. And a shoutout to the team at Oxford University Press—Andrew Chadwick for answering my anxious emails, Angela Chnapko for working with me despite my emails, and Phoebe Aldridge Turner for steering the ship through production.

This book wouldn't exist without the folks who spend their days trying to figure out why franking won't approve an ad, what makes a lawmaker go viral, and how many people is too many for an approvals chain (the Senate proved the limit does not exist). The folks who work in Congress, communication, journalism, digital media, and political advertising are the people who made this book possible. They said yes to hanging out with a nerd for 30 minutes, sharing their world, sharing their joys, and on more than one occasion sharing just why their job might be worse than any other. Your patience is legendary. Shoutout to the digital queens of Congress — thanks for making me feel at home and throwing open doors I didn't even know existed!

There are so many academics who have read parts of this book and provided feedback along the way. It really takes a village. Special thanks to Tiffany Barnes, Jennifer Victor, Molly Reynolds, and Justin Kirkland who picked me up when I was down, offered unwavering support, and mapped out the trajectory of this book. There are not enough bourbon tours to say thank you. This book was also made possible by the support from the Women in Legislative Studies community—never underestimate the power of a room (or binder) full of women. Thanks to my coauthors Stephanie Davis, Joel Reed, Nick Howard, Corinne Connor, Whitney Hua, Libby Hemphill, Angela Schöpke-Gonzalez, Nicole Bauer, Ayla Oden, Cheyenne Lee, Alison Craig, Molly Ritchie, Casey Burgat, Heather Evans, Bryan Gervais, Tanya Gardner, Sarah Smith, Megan Blackwood, Ken Docekal, and Jiebing Wen for doing projects on Congress and communication that you probably didn't ask for (or maybe regretted later).

Thanks to my mentor, Bryan Jones, Wendy Schiller, Craig Volden, Jim Curry, Danielle Thomsen, Frances Lee, Larry Evans, Leah Rosenstiel, Tim LaPira, Rachel Porter, Rachel Blum, Lindsey Cormack, Kelsey Shoub, Amber Boydstun, Ashley Muddiman, Josh Scacco, Trey Thomas, Jon Lewallen, Kathryn Pearson, Lauren Bell, and Julia Marin Hellwege for being sounding boards, friends, and coconspirators. You all saved my sanity.

Academia can be a lot, but I'm lucky to have friends who keep me grounded. Sean Theriault is the one other person whose brain operates on my frequency. Maggie Macdonald is the nerd friend I always wanted as a kid. Rebecca Eissler and JoBeth Surface Shafran keep me grounded and laughing. JD, Ashley, Carrie, and others are the people who keep me coming back to DC.

To my family—both in Oklahoma and in Iowa—thank you for encouraging me, watching my child, and making it possible to be the person I am today. And to Jake, Teddy, and Russell—thanks for being my reason to get up every day. Your support (and constant demands for snacks) means the world!

1
Introduction

On March 11, 2020, Dr. Anthony Fauci, former director of the National Institute of Allergy and Infectious Diseases, testified before the House Committee on Oversight and Reform about the escalating coronavirus crisis. "Bottom line," Dr. Fauci said, "it's going to get worse." While health professionals scrambled for support and parents faced indefinite school closures, members of Congress were left in limbo as to what was going to happen with a looming health crisis and a schedule that originally had the Senate in recess. Then-leader Mitch McConnell had already faced pressure both from within his Republican conference and from Democratic opposition to make a move to stay in DC and negotiate a legislative solution. Congress, like the stock market, was jittery with so many unknowns in the early days of what would become a drawn-out global pandemic.

Congress is not built for rapid response—political institutions are supported by redundant processes and institutional norms that ensure stability rather than expediency. The capacity of Congress to adapt to a rapid information environment was already being tested by 3 a.m. tweets from the president, but the COVID-19 crisis put the firehose of information on full display. Within 24 hours, McConnell announced that the Senate would be in session the following week, seeking a solution to stave off a potential economic and political disaster. While many had expected the Senate leader to make a quick judgment about the recess, the way they found out about it caught them by surprise. At 1:20 p.m. on March 12, the official Twitter[1] account for McConnell announced the return to work and intention to negotiate legislation with the president and Democratic House (Figure 1.1).

McConnell went digital and public without giving staff a warning. Within 30 minutes, *Roll Call* had a story up on their website reporting the return to work—specifically noting that "The Kentucky Republican announced the cancelation via his Twitter account."[2] No prior message was sent through the

[1] In this book, the term "Twitter" is primarily used for the majority of the time to describe the platform which is currently known as "X".

[2] https://rollcall.com/2020/03/12/senate-cancels-recess-next-week-to-work-on-coronavirus-relief-package/

Tweeting Scared. Annelise Russell, Oxford University Press. © Oxford University Press (2025).
DOI: 10.1093/9780197808344.003.0001

Notwithstanding the scheduled state work period, the Senate will be in session next week. I am glad talks are ongoing between the Administration and Speaker Pelosi. I hope Congress can pass bipartisan legislation to continue combating the coronavirus and keep our economy strong.

1:20 PM · Mar 12, 2020

4.5K 3.1K 11K 12

Figure 1.1 Tweet by Senator Mitch McConnell announcing the Senate's plans to address the coronavirus
Source: Twitter.

cloakroom, where updates normally go out. No heads-up was given to the majority of Senate staffers on either side of the aisle. The announcement on Twitter went through the administrative managers "like wildfire," according to one Senate staffer who noted just how out of the norm it was for leadership to first turn to Twitter rather than routing it through the regular channels (Interview 6). Not only was the president going to do everything by Twitter, but also congressional leaders were doing the same and shifting the rules of the information game when offices needed it most. "It always infuriates me when the press talks about McConnell being an institutionalist. . . . It's such a piece of crap," said one former Republican staffer, referencing the leader's recess announcement (Interview 8).

The days of fax blasts were definitely over, but even beyond the machine, it was a choice about how to conduct business and where leadership was going to steer the institution. McConnell and party leaders alike were capitalizing on a digital-first news environment that was changing how information moved through the institution. As the McConnell example makes clear, digital communication and social media are now a vital part of the day-to-day business of Congress. Yet most of what we know about Congress, as an institution, focuses on the legislative behaviors and policymaking processes that exist within this largely unexplored Twitter-driven, digital media ecosystem. We've defined the role of Twitter as a mechanism for representation (Ballard et al., 2022b; Gains & Wagner, 2014; Gervais & Morris, 2018; Russell, 2021a) and electoral politics (Evans et al., 2014; MacDonald, 2021;

McGregor, 2019), but Twitter isn't just a platform for winning elections. Twitter and the shift toward digital communication have vast implications for how Congress governs and who gets to control the institutional agenda. This book uses congressional staff experiences and lawmakers' reputation-building efforts on Twitter to describe the digital communication culture within Congress and explain how the shift to Twitter—despite its tenets of accessibility—reinforced a culture of asymmetric information and resource dependence within Congress.

The central framework for this book is that social media has hastened the race for information and induced a crisis of communication that constrains institutional capacity by furthering power asymmetries in Congress. I argue that social media, notably Twitter as the primary platform for journalists and advocates, has changed the velocity of communication in Congress, precipitating a persistent crisis culture that began long before a global pandemic elevated the necessity for digital communication. The result of this crisis of communication is an information avalanche that requires lawmakers and staff to be professional communicators although they don't have the capacity of a high-functioning legislative and media enterprise. Communications staffers are incentivized to manage a crisis communication operation—regularly preparing for viral disruptions—but a simultaneous and equally debilitating crisis stems from a lack of resources to actually manage that effort. The digital notoriety of Representative Alexandria Ocasio-Cortez or Senator Brian Schatz is the exception rather than the rule. The expectations for effective digital communication paired with the risk of miscommunication incentivizes tighter coordination and control, which prompts centralization by party leaders and furthers unequal power structures (Curry, 2015). Communication hierarchies are maintained by political leaders who can invest in their own communication capacity while also providing what I refer to as a "communication subsidy" to resource-dependent members via graphics, videos, and social media content necessary for digital reputation building. The power of reputation building online has elevated digital communication in a way that ultimately constrains what little capacity lawmakers already had and makes the average member of Congress resource dependent in terms of both policy and communication.

Pairing an analysis of 192 interviews of professionals around Congress with congressional social media data, I explain the Twitter-driven media environment—where misinformation is common and someone is always watching—as the reason that Congress cannot get out of the communication crisis cycle it is in. The demands of social media place new constraints on the capacity of lawmakers, staff, and journalists to function, and Twitter, in particular, has fundamentally changed congressional operations by increasing the velocity of information such that both communication and policy staff are regularly preparing for four-alarm fires that need putting out. When the fire never goes out, how Congress responds has implications for what issues get addressed, the power of constituent input, and the diversity of voices that get heard.

Crisis of Communication and the Realities of Rapid Response

Politics may still be a "slow boring of hard boards," but that no longer describes the daily dialogue among the professionals in Congress whose job can be upended in a matter of minutes with a sentence on Twitter. For example, in 2019, President Trump tweeted about four progressive minority congresswomen—suggesting they "go back" to where they came from—and members of Congress spent the ensuing hours reacting to and responding to calls for comments on the president's language (Figure 1.2). The week's anticipated debate over immigration policy quickly shifted to a conversation about responsible politics and xenophobic attacks as communications staffers managed lawmaker responses.

Congressional staff describe a communications climate where congressional offices continue to make strategic choices but increasingly those choices play out on Twitter and reflect daily digital political debates. Interviews with congressional staff and journalists shed new light on the perpetual problem of deciding how to manage communications when the institution is constantly on alert. Communications staffers are jockeying for opportunities for their boss to be an opinion leader on an issue while also carefully trying to avoid reputational mistakes and digital blunders. This book uncovers the communication culture in Congress over the last 25 years, using a framework of crisis communication to explain how digital and social media have fostered a permanent brand of political disaster communication that tests the capacity of the institution. And while the COVID-19 crisis was a shock to the system in terms of how Congress operates in a digital and remote environment, it reflects a much broader, long-coming shift in how information is shared. On any given day in Congress, a single tweet can set off a political firestorm that burns hot and fast. The president could announce via tweet a new executive order, a journalist could suggest that a pivotal lawmaker may balk on appropriations, or a member might offer a few too many details in a hallway chat that communications staff will have to walk back on Twitter.

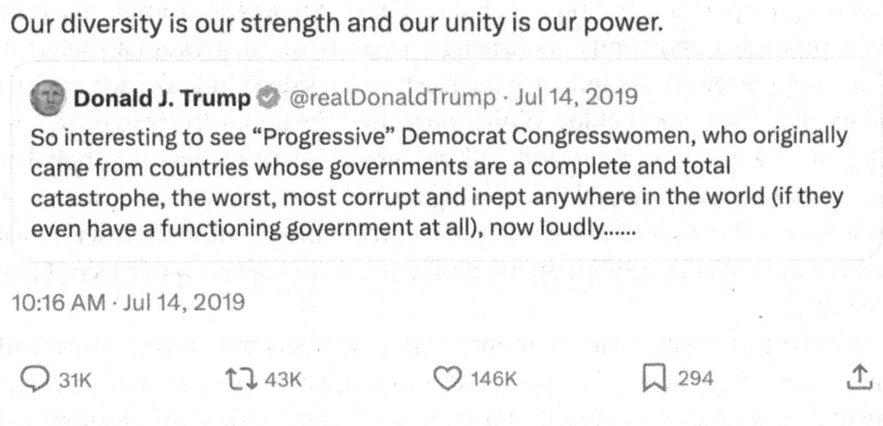

Figure 1.2 Representative Nancy Pelosi responds on Twitter to President Trump's tweet about progressive women in Congress
Source: Twitter.

Congress's daily operations are defined by the rapid cycling of information between political institutions, meaning the logistics of daily engagement in Congress mirror that of a crisis response because staffers and journalists are constantly monitoring the digital political climate, looking for potential crises to exploit for headlines. Lawmakers and senior staff still coordinate their message for the week—organizing around new legislation, upcoming votes, and planned events back home—but the expectation is that the schedule could blow up at any moment and is likely ripe for revisions as conflicts are reframed and political agendas get revised.

I argue that to understand the digital communication culture in Congress, we must consider how social media has induced a cycling crisis of communication within our political institutions that implies constant monitoring and public exposure. That persistent congressional communication means daily tweets, press releases, photo opportunities, and media appearances that test the capacity of a single office. A crisis threatens to make an individual or organization illegitimate in the public sphere (Coombs, 2007), and congressional communication can be understood as a defense mechanism to thwart reputational attacks and bolster legitimacy. Crises are perceived as a threat to one's reputation (Coombs, 2007), and in politics, the choices that elected officials and their staffs make together contribute to reputation maintenance. Political crisis communication has traditionally focused on the agenda-setting setting role of the president to frame and address crises (Coombs, 2011; Windt, 1973), but in an era of social media where the average congressperson can find a digital audience, the weaponization of a crisis as a political opportunity increasingly extends to congressional behavior. For example, amid the industry backlash to President Biden's carbon emissions plans, Senator Sheldon Whitehouse used the opportunity to bolster his climate change bona fides and call out power plant owners for their lazy response to environmental threats (Figure 1.3). For a senator who often likes to write his own tweets, it was an opportunity to insert himself into a political debate and collaborate with digital staff to reinforce his renewable technology priorities.

Similar to a small business or enterprise, members of Congress work with their team (Salisbury & Shepsle, 1981) to mitigate threats to their credibility and seek new opportunities for legitimacy, minimizing any electoral risk and building their political brand. If we consider lawmakers as single-minded reelection seekers (Mayhew, 1974), then the choices they make about how to present themselves and communicate their political brand are directly correlated to mitigating threats to their reputation.

The self-perpetuated crisis that plays out in the ongoing Twitter cycle leaves Congress in rapid-response mode, and this is why some members of Congress decide to invest in the ability to rapidly respond, forgoing legislative priorities in order to build their reputations digitally, which may place them at odds with political foes (Interview 103). A crisis is typically characterized by high levels of uncertainty and urgency, and in a political environment dominated by Twitter narratives, Congress faces persistent uncertainty that requires regular communication. In the early stages of a crisis, often referred to as the initial phase, an organization needs to communicate often with key constituencies and stakeholders. "Early response to crises can limit the extent to which organizations are damaged. Prompt, open responses minimize damage potential" (Brody, 1991, p. 189). According to the Centers for Disease Control and Prevention, the initial phase of crisis and emergency risk communication should include simple and concise engagement on social media to get a sense of what people are thinking and establish credibility with regular updates. Cooperation, nuance, and background information are usually involved in the next phase of crisis maintenance, but Congress rarely gets to this second phase because new crises continue to gain traction as the rapid

This is the part where an industry too lazy, negligent and greedy to capture its own emissions now complains that it's not technology in common use — oh, right, because they were too lazy, negligent and greedy to use the technology.

From reuters.com

5:33 PM · Aug 8, 2023 · **9,551** Views

11 120 339 3

Figure 1.3 Democratic Senator Sheldon Whitehouse tweets about industry emissions
Source: Twitter.

exchange of information continues on social media. The media play obvious informational and amplifying roles in disasters (Kasperson et al., 1988), and those roles can be central to working through crises; in Congress, however, the media and journalists are part of the information cycle where minor disruptions become major news on Twitter and their amplification means repeating the initial phase of a crisis cycle. Prior research shows that media venues like blogs can serve community-building functions during a crisis or disaster (Macias et al., 2009), but in Congress that function is complicated by Twitter being both a community-building mechanism and the source of many potential political disasters.

Similar to political scandal, the risk of miscommunication fosters coordination and consistency, precipitating control (Baumgartner & Jones, 2018).

Communication becomes even more fundamental to congressional operations when everything is moving through centralized channels and the inputs are being monitored more than ever before. This emphasis on coordination and the resulting power asymmetries (Curry, 2015) mean that powerful voices become louder and those with resources are better positioned to shape the narrative. Communication hierarchies are maintained by funneling information through the same channels, further testing capacity by constraining inputs and outputs that only momentarily slow the exchange.

Congressional policymaking has only gotten more complex over time, and the breadth of what Congress can do has expanded (Jones et al., 2019); digital communication is part of that complex dynamic. The realities of a fire-alarm response driving congressional behavior are nothing new (McCubbins & Schwartz, 1984; Scher, 1963), but social media fuels that fire with increased attention, more information, and a news cycle that churns fast. This information-rich environment with high expectations for rapid response challenges Congress's ability to do its job when the norms for policymaking remain unchanged. In the House, communications are often managed by a single staffer (Macdonald & Russell, 2024). In the Senate, that effort is shared by three to six people—but even with additional staff, the chamber remains similarly constrained by outsized demands from journalists and larger constituencies. Congress is not allocating new resources to meet the demands of digital engagement, meaning trade-offs that limit legislative capacity and reorient priorities. Congress needs greater capacity in terms of its lawmaking abilities (LaPira et al., 2020), but addressing that demand is made more difficult by the pace of information being channeled through these political institutions.

Centralization and Asymmetric Resources

Congress legitimately handles multiple natural disasters and health crises, but the Twitter-perpetuated crisis continues to leave Congress in rapid-response mode, which motivates offices to rely on established measures of communication support and information exchange. In today's Congress, information is centralized by powerful voices, and paired with that information advantage are more resources to manage the communication crisis. The resulting centralization and coordination by lawmakers and their staff reflect a challenging dynamic in congressional communication where professionals must sort through the information influx but also synthesize the information going out in ways that perpetuate the cycle. Stakeholders are monitoring the content and quantity of information released while journalists simultaneously attempt to acquire as much information as possible (Arpan & Pompper, 2003). The crisis climate also fosters centralization within offices, which creates a firewall between policy and communications while simultaneously centralizing information through resource-rich entities like party leadership, caucuses, and committees that provide offices with the necessary communication support.

The centralization of power by parties and party leadership leads to a resource asymmetry that shapes the diversity of voices and the information flow in Congress. The notion of "all hands on deck" to respond to a crisis captures the way in which communications professionals respond to information, but the ability to respond to any emergency is constrained by resources. I argue that the centralization of power by parties and party leadership leads to an information and resource asymmetry that shapes the information flow in Congress. Research suggests that party power has been centralized in congressional offices where lawmaking is primarily unorthodox and managed by leaders who benefit from resource advantages (Curry, 2015; Curry & Lee, 2019; Sinclair, 2006). Political power is centralized by party leaders with strong decision-making power, but I explain that additional power stems from the professionalized communications operations, where the information advantage coupled with the resources to circulate that information leads to sophisticated press shops that are able to shape the narrative. Rather than trying to control party members, the power to dominate the message going out gives leaders the advantage. Even in a fragmented media climate where the venues for agenda setting are vast, the resource advantages by leaders, senior senators, and so forth offer powerful tools to combat that information surge and demand. Research suggests that the centralization of power by congressional majorities doesn't necessarily equate to more preferred policy outcomes, but they do set the rules of partisan conflict and engagement (Curry & Lee, 2019). Similarly, party leaders are not necessarily able to control the narrative coming out of Congress while also balancing majority power and policy goals (Smith, 2007); but I explain how they do use their resources to spur the conversation, communicate the terms of debate, and fuel the information exchange in ways that affect the narrative both inside and outside Congress.

Lawmakers have unprecedented opportunities using digital communications to drive their own success; not only do those choices affect communication but also, as congressional staff argue, a Twitter-driven culture shapes how lawmakers and staff engage in the policy process. Powerfully positioned lawmakers can benefit from this social media environment, but amid the limited advantages for a few is the greater threat to the function of Congress as an organization. A crisis curbs an organization's performance and generates negative outcomes (Coombs, 2007). One of the negative externalities of this crisis of communication is the threat to congressional capacity, incentivizing further divestment in legislative operations by the average member of Congress (Crosson et al., 2021). Sufficient capacity is already lacking from the policymaking structure in place, but further complicating any semblance of functionality is the increased velocity of information. Congressional offices face a flood of information, and this excess constrains how offices prioritize their time and resources. We often consider congressional capacity in terms of policymaking personnel (LaPira et al., 2020), but how Congress adapts to the communication climate has a direct impact on the ability of Congress to function. The influx of information and the associated risks mean information is shot through a central tube. As told by staff, capacity is tested when you shoot too much water through a single hose. Digital technology—from satellite trucks to social media—has changed the relationships that form the foundation of Congress, and this new environment means we must reassess how we understand our political institutions.

Good public policy and power are two essential goals for members of Congress (Fenno, 1977), but these simultaneous goals are more often at odds when power comes in 280-character narratives with hashtags and followers that have the power to disrupt and distract from policy. Collaboration in Congress can be tenuous even in the best environment, and in a world where policy must be both correct and consumable at any given moment, that tests the traditional policymaking capacity of Congress, which has often relied on back-room deals and behind-the-scenes efforts to move an issue forward.

Tweeting to Stay Ahead of the Information Game

Information is powerful, and within political institutions, that power is magnified by the digital exchange of news and conflict. Congressional offices and journalists are able to use social media to track an evolving news cycle, but that same platform begets more information and a need to prepare for the next social media–driven crisis. Twitter's networked platform provides a daily ticker where congressional staff and journalists aggregate sources and track the progression of political content for new, actionable information. Even at the country's founding, James Madison wrote, "No man can be a competent legislator who does not add to an upright intention and a sound judgment a certain degree of knowledge of the subject on which he is to legislate." Congressional offices face a flood of information fueled by digital sources, largely defined by policy and political information. Regardless of whether they are evaluating a policy proposal or juggling signals between political actors about voting decisions, this information overload shapes lawmaker behavior and constrains the actions of those professionals managing schedules, developing policy memos, or typing up press releases.

Information is abundant and moves at lightning speed, affecting the jobs of not only communications professionals but also those working on policy as the rapid cycling and exchange of information can shape policy preferences and legislative negotiation. The problem isn't just too much information. Congress isn't a world where information is costly; rather, the costs of ignoring information are what really matter. And while those choices are often framed in terms of electoral costs and political incentives, the cost of doing business is a reality that all who shape the information flows in Congress must grapple with. The breadth of what Congress can do and what is expected of policymakers has grown—in a sense, the river is increasing in both width and depth. But in addition to these concerns, we also have to consider how fast the water is flowing. The capacity of Congress and its ability to function is based not only on the institutional infrastructure and resources allocated but also on the nature of the information flows and the velocity of that exchange. Regardless of whether any issue rises to the level of a true crisis, those in Congress still have to prepare for that eventuality and remain on heightened alert. This constant demand for news and the high-stakes game of political agenda setting on Twitter test the capacity of Congress to handle the bottleneck of information when the pressures for transparency are high and the demands from constituents and advocates continue to increase. Twitter is the primary vehicle for social media communication in Congress. Staff and lawmakers may use Instagram and Facebook to connect with constituents outside of the Beltway, but for the daily dialogue of Congress, one need look no further than Twitter to gauge the pulse of Congress.

For many journalists and communications staffers, their email inbox is a black hole. One journalist who covers her congressional delegation reported more than 100,000 unopened emails in her inbox (Interview 21). In a world where email can no longer contain the deluge of information, Twitter is an alternative venue for trying to track legislation and the daily schedule and connect with sources. "It's all Twitter, all the time," confirmed one journalist about the way social media has inserted itself into the daily routines of the journalists covering Congress (Interview 49). An essential piece of Congress is the narrative, and while senators are often trying to direct that with their own tweets, there is an undercurrent and daily dialogue with journalists that tell the story of both the institution and its dynamics. Journalists are part of the information game, where they both fuel and react to the fires in Congress while also adapting to a world where their power comes from followers rather than proximity. Social media strengthens relationships between journalists and sources, where leads begin online and reputations are defined digitally. The 24-hour news cycle goes minute by minute, and sustaining that cycle is both difficult and dubious.

The communication that fosters the information exchange in Congress occurs over text message, email, and Twitter, but amid a global pandemic, those digital connections become even more necessary. The opportunities to connect while waiting in line for coffee or standing in the hallway waiting on a lawmaker mean that both staff and journalists are relying on virtual connections. For some, those connections are equal to or better than in-person interactions, but for many, the loss of a personal connection makes it harder to track people down. A number of journalists report that it is easier for staff to ignore an email or phone call than a journalist staring them down in a committee hearing.

Velocity of Communication and Congressional Capacity

A crisis can threaten what's expected of stakeholders and can hamper an institution's performance—generating a surplus of negative outcomes (Coombs, 2007). One of those negative outcomes is the threat to congressional capacity. Social media has escalated the velocity of communication in Congress, creating a sense of urgency with the rapid exchange of information that largely occurs online. Members of Congress invest substantial capital—human and monetary—to communicate with journalists, constituents, and copartisans through digital platforms (Cormack, 2016; Evans et al., 2014; Russell, 2021a). The role of digital directors and communication directors has increased as information has become centralized; these professionals are the gatekeepers of information for each office. The days of turning to policy staff, even for background information, are quickly fading as the need to control the narrative and limit potential gaffs reigns supreme. And as news moves more quickly, journalists are writing stories and tweets on the fly as the digital audience expects immediate satisfaction such that all participants in this congressional dance must remain alert despite the deluge of information. Social media becomes an alternative space for sorting through that information while also offering noise and its own dialogue that fundamentally shape the daily routines of staff around Congress.

We often consider congressional capacity in terms of policymaking personnel (LaPira et al., 2020), but how Congress adapts to the communication climate has a direct impact on its ability to function when the need for effective communication outweighs the capacity to provide it. Digital technology—from satellite trucks to social media—has changed the relationships that form the foundation of Congress, and this new environment means we must reassess how we understand our political institutions. Today's communication culture challenges congressional capacity in three distinct ways. First, the persistence of information means constant engagement by all, which tests the ability to respond, filter out less important news, and remain on top of the narrative. Second, the rapid pace of information tests the ability of all to maintain communication and legislative norms. Third, new technology reinforces powerful voices, positions of power, and individualization among staff and journalists.

Measuring Congress's adoption and normalization of digital media has never been easier due to an abundance of publicly accessible data. Between 2013 and 2018, members of the House of Representatives sent more than 1.37 million tweets, and in the race in 2020 they had more than 20,000 posts on Facebook. Members of Congress, especially senators, are political celebrities online, with followers in the hundreds of thousands and millions. Lawmakers use social media to define themselves and build a national reputation (Russell, 2021b), but behind those messages is a network of professionals whose daily lives and professional success are tied to that information flow. The mechanisms behind the 240-character tweets remain comparatively unknown, yet they signal the ability of Congress to adapt to new media environments and test the capacity of the institution. What a lawmaker says on Twitter or CNN can illuminate a lot about representation, but to understand how the minute-by-minute information exchange shapes the business of communication in Congress, we need the first-person perspectives of those trying to adapt to the new information environment to shed light on their strategies.

Interviews with more than 190 communications and policy staff as well as journalists, conducted between 2020 and 2023, illuminate how social media has tested the capacity of Congress by elevating digital communication to a level that necessitates resources and a communication subsidy. A series of semi-structured interviews reveal how communication norms have changed in light of social media and what daily routines around these platforms look like. Respondents were asked about how the office uses social media to foster reputations, the role of policy as a messaging strategy, and how social media tests relationships between reporters and staff. I analyzed responses using an inductive approach to thematic analysis to allow patterns, common themes, and variations to emerge from their statements. Significant and meaningful statements were collected and categorized into similar clusters of meaning (Kvale, 1996), and I used those clusters to organize four subsequent chapters for this book, covering the four decades of digital media transitions, the normalization of digital tools into press shops, collaboration and centralization in digital communication, and partisan-driven conflict communication.

Organization of the Book

Political institutions adapt and respond to both internal and external pressures, but as the media climate changes, Congress's capacity to handle this new communication environment is tested by new norms for engagement. The rise in digital media has changed how lawmakers pursue success and power in Congress (Russell, 2021a), but behind-the-scenes social media is just the newest technology to test the ability of lawmakers, their staff, and the press to develop relationships that evolve to meet the speed of the information exchange. This book uses a mixed-methods approach to understand the relationships central to congressional communication, taking advantage of a multiyear dataset of lawmakers' social media messages and interviews with more than 190 communications and policy professionals in Congress to provide context for how social media became the latest test of institutional norms. Using interviews and Twitter data to illustrate how digital media has fueled the very same power asymmetries we expected it to disrupt, I argue that Congress is experiencing a crisis of communication.

I present (Chapter 2) a new crisis of communication framework that examines how the velocity of information and the pressure of Twitter force journalists, press professionals, and policy staff to reassess how they operate and form new routines for the daily operations in Congress. Congress has adopted a rapid-response communication strategy to meet the speed and volume of the information flow in Congress. This organization-based perspective reflects how offices have structured themselves to address the increased attention to communication and persistent preparation for any incident to become a crisis through viral content or collective responses by political stakeholders. The response by congressional communicators fuels this crisis cycle, where offices continue to function in the precrisis and initial response phase such that postcrisis analysis, situational assessments, further explanation, and adaptive messaging are rarely realized as offices persistently triage new information. The implications of that crisis go far beyond how an office operates and affect how Congress operates, its capacity to do so, and the power of individual actors to shape the debate and dialogue. By considering the crisis as a social construct propelled by social media, we can take a more holistic approach to understanding how Twitter and technology have induced new communication strategies and influenced the persistence of crisis communication as a tool for powerful voices in Congress.

Twitter has become the most consistent platform for the communication ecosystem of the professionals tasked with the daily operations in Congress, and I explain (Chapter 3) the origins of that Twitter-driven culture and what that communication environment looks like in today's Congress. In the 1980s, Congress adapted to C-SPAN and updates to electronic voting. In the 1990s, members moved from making news via TV satellite trucks to novel attempts at engagement as the internet took hold. Since then, the evolution of websites, blogs, podcasts, and social media has ushered in a digital era that both continues the technological evolution and tests the institution's capacity to readily adapt. Lawmakers have always looked for new opportunities to take advantage of technology. As Speaker, Newt Gingrich's conservative movement was built on his ability to find new ways to get his message out—taking advantage of television coverage and one-minute speeches. A decade later, Senate Majority Leader Harry Reid would further invest in consistent and robust communications, establishing a "war room" in the Senate that tried to integrate "new media" into Democratic messaging. Twitter is the latest in a series of media shifts that change the landscape for political communication and require further investment in congressional communications. This investment means there are more journalists covering the Capitol than ever before, and press staff are tasked with not only sorting and filtering information but also creating content that drives the information exchange.

The nature of that press exchange is defined by the daily routines of press shops in Congress, a largely unknown operation within the legislature that is fundamental to how information moves through the institution. I detail (Chapter 4) what the average communications office looks like, how digital is integrated, and what it means to work in a position subject to a nonstop news cycle. As more offices prioritize digital, this creates new opportunities for content creation, but at the same time, communications staff are asked to do more tasks with minimally more resources. This expectation and crisis climate mean that staff burnout is common, outside support is (mostly) valued, and many digital staff are making up the rules as they go without a standard for how digital can and should be utilized. The reader learns in Chapter 4 just who is in charge of the tweets and press releases going out daily and how offices decide when to enter the digital dialogue.

For a minority member or a junior senator, using Twitter to craft a narrative can be a powerful tool that bypasses institutional constraints, but the implications of that investment mean trade-offs elsewhere. Successful policymaking is often linked to successful communication; however, the costs of doing both in Congress are far too high for many members. The central role of digital in congressional offices presents a dual problem—the average congressional office doesn't have the time or resources to invest in policymaking, and even when redirecting attention to press, the perpetual news cycle online requires more content creation than a single office can afford. Research shows that party leaders have an asymmetrical information advantage when it comes to policymaking (Curry, 2015), but those resource advantages are buoyed in a Twitter-driven Congress by (1) less policymaking attention by rank-and-file members and (2) the ability to provide a communication subsidy to copartisans. I explain (Chapter 5) how Twitter—once thought of as an equalizer for political minorities—has been normalized by powerful voices to fuel asymmetric resources in policymaking and communication. As members redirect attention to the crisis communication environment in Congress, the trade-off in what Fenno described as "good public policy" means they are more likely to rely on party and committee leaders for policy information (Chapter 5). Over time party leaders have centralized spending within the Legislative Branch Appropriations Acts, providing them with outsized resources that shape both legislative and communications behavior. Semi-structured interviews and a content analysis of Senate tweets from the 113th to 115th Congresses suggest a distinct digital style for lawmakers with resources, particularly in terms of their political and policy rhetoric. Similarly, the added emphasis on content creation and digital engagement gives party leaders new tools to supply what I term a "communication subsidy" to members who cannot alone produce the graphics, videos, and social media content they want for digital reputation building. Communications staff report that they meet weekly with party leadership and caucus staff to go over messaging strategy, exchange ideas, and gain support from the dozens of communications staff employed by party leaders or committees. While not all offices use the material, the coordination allows for a sharing of best practices, technology trainings, and institutional digital knowledge that only the caucus and committee resources can logistically provide.

But as the Twitter-driven media environment demands more attention with fewer resources, this semi-permanent crisis operation has implications for policymaking and institutional organization. Twitter, and digital engagement more broadly, offers lawmakers new tools for representation. Members are less reliant on policymaking prestige or party favor to build a reputation. Lawmakers use conflict, party-polarizing rhetoric, and provocative messaging to propel themselves on cable news and build a political brand. In Chapter 6, I explain how and why Twitter has contributed to a prevalence of angry, negative rhetoric that is both perpetuated by communications staff and covered by journalists. Using a dataset of House members' tweets and interviews with communications professionals on the Hill, I explain the rise in Twitter as a tool for publicity and how taking advantage of this communication crisis culture has perpetuated a style of reputation building on social media that fuels conflict and partisan divisiveness. I show how the partisan divide in Washington, in addition to electoral security, is linked to representatives' angry communications online. Press staff are increasingly part of the digital content creation process, which supplies journalists and activists with divisive rhetoric that shapes the reported narrative about Congress.

Finally, I assess what the crisis communication cycle and digital information flow mean for lawmaking and Congress's capacity to function in our partisan political environment. The party-polarized institution, paired with Twitter updates that can derail negotiations, means that even policy and committee staff adapt to the rapid rhetoric (Chapter 7). When information gets "tribalized" in the media, that can derail the policy process (Curry & Lee, 2020), and those ideological networks are inherent to new media where information is abundant regarding congressional behavior. The pressure to be able to write policy that both is meaningful and can be consumable by journalists and constituents is constant, emphasized even more in a world of policy prioritization by Twitter. Policy rhetoric accounts for more than half of all tweets sent by members of Congress (Russell, 2021a), and the communications and policy staff must collaborate to feed the media machine. While most members use their policy priorities as fodder for their reputation building online, those with the resources and incentives to promote those messages will pattern the policy narrative coming out of Congress.

Conclusion

Research has begun to unpack the implications of social media for partisan politics and policy debates in Congress (Barberá et al., 2019; Straus & Glassman, 2016; Theocharis et al., 2020), but this book looks to the institution and the people within it to understand the relationships at the core of that communication. Scholars and politicians once lauded Twitter's utility in connecting constituents to what is going on in Washington, but in reality, the impact of digital media is felt far beyond what a lawmaker wants to say to folks back home. For an institution in the 1990s that went from primarily trying to triage the influx of constituent mail to the 2000s where email has sent constituent contact into the hundreds of millions (Shogan, 2010), Congress has adapted but also had its capacity to channel that information stretched to a breaking point. The media landscape has fragmented audiences, and members of Congress, along with staff and journalists, have become even more entrepreneurial in the face of an accelerating news cycle (Sellers, 2000). Members of Congress face individual and collective responsibilities that compete for their scarce time and attention, and congressional capacity is tested by new and sophisticated digital operations, fewer staffers, and increasingly complex policy. In addition, the demands of social media and digital technology place new constraints on how lawmakers, staff, and journalists function on a daily basis. New tools for engagement offer new opportunities to redefine what it means to be successful in Congress, but the costs of digital content creation and customizing a message to match the preferences of variable audiences are increasingly more than lawmakers or their staffs can afford. The changing velocity of information in Congress has implications for what issues get addressed, the power of constituent input, and the diversity of voices that get heard. Social media has fundamentally changed expectations about accountability, engagement, and transparency, but it has also reinforced political hierarchies that have elevated leadership, made long-term policy collaboration tenuous, and raised the stakes of political soundbites. The political dialogue on Twitter is accessible to anyone with a smartphone, but new technology doesn't necessarily mean the voices at the decision-making table sound any different.

2
A Crisis Framework for Congressional Communication

> Congress is overwhelmed and overmatched. It lurches from crisis to crisis and is unable to effectively "think," be strategic and proactive, and look ahead to future, or less pressing, problems.
>
> —***Staff director, House committee***[1]

Congress isn't a stranger to crises, political or otherwise. Lawmakers have overseen wars, managed recessions, responded to a global pandemic, and experienced the horrors of an insurrection. But as *The New Yorker* described it recently, many of the crises Congress faces today are self-imposed and a function of how the institution operates. Self-inflicted wounds aren't the only thing constraining the capacity of Congress, but for the men and women at the front lines of lawmaking, operating in a crisis environment has become the norm. On May 19, 2022, *Bloomberg Law* reported that congressional attention was "scattered" amid crises, rushing to tackle one after another. Two days earlier, *Politico*'s "Huddle" titled their morning congressional update with "Crises drive Congress' to-do list." The morning report told the long and short of high-priority items that were testing the capacity of Congress to manage an unmanageable list of mounting policy and political problems—aid to Ukraine, domestic terrorism, a baby formula shortage, and escalating gas prices. The "tangled web of crises" reflects the complexity of policy solutions in a hyperpartisan political climate, but when cooperation and consistency are tested by 280-character Twitter statements, political realities become even more complicated.[2]

Congress manages important policy and operational problems on a regular basis, but more frequently and unending are the reputational crises and socially mediated communication crises perpetuated on Twitter that have

[1] Survey of Congressional Exemplars by the Congressional Management Foundation, 2022.
[2] *Politico*'s "Huddle," May 17, 2022.

Tweeting Scared. Annelise Russell, Oxford University Press. © Oxford University Press (2025).
DOI: 10.1093/9780197808344.003.0002

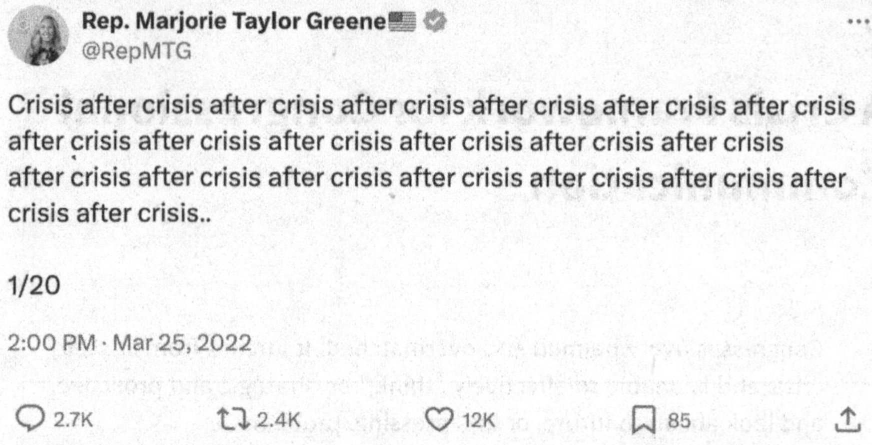

Crisis after crisis..

1/20

2:00 PM · Mar 25, 2022

2.7K 2.4K 12K 85

Figure 2.1 Representative Marjorie Taylor Greene sharing a tweet about crises
Source: Twitter.

implications beyond digital practices and shape the organizational behavior of Congress. Digital-driven crises aren't just the norm (Figure 2.1), but rather reframed as opportunities—or, as Homer Simpson famously labeled it, a "crisitunity"—for engagement, reputation building, and political jockeying for the first or final word on an issue.

Congress may be in an endless cycle of trying to figure out if Chicken Little was right and if the sky is really falling,[3] but in terms of Congress's ability to mitigate the slow-burning information crisis, that sky has been falling for some time now. New technology and an evolving media climate have regularly prompted Congress to adapt to new information environments and figure out how to manage the benefits of new tools, new levels of accessibility, and the challenge of channeling new information and addressing new audiences. From radio to C-SPAN, satellite trucks to cable news, and now the transition to a fast-paced social media climate, Congress has managed to play catch-up when it comes to figuring out how to integrate increasingly digital information into an institution that formerly embraced the novelty of the fountain pen. But at some point, the information overload became more than just a feature of Congress and evolved into a persistent crisis of communication that Congress must reckon with. Offices accept the elevated role of digital communication with the press and voters, but many outsource the logistics of that engagement or limit their reach due to capacity and resource constraints.

[3] https://nymag.com/intelligencer/article/crises-congress-self-imposed.html?regwall-newsletter-signup=true#;

I argue that the evolution of digital media, headlined by the normalization of Twitter as a means for tracking information in Congress, fundamentally shifted congressional communications into a crisis management operation to address digital uncertainty. Prevention and preparedness are commonly accepted, basic principles of crisis management, but when the information cycle moves so quickly that it also spins new information into problems, that prevention effort is rarely realized. Compounding informational failures can create new dangers, and the high-speed information exchange in Congress facilitates that perpetual threat.

This chapter lays out how congressional communication came to mirror that of a crisis response where communications professionals are persistently at the intersection of urgency and uncertainty. Communications staffers and journalists alike operate in a media environment where new information could arise at any moment, reorient the agenda, or create new opportunities for performative politics. In May 2022, when the majority opinion in the *Dobbs* case leaked and signaled the end of federal abortion protections, decisions about how to respond dominated the next 24 hours on congressional Twitter, but then everyone was back to doom scrolling the following day for another political predicament (Connor & Russell, 2024).

I use a crisis communication framework to explain how the incentives of social media contribute to a high-speed, high-volume information exchange that has the potential to overwhelm a congressional office. Many offices have a single staffer designing digital content, drafting tweets, writing newsletters, and writing remarks for the next constituent event or congressional hearing. When offices are burdened by being both digital media consumers and producers, they maintain a dependence on those with resources for communication support—reinforcing asymmetrical power dynamics within Congress. Twitter may be cheap, but effective digital production and media monitoring require an investment that very few within Congress have the resources to make happen. The irony of this crisis climate is that social media was originally lauded for its ability to disrupt institutional norms and give rise to new voices, but in reality, the partisan political conflicts and information inequities that characterize Congress are actually further reinforced as many staffers rely on tweets by reporters and toolkits by party leadership or political allies for the most accurate information. Social media data and interviews with congressional staff and journalists show how resources shape both the communication operations in Congress and the output on Twitter. Those working in Congress rely on social media to cultivate political narratives, using its viral tendencies and power for reputation building and further partisan entrenchment. Twitter, the dominant digital platform for communicators in Congress for over a decade, transitioned from just an opportunity to a requirement, and with that shift came new challenges for congressional offices to meet the demand of being effective digital communicators, tracking shifting narratives to remain central to congressional agenda setting.

Congressional Communication as a Crisis

How we understand the operation of Congress and those individuals who manage the daily policymaking is primarily through the perspectives of the lawmakers themselves or the legislative staff who are tasked with issue research and policy memos. This narrative of Congress as a policymaking institution spurred by variable levels of effective partisans is shared both publicly and among those who study the institution (Adler & Wilkerson, 2013; Esterling, 2007; Russell, 2021a; Volden & Wiseman, 2014). But increasingly important to understanding both the capacity of Congress and the mechanisms that shape its daily operations is the communication culture that moderates the flow of information, policy or otherwise (Furnas et al., 2021; Lee, 2016; Russell, 2021a; Gaynor, 2022). Self-presentation has always been a fundamental component of representation (Fenno, 1977), but that reputation building goes beyond constituent service and credit claiming in a digital media environment where presentation is less a choice and rather a mandate. The decision is no longer between a "show horse" and a "work horse"; rather, the question has become, what kind of show horse does a lawmaker want to be?

The evolution of news on political Twitter is akin to a lightning strike where disproportionate attention persists as a norm and communications professionals are constantly monitoring for new threats. I offer a new framework for how we conceptualize the digital-driven communication culture in Congress. I use data from staff interviews and social media outputs to explain *how social media hastened the race for information and induced a crisis of communications that constrains institutional capacity by furthering power asymmetries in Congress.* The principles underlying this framework proceed in four parts, detailed in the chart below (Figures 2.4). First, lawmakers and staff operate in an environment of information overload, and second, those offices and journalists use digital tools like Twitter to manage and track the rapid-response information exchange. If you want to know the latest on Speaker negotiations, Twitter and *Politico* e-newsletters are primary tools. Digital media influence congressional operations by

Hunter Biden has no marketable skills. His business was selling access to Joe Biden.

These were Joe Biden's business dealings—shaking down corrupt oligarchs for millions of dollars for political favors.

5:27 PM · Aug 13, 2023 · **226.9K** Views

2.1K 2.1K 8K 26

Figure 2.2 Tweet by lawmaker discussing ongoing investigations in Congress
Source: Twitter.

increasing the speed, volume, and visibility of information and simultaneously creating new communication opportunities. Lawmakers scroll Twitter for the latest updates on congressional investigations and use new information as a golden opportunity to shoot their shot. See Figures 2.2 and 2.3.

But third, that daily speed and volume of information exchange online overwhelm the communication capacity of many offices and create a risk-averse communication operation that mirrors a hierarchical crisis response. The incentives for digital engagement place increased strain on the professionals working in Congress because that means increased information filtering, new risk assessments, and a transition from being content moderators

No one is above the law: not Members of Congress, not the President, and not Justice Clarence Thomas.

Today @AOC @RepJerryNadler @RepHankJohnson @RepRaskin and I requested the DOJ to investigate Justice Thomas' alleged staggering violations of the Ethics of Government Act.

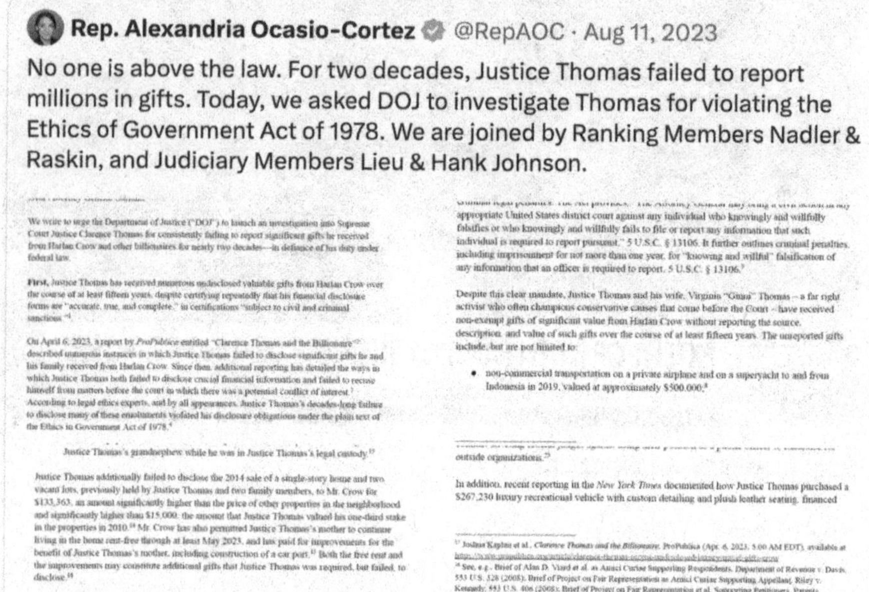

Figure 2.3 Tweet by lawmakers discussing ongoing investigations in Congress
Source: Twitter.

to digital content creators. Lawmakers put in place a cumbersome approval process—the internal process for green-lighting communications—for digital content because the expectation is that anything on Twitter or Facebook is an official statement. Fourth, the increased incentive for rapid response induces offices to seek what I term a "communication subsidy," forcing offices to rely on individuals and organizations with the information and resources to support the need for digital content and efficient communications. Committees put together toolkits for pending legislation, policy advocates share sample text, and some lawmakers outsource their paid advertising to navigate tricky technology and ethics regulations.

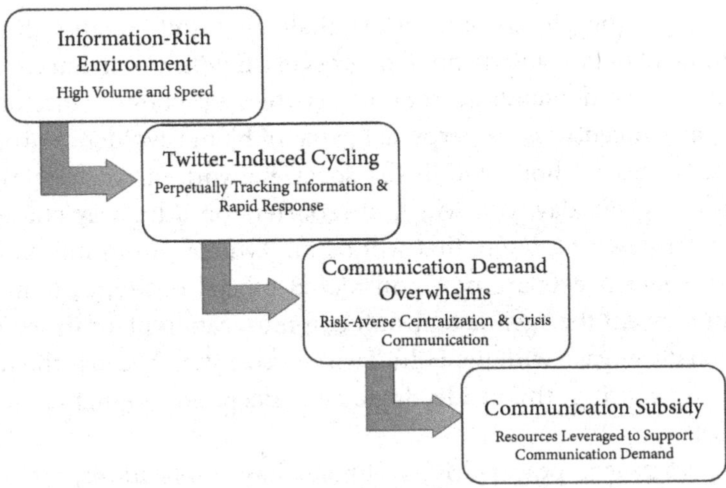

Figure 2.4 Flowchart for congressional communication

My conceptualization of this crisis communication climate builds a new line of research that explores the central role of digital communications within Congress and the implications of that prioritization for congressional capacity. The role of communications within the institution has gained unprecedented prominence, and the emphasis on presentation places additional demands on congressional offices to maintain a professional press and media department without sufficient resources. For example, some House offices are unwilling to invest in digital tools like Adobe Creative Suite, while other Senate staffers are using their own camera equipment to produce professional photography.

The concept of information asymmetries and resource dependence within Congress is not new to political science or legislative studies, but unlike previous research centering asymmetries on lawmaking (e.g., Bimber, 1991; Curry, 2015; Lupia, 1992), these limitations extend to information exchange and communication norms. The firehose of information spurred by Twitter and digital media has revealed an equal weakness of communication capacity that many legislators and staff are not equipped to solve on their own.

Finding support for congressional communication and new ways to elevate a lawmaker's voice amid the noise leaves many offices relying on familiar, traditional tactics to navigate this digital climate. For many, successful engagement means turning to political shots that mirror partisan talking points, turning anger and partisan conflict into reputation-building efforts, or simply posting photos of local townhalls that don't require the research and vetting of policy statements. Congress exists within a digital communication climate that demands accessibility, enables a preponderance of partisan attacks, and incentivizes a perpetual game of blame avoidance. And all that happens in just an hour within the social network of congressional Twitter. On any given day, you will find reporters on a hallway chase looking for an interview or a quote that will be on Twitter within minutes. And in a world where tweets are now considered official positions, that information can reorient the agenda and shift communication plans in seconds. You can't casually engage with the Hill's Twitter ecosystem because the narratives are rapidly shifting, the insider logic runs deep, and digital clout conveys influence.

This fast-paced, power-driven climate has implications for a healthy democracy, but just as important is the capacity of the political institution to function daily at this breakneck speed. Lawmakers are expected to be effective policymakers, managers, and communicators—and the lion's share of that responsibility falls to the staff who support and sustain each office. The increasing demands, though shared, are felt most readily by the staff who organize and manage congressional offices. Congressional offices are always preparing for a bill to drop or a stakeholders' meeting, but multiple policy staffers suggest it's the communications staff—the people managing the information exchange—who are always "on the clock." Press staff are routinely texting colleagues at 9 p.m. asking for an update on a press release because a journalist is inevitably waiting on a statement. There's a "burn and churn" reality among those whose job has become managing the information deluge that moves through Congress, mirroring the role of a crisis manager in addition to that of a communications professional or press relations expert. Digital staff are the first line of defense against online misinformation, hate speech, and comments that would leave anyone disgusted and shamed. Communications staff work, ideally, in a collaborative way with policy staff such that they create, as one policy staffer described, "fail-safes" in a risk-averse endeavor to protect the reputation of the office and its message.

Lawmakers and staff face an unprecedented number of demands on their time and attention, and the reality of a Twitter-driven political ecosystem leaves the average office ill-equipped to manage the information deluge. Brian McNair (2016) refers to this new communication climate, spurred by digital, networked media, as "chaos culture." The hyperscrutiny of democratic governance in a new media environment where secrets are well known creates a crisis logic that crisscrosses the public sphere. This socially constructed crisis of communication—elevated to a crisis because political actors perceive it as such—forces those in Congress to behave accordingly within that crisis climate. The crisis perception stems from the consistent uncertainty about where information is coming from, how fast, and the policy and political implications of that new information. A crisis can seemingly come from nowhere, and in Congress those process-driven pseudo-crisis events are often fleeting by the hour; however, the perpetual nature of these events keeps that crisis communication operation cycling. The uncertainty of emergent issues and new information has always been present in political institutions, but the speed of information and demand for swift action perpetuate a cycle of crisis preparation and mitigation. There is very little nuance in the 140 or 280 characters on Twitter, such that a major crisis and a minor crisis prompt similar, extensive filtering by professionals to prepare for all eventualities while simultaneously anticipating where that crisis might fall in terms of severity. For Congress, the speed of social media and demand for rapid response minimize the potential for a long-run crisis response, where sometimes the best tactic is to say nothing. But saying or doing nothing is also a choice and has the potential to prompt new stories about "why leadership is stalling" or members are refusing to act. Journalists expect a quick turnaround for inquiries, and in online media, stories go live with or without a lawmaker's perspective. The perpetual engagement online by journalists and their audience furthers quick, blunt responses that again fail to fully mitigate a perceived crisis and further perpetuate the cycle.

As we conceptualize Congress and its capacity for governance in the 21st century, we have to consider how information moves through the institution, just as we consider the effects of policymaking capacity and party polarization. We must try to understand the communication climate that has steadily and over time become central to institutional organization. In 2009, the word "digital" came up in the US House office expenditures 28 times—mentioning digital goods, technology services, and office products. By early 2022, expenditure reports included the word "digital" approximately 1,369 times—now most often referencing digital directors, digital assistants, and contracts for digital services. The institution has always adapted to new media and new technology as new tools for representation and personalization offered lawmakers greater agenda-setting capabilities, but the framework for how we understand congressional communication in an era of Twitter and rapid response is best described by the crisis climate norms that shape the day-to-day operations of Congress.

What's a Crisis and Its Implications

A crisis, catalyzed by a number of factors, can be devastating to any organization, and Congress has to persistently prepare for anything that can reorient schedules or disrupt the political process. A crisis, while easy to identify post hoc, is notoriously difficult to define within the social sciences (Eastham et al., 1970). Also, inside each of these social science disciplines, there have been disagreements regarding how to define "crisis." A crisis can be defined as an unpredictable event that threatens stakeholders' expectancies and can seriously impact an organization's performance and generate negative outcomes (Coombs, 2015, p. 3). Additionally, a crisis can either be a small- or large-scale event that represents a biological/natural or a social/organizational threat (Frandsen & Johansen, 2022), with the latter being more common within a legislative setting.

In Congress, the capacity for managing digital communication has become the perpetual crisis that propels offices to engage with reporters and one another as if the routine exchange of information is a disaster response. Staff tasked with tracking information and monitoring Twitter for some new issue are constantly preparing for something to go viral that threatens their political agenda, the political calculus, or the reputation of a member. Some crises are operational—things happening around you like a global pandemic, a flood, or a terrorist attack—and draw in stakeholders to resolve the many externalities related to the crisis. Most notably, government agencies like Federal Emergency Management Agency have used social media as a tool for information dissemination amid natural disasters. In the wake of the COVID-19 crisis, lawmakers used their digital platforms to provide updates on health recommendations, economic relief, and emergency funding for families and businesses. But in Congress, the primary reason the institution operates using a crisis model has less to do with external crises and more to do with the images of those within the institution and the conflict inherent to a partisan political climate. These types of crises—also described as event-driven communication—are reputational, where there isn't necessarily anything physical that has happened, yet some response is still required, and often this type of crisis "breaks the digital world" as events unfold on social media (Coleman, 2020).

Situations do not create crises; rather, perceptions and rhetoric define these events (Windt, 1973). Perceptions are more important than reality in terms of how an audience or the public responds (Strömbäck & Nord, 2006), and the perception of high-stakes engagement online feeds that crisis framework.

Crisis communication in a political setting is patterned by politicians and the media contouring perceptions of the crisis and assigning blame or responsibility (Strömbäck & Kiousis, 2013). In turn, political communication crises are rarely about objective conditions, which matches the nonrepresentative reality of Twitter. Lawmakers and their respective political organizations are more likely to find themselves assigned responsibility for and tasked with mitigating crises outside their control (Strömbäck & Kiousis, 2013). The speed and viral nature of digital platforms mean that shifting blame persists without corrective action being taken or apologies being made—one reason the rapid cycling of digital communication continues. The power to address conflict in real time is one of the most appealing advantages of social media, but the high-velocity information exchange incentivizes risk-averse behavior that often perpetuates news cycles and introduces new information that could reorient schedules.

Crises can fall into three stages: precrisis (prevention and preparation), crisis event (recognition and containment), and postcrisis (evaluation and follow-up) (Cheng, 2018; Coombs, 2015). In a crisis, you traditionally have a prearranged plan that you can put into motion when disaster strikes. The basic tenets of this preparation involve a prepared statement and carefully constructed communications ready to acknowledge that you are finding and gathering information. But this precrisis planning does not occur in reality in Congress, where journalists demand quick action and Twitter drives the narrative.

For lawmakers and staff, responses beget more information and more unanswered questions that make it hard to create a consistent statement. For instance, in February 2022, the future of Democrats' "Build Back Better" legislation—$1.7 trillion in proposed social investments—was left in limbo amid conflicting messages by Senate Democrats. Before lunch one day, *Politico* reported that Democratic Senator Ron Wyden was talking to reporters about finding common ground on the proposal and working with West Virginia Democrat Joe Manchin, who became a vocal skeptic of the framework.[4] By the end of lunch, another reporter had caught sight of Manchin, asked him about what could go in the Build Back Better bill, and quickly turned to Twitter to report that Manchin confirmed Build Back Better was "dead." Within an hour and a couple tweets later, the narrative about potential legislation, what Democrats were focused on, and how we should think about next steps was changing again. Whatever prepared statements or

[4] *Politico*, https://www.politico.com/newsletters/playbook-pm/2022/02/01/manchin-on-bbb-its-dead-00004181.

language offices had about the progress on Build Back Better was no longer useful.

If you say that Build Back Better is "dead," that will drive the news cycle regardless of whether it is correct or is any different fundamentally than the information reported one month prior. Even with clarification or follow-up—which Twitter isn't really built for—the information exchange, however minor, still reorients the day for staff such that proactive messaging for that day or week gets pre-empted by lawmakers, and their staff have to respond to a sentence on Twitter.

In the case of the statement that "Build Back Better is dead," the senator was referring to the bill that had not advanced over a month ago, reiterating what had been true for a month, rather than forecasting any new developments on the issue. The context of his comment was irrelevant because it set off a chain reaction where both Manchin's office and party leadership had to provide further context and clarity, countering the narrative that their efforts to make legislative progress were all but dead on arrival. This type of media and Twitter-induced crisis, whether small or large, is a constant in Congress and often drives the dialogue in a Twitter ecosystem that is divorced from the realities of local communities and the mass public. And even without that spillover effect—even if this dialogue never affected a single message that ever reached a voter—it forever shapes how the political institution behaves, and those norms have indirect effects on both policymaking and representation.

Thinking about Congress as experiencing a crisis of communication considers both the operational perspective of crisis communication and a social constructionist view of strategic communications. Among US scholars, crisis communication is considered a subdiscipline in public relations and corporate communication—a function of organizational information dissemination (Coombs & Holladay, 2010, p. xxvi). Crises create a sense of immediacy and urgency (Kiewe, 1994). Congress has adopted a rapid response communication strategy to meet the speed and volume of the information flow within it. This organization-based perspective reflects how offices have structured themselves to address the increased attention to communication and persistent preparation for any potential crisis through viral content or collective responses by political stakeholders. Responses by these organizations fuel this crisis cycle, where offices continue to function in the precrisis and initial response phase such that postcrisis analysis, situational assessments, further explanation, and adaptive messaging are rarely realized as the cycle moves from one crisis to another.

Considering this crisis cycle from the social constructionist perspective is also key to understanding the context of congressional communication and how the era of Twitter has fueled these communication dynamics and incentives. The types of crises that perpetuate via social media are routinely organizational crises and crises of reputation that reflect the operations of the political institution and are socially constructed within this policymaking environment. Twitter offers a platform for a unique congressional communication ecosystem where crisis may arise and dissipate, with the potential for a within-network crisis to go viral online and spread beyond the stakeholders involved. This type of social media–driven crisis is defined by the many actors engaging online, and there are multiple meanings and frames for the crisis as lawmakers, journalists, and political actors attempt to define the scope of the issues and provide context. The implications of that crisis go far beyond how an office functions and affect how Congress operates, its capacity to do so, and the power of individual actors to shape the debate and dialogue. By considering the crisis as a social construct propelled by social media, we can take a more holistic approach to understanding how Twitter and technology have induced new communication strategies and influenced the persistence of crisis communication as a tool for strategic communications in a digital space.

Digital Adaptation to the Information Overload

Information is an abundant resource in Congress, with various stakeholders trying to advance their particular agenda or preferred narrative, but being able to triage that information and use it effectively is the key for communication managers. Members of Congress, staff, and journalists are part of an ongoing exchange of information that can disrupt the decision-making process and narrate the terms of debate. In Congress, information is powerful because stakeholders can leverage that information for political power and personal success (Curry, 2015). Private businesses, lobbyists, federal agencies, and other elite actors compete to supply information to Congress (Baumgartner & Jones, 1993; Jones & Baumgartner, 2005; Jenkins-Smith & Sabatier, 1993), and that information increasingly moves through digital networks with the capacity to gain more volume and speed. For many offices, the choice is less about what to engage with but rather what to ignore. Congress has adapted to the digital information climate, utilizing limited resources to develop digital practices and bolster creative content in ways that align with their policy, political, and personal preferences. Lawmakers and their staff are faced with a never-ending list of demands on their time, so what information they choose to highlight through their many communication channels signals what matters most to them and conveys important information about the priorities of that office.

Twitter and digital tools are central to how congressional offices track the high-speed information flow in Congress. Congress's persistent readiness mirrors that of a crisis or disaster response, yet many crisis communication theories and models do not traditionally consider the impact of Twitter despite the many ways the platform fundamentally shapes engagement, offering both new incentives and new threats. More recently, social media platforms such as Wikipedia, Twitter, Facebook, Pinterest, and Google Plus have been ushering in a "new era of crisis communication" that shapes the relationships between organizations and stakeholders (Cheng, 2018). Crisis information spreads rapidly and influences society through social media (Cheng, 2020), and Congress is no exception to this phenomenon. In many ways, platforms like Twitter present a unique challenge, a "double-edged sword" that brings both opportunities and challenges for communication (Cheng, 2018). From one perspective, social media can help an institution monitor crises, spur new conversations with variable audiences, cultivate trust and maintain relationships, and create greater transparency (Cheng, 2020; Jin & Liu, 2010; Macias et al., 2009). For example, the Select Committee to Investigate the January 6th Attack is a notable instance of congressional communicators using a platform like Twitter to bolster their institutional operations. Throughout the hearings conducted in June and July 2022, the committee's Twitter account regularly promoted its work and paired digital content in real time with hearing testimony. On the Sunday before a hearing in July, the committee's Twitter account promoted appearances on *Meet the Press* and *Face the Nation* to preview the following week's hearings, connecting traditional media and social media as part of its larger communication strategy. During the hearings, the account shared key video clips and graphics detailing new information. During the interview of former White House aide Cassidy Hutchinson, the account shared a live feed and video highlights of the witness testimony that garnered tens of thousands of likes and shares.

But also inherent to social media is misinformation, nasty rumors, negativity, and amplified emotions that threaten crisis managers' ability to control official messages when new content emerges (Liu et al., 2011; Wigley & Fontenot, 2010). During the first Trump presidency, Delaware Representative John Larson warned that angry political rhetoric in Congress can have dangerous consequences, and the events of January 6th are evidence to that cautionary tale. But even beyond physical violence, Twitter is regularly the place for lawmakers to "let 'er rip" when it comes to taking political jabs at partisan opposition. Social media has become a vehicle for political anger that can fuel partisanship, racial resentment, and misinformation (Ballard et al., 2022a; Russell, 2018). For example, some senators suggested they were "just asking questions" when spreading misinformation about COVID-19 vaccinations.[5]

Twitter is both the problem and the solution in this type of communication scenario where the ability to quickly address one issue is also just as likely to create additional concerns. And the mere potential for content to become viral at any moment requires a permanent sense of readiness. But the transition to this digital crisis climate is not an abrupt shift or reflection of drastically evolved norms in Congress. For decades, lawmakers have been carefully crafting their own media presence, increasingly independent of political parties (Kernell, 2006). The media landscape is continually evolving and splintering audiences such that politicians are constantly trying to become more entrepreneurial and efficient with their presentation efforts, whether on television, on radio, or online (Sellers, 2000). The power to disseminate news and shape the narrative is central to lawmakers' efforts to brand themselves both within and outside of Congress (Manheim, 1991; Sellers, 2000). The ability to shape public information has long been tied to electoral goals; with YouTube and livestreamed events having become the reality, lawmakers now have to increasingly juggle content across multiple public relations platforms (Cook, 1989; Cormack, 2016; Evans et al., 2014; Grimmer, 2010).

Implications of Crisis Communication

Social media is both the accelerant and the extinguisher when it comes to the crisis of communication in Congress. In the era of social media, the ability of organizations and individuals to quickly respond to a crisis is unmatched (Bennett & Iyengar, 2008), but new platforms also generate new risks and new opportunities for crises to take hold (Coombs, 2014). In Congress, this crisis of communications threatens the institution's ability to function, in terms of both the resources required to manage a digital operation and the political incentives that a platform like Twitter integrates into the norms of Congress.

[5] https://www.cnn.com/2021/05/07/politics/ron-johnson-vaccine-misinformation-fact-check/index.html

Asymmetric Resources and Priorities

In a digital congressional environment, the autonomy to set and promote an agenda remains constrained by available resources and institutional design. Congressional rules, structures, and norms affect legislative outcomes by directing the distribution of power and resources (Anzia & Jackman, 2013; Wawro & Schickler, 2007), which extends to lawmakers' communication efforts. For the average member of Congress, the cost of information paired with limited resources makes it difficult to stay informed about pending policy (Curry, 2015). Party and committee leaders have an informational advantage (Bianco, 1997; Box-Steffensmeier et al., 2015; Stratmann, 2000) because of their additional resources. These policy and information asymmetries extend to the communication strategy because being effective and visible across multiple digital platforms is increasingly prioritized. Success in office and within the institution is now pursued through digital communications in a way that seeking out local newspaper coverage or airtime on radio could never sustain. Members pick their battles about prioritizing issues and devoting attention to policy and representation (Furnas et al., 2021; Hall, 1998; LaPira et al., 2020; Russell, 2021a). These resources both directly and indirectly shape their policymaking behavior, their relationship with party leadership, and their communication strategy (Anderson et al., 2020; Curry, 2015; Russell, 2021a).

Communication plays an increasingly important role in lawmakers' success or failure in Congress. As one congressional staffer described it, they are constantly watching the analytics of their message, just like when selling a product, except this time they are selling legislation rather than a product (Interview 116). But the public relations costs of promoting legislation and political brands often exceed the capacity of a single office and lead lawmakers and staff to look for communication support—what I term a "communication subsidy." The emphasis on professionalized communications combined with the limited resources within each office facilitates party leadership's communication influence, distinct from their policymaking influence, based on their ability to provide information to congressional offices via their digital communication efforts. In reality, this means that party and committee leadership have the digital and communications staff required to provide materials and training to rank-and-file offices that lack the capacity to staff and fund a digitally minded communications shop. Materials come in the form of shared press toolkits, digital graphics, sample text, and prioritized messaging by the party. Support and training for digital communication are also managed by party leaders, as they provide invites for Google and Facebook platform training or produce digital fellowship programs to slowly build a capable cohort of digital staffers. The asymmetry in communication resources places party and committee leaders in a position of power because it allows them to lead the messaging for the chamber, advance their own priorities, and create dependency through the support they offer to those resource-poor offices. Congressional offices are given a fixed amount of money for staff, communications, and office management such that even with the rise of electronic communications, the budget remains a constraint on representation. I further flesh out the implications of leadership's communication power in Chapter 5 by delving into the ways leadership can supplement digital efforts and how those lawmakers with resources present a fundamentally different rhetorical agenda on Twitter.

Perpetuating Partisan Conflict

Some scholars refer to a crisis as a political weapon (Coombs, 2007), and in Congress, tools that convey power are most prized. Situations become crises because political actors define them as such. One tactic, crisis exploitation, relies on the strategic use of crisis rhetoric to alter levels of political support for elected offices and associated political agendas (Boin et al., 2008, 2009). A crisis has the potential to delegitimize the authority of those in powerful positions, and for those seeking to disrupt the political status quo, a crisis can be a useful environment for politically delegitimizing rhetoric (Klein, 2007). A culture of crisis communication leads to political opportunity windows for those challenging established policies or powerful political opposition (Birkland, 2006; Keeler, 1993; Klein, 2007). In other words, a crisis can become a political weapon used to hurt political careers or promote policy changes. The ability to meet the information demand creates an opportunity to wield power as what it means to be successful in Congress can be increasingly defined through digital presentation. A crisis climate isn't conducive to creativity or fresh thinking, so to meet the information demand during a crisis, lawmakers and their staff rely on familiar tactics like partisan politics for engagement. Polarization and partisan conflict are pervasive within Congress, and the changing media climate and new digital tactics for engagement both reinforce and provide new venues for that partisan warfare. Hyperpartisanship in Congress extends from the legislative process into lawmakers' strategic communications. Those working in and around Congress have watched as this conflict and partisanship have become the primary frame for congressional narratives. Describing the changing political climate during the mid-2000s, one staffer noted a reporting style that placed a higher emphasis on conflict than policymaking accomplishments (Interview 7). The partisan conflict and the back and forth between majority and minority lawmakers are not new, but during the shift to a Twitter-driven information climate, "the sensationalism, the ideological leanings, and partisanship all went through the roof" (Interview 135).

Those staff who are tasked with tracking the daily dialogue on Twitter believe that "there's always a certain amount of partisanship, but I think the partisanship is, is a lot starker," and they attribute that in equal parts to media change, changing communication norms, members' self-perceptions of their success, and what those members think they need to do to get reelected (Interview 137). When you combine those dynamics with the resource asymmetries inherent to congressional offices, staffers don't mince words: "Lack of investment, that lack of capacity and resources given—combine that with hyperpartisanship—it's a recipe for disaster" (Interview 65).

A Twitter-driven communication climate has incentivized rapid responses and limited time for detail-oriented policies while appealing to specific digital constituencies that fuel partisan conflict (Tromble, 2018). Senators' choices about how to make partisan appeals to a digital constituency shape not only representation but also the institution itself and the type of information that is valued among stakeholders. Congressional cache and clout are a function of power not only within the institution but also within the broader political dialogue. Adding digital power to the established norms for institutional and party power fuels a crisis climate as members and their staff inevitably have to look for ways to manage their work or seek advantages given the new norms for engagement and communication. In Congress, being able to kill opposition legislation is just as important as building it, and increasingly that effort to quell a political agenda is done over social media or digital communication (Interview 114). Finding ways to elevate a lawmaker's voice amid the noise leaves many relying on familiar, politically divisive tactics to navigate a still relatively new digital climate. Twitter is where the policy and political game collide as policy presentation and political posturing can easily go hand in hand. For many lawmakers, this can take the form of turning to political shots and familiar partisan talking points, turning anger and partisan conflict into reputation-building efforts that don't require the research and vetting of policy statements. Congress exists within a digital communication climate that demands accessibility, enables a preponderance of partisan attacks, and incentivizes the perpetual game of blame avoidance.

Conclusion

Scholars have increasingly studied the effect of social media on our elections, our democratic norms, and effective partisanship, but just as impactful is the integration of social media into our policymaking institutions. New technology has persistently disrupted institutional norms and forced policymakers to adopt new practices, but the digital shift toward Twitter has prompted lawmakers to turn further inward, speaking to advocates and political insiders rather than making constituent connections. In 2009, the Congressional Research Service published one of the first assessments of member use of Twitter—"Social Networking and Constituent Communications"—framing digital tools as a mechanism for constituent outreach. They argue that new media technologies could "enhance the ability of Members of Congress to fulfill their representational duties by providing greater opportunities for communication between the Member and individual constituents."[6] But that constituent-centered digital reality never came to be. Members are certainly "spreading information about public policy and government operations," but they do so among an elite community. More than a decade later, the fable of courting constituents on Twitter has all but disappeared as most lawmakers and staff see reporters and copartisans as the primary audience.

Social media and digital platforms bring new challenges for government, including image management issues and fragmented media channels, that fuel the climate of crisis communication (Gilpin, 2010; Liu & Fraustino, 2014). A key to understanding digital media's effect on American political institutions is acknowledging and explaining its ramifications for congressional capacity and representation. Congress is one of many institutions where the everyday norms of governance have adapted to the digital trends in media, and policy staff track Twitter to consider the news of the day and the schedule of votes. Social media is not an outlier in the impact that technology can have on our political institutions—C-SPAN forever changed accessibility to Congress more than 40 years ago. The fundamental change with social media is not in the novelty of access or direction of change but rather its scope and magnitude. Social media, specifically Twitter, has neither redirected communications nor reoriented relationships but rather brought them to the brink and fueled a speed of interaction that is unprecedented for an

[6] Congressional Research Service Report R43018, https://www.everycrsreport.com/reports/R43018.html.

institution that was never designed for speed or efficiency (i.e., the Senate filibuster). But each time political institutions adapt, information flows change and actors engage with one another in new ways to reflect the changing political environment. The changing nature of digital political engagement is most readily visible during the campaign cycle, but those changes also bring new transparency and immediacy to the work done by lawmakers long after the election is over.

3

A History of Playing Catch-Up in Congressional Communication

It's no secret that Congress is an 18th-century institution using 20th-century technology to solve 21st-century problems,[1] but when you add in an evolving digital media climate, the story about how Congress communicates gets complicated. The Twitter-driven norms for daily engagement within the institution didn't come out of thin air, as lawmakers have always adapted, albeit slowly, to new opportunities for media access, engagement, and, ultimately, added autonomy. In the 1970s, districts were clipping local papers and faxing them into DC. In the 1980s, C-SPAN became a regular feature, offering new access to the policy process, while newspapers like *USA Today* were moving quicker and with shorter stories. In the 1990s, satellite TV and the internet brought changes in accessibility that continued into the 2000s as websites, blogs, and "new media" became regular tools for reputation building. It's not that Congress is averse to new media technology—the appeal of new constituencies, both at home and globally, continues to drive lawmakers to explore alternative mediums for their message. The national reputation and successful strategy of Representative Alexandria Ocasio-Cortez would not have been plausible without a media climate that increasingly enables members of Congress to shape their message from within rather than relying on gatekeepers from the outside.

But Congress was not an institution designed with digital in mind, so carving out space for lawmakers and their offices to become individual news dissemination operations means a protracted effort by political leaders and their staff to keep pushing the ball forward. Digital advancement in Congress has more to do with how party leaders leverage advantages, how rank-and-file members jockey for attention, and how journalists master the art of a "scooplet"—a tiny news nugget—on Twitter. Over the last 40 years, Congress has adapted to satellite television, cable news, email, and online blogging—all examples of an institution attempting to retrofit its historic norms for a

[1] https://twitter.com/ModernizeCmte/status/1173699852947066883

Tweeting Scared. Annelise Russell, Oxford University Press. © Oxford University Press (2025).
DOI: 10.1093/9780197808344.003.0003

modern media atmosphere. Much of this change stems from party leadership with the resources and capacity to navigate new technology, seek out new agenda-setting measures, and provide a roadmap for offices. Digital politics and communications shifts have long been fueled by party leaders and their priorities—contributing to the constrained communication capacity of members who comparatively lack the resources or time to make a similar investment in digital. Gingrich and C-SPAN both arrived in Congress in 1979, and over time the former Speaker learned "how to exploit the unblinking television eye in the House . . . revealing himself to be one of the smartest chiefs in the global village" (Seelye, 1994). Nancy Pelosi made more subtle yet equally impactful moves as Speaker when she embraced "new media" to consider messaging across blogs, YouTube, and an increasingly fractured media climate. Pelosi carved out her own niche in the blogosphere and "rivaled President George W. Bush and the presidential candidates through much of 2008" (Peters & Rosenthal, 2010). In the Senate, Chuck Schumer had to corral his own media operation, reconceptualizing the Senate Democratic Media Center, to respond to the Twitter-driven Trump presidency and the increasing digital demands within his Senate caucus.

Changes are not always easy, and they aren't always welcome. In debating whether Senate proceedings should be covered live, Rhode Island Democrat Claiborne Pell once proclaimed, "Television will lead to more, longer, and less relevant speeches, to more posturing by Senators and to even less useful debate and efficient legislating than we have today." Fast forward to Twitter, and the late senator looks like a fortune teller. If you listen to podcasts, watch cable news, or even watch late-night comedy, social media is central to your information diet because tweets become fodder for political and policy news. Journalists, writers, and celebrities—a network of "interest actors" (Moses, 2023)—use Twitter to redirect information for the masses, which becomes part of the public dialogue.

The uptake of digital tools for communicating within and about Congress began years before President Trump normalized Twitter as a policy tool, and understanding what led to a disinformation-fueled January insurrection on the Capitol is just as critical as knowing what comes next. In this chapter, I explore the evolution of new media adoption in Congress and use interviews with congressional staffers and journalists to explain how party leadership has guided their members through different eras of digital advancement. Even as new technology expanded the reach of members to a national audience, the power of access and the technology tools necessary to achieve access have always been tied to party leaders' priorities. Party leaders are not the causal mechanism in digital media adaptation, but they grease the skids along the way. I explain why Newt Gingrich selling his "Contract for America" on national TV and the ability to build a political persona via the internet are both part of a longer story about how a political institution evolves while also forgoing any sort of restructuring or meaningful resource allocation to meet the actual demand of that technology revolution. Communications staffers have persistently adapted to new roles and new platforms, constantly being expected to pull in new audiences and build a more robust brand for their bosses. I expand on previous scholarship on digital technology adoption to explain how Congress reached this crisis of communication that asks elected officials to be media producers on top of their policy and constituent service responsibilities. Lawmakers and their staff have been systematically presenting themselves to constituents through their messages for decades but also taking advantage of technology to change the definition of "constituents" beyond just registered voters in a specific district. I detail how Congress has consistently broadened opportunities to present policy and political priorities to an expansive audience.

Satellite TV Changes the Rules of the Game

For most of history social interaction has been face to face, but in a political world that is increasingly mediated, we search for new interactions that shape the ways we understand one another. Political leaders are now visible—and have the capacity to increase visibility—in ways never before realized. Simply watching television is a form of interaction, and the normalization of television within the halls of Congress reshaped the way members interacted with each other and the public. Even today, the choices that members make about how they present on the floor are conditioned by the potential for increasingly national media coverage, for example, Representative Katie Porter color coordinating while subtly throwing shade during a highly publicized vote for House Speaker (Figure 3.1).

The biggest technology changes in the institution have not come from within but rather from a transition from the media environment that extends outside Congress, and that started with television (Interview 2). The shift toward mass media and radio has changed the political calculus for many politicians over time. President Calvin Coolidge's "Silent Cal" persona was carried out on radio, giving him an effective platform for his message that matched his preferred presentation style. Digital shifts in congressional communication are similarly punctuated by lawmakers positioning themselves for TV coverage and entering people's homes on a regular basis.

Figure 3.1 Democratic Representative Katie Porter of California reads a book during the January 2023 House of Representatives Speaker vote
Source: Twitter.

The scariest place in Congress quickly became the narrow space between a communication-savvy member of Congress and a camera as they realized the power to shape and narrate their priorities for a mass audience. Technology changes people's behavior, and in the 1990s, Newt Gingrich changed the rhythm of Congress in more ways than just through his conservative politics or policies. It's hard to tell a story of congressional development throughout the modern era without noting the effect of Speaker Gingrich and how he built (and potentially lost) a powerful political persona based on attention and spectacle.

As a member of the Conservative Opportunity Society, Gingrich, before he took over the House, and his colleagues capitalized on the relatively new C-SPAN cameras by using provocative partisan language that generated thousands of voter phone calls. As *The Atlantic* described it, "Gingrich recruited a cadre of young bomb throwers—a group of 12 congressmen he christened the Conservative Opportunity Society—and together they stalked the halls of Capitol Hill, searching for trouble and TV cameras."[2] The former Speaker left an outsized legislative and messaging footprint that continues to pattern behavior in both the House and Senate (Green & Crouch, 2022; Theriault, 2013). The partisan warrior behavior and the notion that positions of power were something to publicly campaign for shifted the norms of these institutions. Power and position were not just something to be earned but something to angle for such that the political gamesmanship was unending. "Chairman don't get chosen, at least on the Republican side, purely on seniority anymore. They get chosen because they have to campaign for it and get, you know, other members to support them" (Interview 37). Gingrich reoriented party leadership and centralized decision-making—shaping the trajectory of policymaking within the House of Representatives for decades.

> With the Gingrich era, a lot of the rules, reforms that were enacted in that time in 1995, moving forward, really got rid of a lot of the policy and steering committees that had a lot of legislative power and leverage. And when you do that, you weakened individual offices, and they became "yes or no" people as opposed to individual lawmakers that can really work together. (Interview 65)

He infused a sense of partisanship in the procedural action within the chamber, and those choices were carried over to the Senate by the members who lived through and experienced the power of those House shifts (Theriault, 2013). But the power of those changes and the reason they remain salient today are related to how Gingrich sought and captured media attention. Gingrich told supporters, "The No. 1 fact about the news media is they love fights.... When you give them confrontations, you get attention; when you get attention, you can educate." (Coppins, 2018) Former leaders like Tip O'Neill took an "all politics is local" approach, while Gingrich proved that traditional power structures could be countered by nationalized media highlighting partisan conflict (Green & Crouch, 2022). Previously, the visibility of Congress was often the purview of AP and Reuters stringers who sat in smoke-filled rooms with congressional committee leaders who wielded ultimate power over both policy and political levers. Local journalists would wait for faxes from representatives who could comment on a new project or what legislation meant for those in the district. Gingrich flipped the script and used technology to do it all. Gingrich believed that reporters preferred to cover partisan

[2] https://www.theatlantic.com/magazine/archive/2018/11/newt-gingrich-says-youre-welcome/570832/

conflict and that a skillful member of Congress could use that to their advantage (Green & Crouch, 2022). Conflict, and the growing audience for that conflict, could be used as a political weapon. "Gingrich found ways to put on a show. He recognized an opportunity in the newly installed C-SPAN cameras, and began delivering tirades against Democrats to an empty chamber, knowing that his remarks would be beamed to viewers across the country" (Coppins, 2018).

Political entrepreneurs need resources to pursue their goals, and for Gingrich, television was a powerful tool to capture attention and audiences. Weeks after Gingrich was elected Speaker, the famous O. J. Simpson trial began, capturing the attention of hundreds of millions. Gingrich used the accessibility of satellite TV to tap into the ongoing digital transition the country had been adapting to throughout the modern political era. For those in Congress, the pace of news and information picked up after Gingrich became leader, such that many House Republicans had more press calls than they ever had before. One former staffer described this transition as "PTSD" just a week after taking the majority under Gingrich (Interview 132). These members had long been in the minority, and staff were unprepared for the information deluge they faced. Gingrich amplified the information overload by normalizing new communication avenues, newsletters, audiotapes, and lectures that allowed him to construct and shape the political agenda coming out of Congress (Green & Couch, 2022). Pairing his investment in messaging with his skills for oratory and debate proved to be a watershed moment for how leaders prioritize messaging and support their own initiatives. And with the transition to a more media-savvy Republican conference came a new generation of press staff, many of whom only had experience in a campaign setting and often didn't have the background to engage with the journalists on the Hill. This disconnect between lawmaking and communication expertise frustrated many journalists early on: "Under Gingrich, because what I suddenly saw was insane, were a lot of new, young, inexperienced press people. They had no press back background. They were uninterested in learning exactly how the press [in Washington] worked" (Interview 44).

The news frenzy became the new normal and over time evolved into today's digital crisis of communication, but the effect of party leadership becoming both a policy and messaging force reflects the further centralization of leadership where leaders wield both policy and presentation power. No longer were committee leaders pulling rank by controlling the number of opportunities their members got in front of a TV camera (Interview 42). The political circus had come to stay, and that provided easier and more compelling television than updates on House Committee on Energy and Commerce hearings.

Gingrich was able to use his attention-grabbing tactics to propel him into leadership, but for the average member of Congress, these tactics remain beyond their capacity, and the power went with Gingrich. Despite the satellite transmission capability that gave individual members the chance to go on camera for the local TV station, members largely lacked the capacity to create the personas and fodder that would garner media attention. Gingrich centralized leadership via a cult of personality, but even after Gingrich left, the messaging power never diffused back out to the members of their conference. As one former staffer noted, "That centralization of leadership—it makes it more difficult for members to either stand out, make a name for themselves, so that they can move up slowly. . . . It's not a Republican problem. It's not a Democrat problem. It's a both parties problem because it's the way our system incentivizes lawmakers' sustained power" (Interview 65).

Future leaders in the House and Senate took many lessons from Gingrich's rise to power, and while many of them chose a less obvious attention-seeking press strategy, they realized just how much power could be gained from shaping and controlling the narrative coming out of Congress. Other members would adopt and carry forward Gingrich's procedural tactics (see *The Gingrich Senators*), but the role of a party leader in navigating the political agenda in an increasingly digital and networked media climate is strongly tied to the experience of a Gingrich-led House.

New Access: The Internet, Email, and "New Media" in Congress

In the summer of 1993, the House of Representatives entered the internet era by setting up an email pilot program that allowed seven members of Congress to communicate with their constituents through email—and no surprise, one of those members was Newt Gingrich.[3] When external email began in the mid-1990s, this permitted the public to contact member offices 24 hours a day—providing a new level of accessibility to Congress. But just as important as the ability to connect the public to member offices was the ability for member offices to connect with each other and the other policy actors within the federal government and policymaking subsystems. Twenty years after the pilot program began, members were getting thousands of digital messages per week. "I would say, if we got of those, you know, 2,000, 3,000 incoming messages a week, probably 90% were email and then maybe 10%

[3] https://thehill.com/policy/technology/235344-a-brief-history-of-congress-and-email/

physical mail. And so definitely, mostly email" (Interview 40). The addition of digital options, even for traditional press tools like press releases, didn't replace a press shop's activities but rather expanded them. As one journalist described, the amount of press releases became unending and often ended up in reporters' inboxes (or trash) on a daily basis.

> When I started out, you got information, either from press releases, or being on Capitol Hill, either for a hearing or to do, to go to a scheduled interview. And we were highly dependent on interaction with both members and Hill staff. To me, the big difference today is that I guess I'd say there are more press releases than ever. You know, it's hard to even think back that far, where, you know, you know, press releases, if you use them, came in mail. Not a, not an email . . . so to me, the biggest change is, first of all, you get all these press releases by email. (Interview 45)

The next digital media test leaders faced was both the promise and threat of the internet, where traditional media and "new media" were coming together to present lawmakers with new options for messaging and engagement. New access meant new kinds of internal monitoring and information sharing. Most communications staff were monitoring local news, radio stations, and television, but with the internet, the way that offices could monitor information—and engage with it—changed. The days of *USA Today* throwing parties with "big shrimp and more food" were gone as newspapers struggled to move online and Congress began looking beyond print pages (Interview 1).

When it comes to digital transitions, many people point to the role of the Howard Dean campaign in utilizing digital for political purposes. From the Dean to the Obama campaign, that transition ushered in an era of "new media" where things like blogs, early social media, and online fundraising took hold. Additionally, congressional leaders had noted Gingrich's successes and failures with this media onslaught and made cautiously optimistic moves to engage a digital community. Individual member offices tried new things and offered anecdotal accounts of what was possible online, but leaders were the ones with the capacity to reorient communication norms and shift communication strategies for the caucus and institution more broadly. Nancy Pelosi was the first to upload content to YouTube while she and her Republican contemporaries were trying to figure out how to manage the influx of "new media" journalists and online outlets.

The internet as a primary mechanism for information sharing wasn't a given, as many were skeptical of its appeal for strategic messaging. In 2006, former Alaska Senator Ted Stevens famously noted that the internet was just a "series of tubes," and journalists labeled the federal government a "technology skeptic."[4] Representative Patrick McHenry noted in 2014 that government is usually a decade behind in technology and that a "lurching bureaucracy" is not doing anything to speed up the digital advancement (NextGov, 2014). But aside from Representative Darrel Issa crawling under desks to serve as impromptu tech support, the institution adapts to engage with and filter the deluge of information pouring into and around Congress via digital means.

Despite the hesitancy of some members, a number of leaders across both parties saw advantages to using digital tools. Leaders perceived new technology as a way both to harness a political narrative that would lead to political success and to exert political power and maximize their reach. While Nancy Pelosi is not known for her oratory skills and certainly does not have the same skill set as Gingrich, she was able to pull a "Calvin Coolidge" so to speak by taking advantage of technology to fit her own goals and her personal skills as a lawmaker. Coolidge didn't have the impassioned speechmaking of his predecessors, but his more constrained rhetorical style perfectly fit the incentives and constraints of radio.

Senator Harry Reid, in response to losses in 2004, put together a "war room" to bring progressives together and speak to the local bloggers back home. According to one former Senate communicator, "The Senate is always quick to break any kind of new technology that allows them to communicate to their constituents" (Interview 2). Reid's war room brought together senior staffers across the Senate to counter the bully pulpits of the Republican-run White House, Senate, and House. Through these efforts, Reid used his resources to support communication with online reporters. The Senate had shifted from an era marked by great statesmen like Teddy Kennedy who couldn't work a Blackberry to save his life to one marked by senators looking for new ways to engage online communities (Interview 108).

Digital communication is often thought of in political or partisan messaging, but much of the early logistics of messaging was actually bipartisan in the effort to revise congressional rules to allow for digital messaging. "Republicans and Democrats, particularly in the early years and on the staff side, were trying to rewrite the internal rules to do stuff. It was a united front" (Interview 173). Many of the staffers and early digital staff came to DC with interests in websites or computer science, so the political-driven narrative of digital emerged later. The messaging largely evolved with the technology,

[4] https://www.nextgov.com/ideas/2014/09/congress-basically-still-your-grandparents-when-it-comes-internet/95468/

particularly between 2000 and 2010, when there was shift from a limited digital presence to full engagement online. That limited digital presence was not just a matter of public-facing communication, but also internal communication, where recently elected Whip Nancy Pelosi realized that there was a niche to be carved out in internal digital communication as well. Whereas Gingrich's media presence often ruffled feathers within his own conference, Pelosi aimed to build greater connections.

> She understood the power of that type of technology changing, and you can't live in San Francisco without seeing that in every element. And so she knew that technology was changing. And that Congress was not taking advantage of it. And so as kind of a first step, the first thing we did was build the first house intranet, which was literally like a Craigslist for House bills and talking points and democratic policy committee materials. (Interview 173)

The ability to share information across the institution, without going through traditional channels or in-person meetings, was a relatively novel change of pace in Congress. As one staffer described it, "Every member and every staff want different levels of information. And at that time, there was no way to make information accessible to people in the format that they wanted" (Interview 173). For Pelosi, as a prospective leader, she was able to bring that to the table and meet the needs of the caucus as a whole. Her investment in digital both served her own purposes of message maintenance and laid the foundation for digital investment that would play out for the next 20 years.

Republican leaders such as Eric Cantor, Steve Scalise, and Paul Ryan were proactive in hiring press and strategic communications staff who recognized how digital platforms could further their goals, and those staffers actively worked to realize that potential within the GOP conference. Cantor's office, for example, targeted staffers from the Heritage Foundation to bolster the conference's social media efforts, strategically leveraging digital tools to promote the party's agenda (Interview 115). The Heritage Foundation was building a robust digital presence, and Cantor was attuned to the shifting media landscape and saw the value of social media in engaging with journalists on Capitol Hill. A former Republican staffer noted that Cantor grasped the reasons behind their digital initiatives and viewed social media as a crucial channel for communicating with the media (Interview 115). Eventually frictions between Cantor's and Boehner's staffs lessened and there was a collaborative effort among House GOP leadership to establish more sophisticated communication norms. Cantor's commitment to digital innovation was evident in his collaboration with Democrat Steny Hoyer to organize the inaugural Congressional Hackathon in 2011. This event aimed to encourage the integration of digital technology into congressional practices.

For leaders and their caucuses to engage the way they wanted to, the antiquity of Congress proved problematic. New technologies have repeatedly tested Congress's adaptability; they create challenges in the form of new expectations, perverse incentives, and disruptions.[5] Many of the rules in Congress did not initially allow for the type of digital presentation we have come to expect today. "There were staffers who understood platforms like YouTube, there were staffers who understood kind of what was going on. But none of the institutional rules provided for the changing media landscape" (Interview 173).

For example, the rules on franking—official communications funded by members—limited pictures in newsletters such that no more than one-third of a page could be a photo, and those rules were applied to websites such that there was no capacity for flashy splash pages with photos. The institution was using analog guidance for digital performance. The rules were largely based on an institution where, in 1969, there were only three computers on the entire Capitol campus. By the start of the 106th Congress (1999–2001), freshman member orientation was supplemented with a computer tutorial featuring House office buildings and the Capitol.

Blogs were one of the next changes in technology that drove many in party leadership to consider the role of "new media" as a means for moving their message. Blogs were considered a way to reach new communities—much in the same way that lawmakers today reach out to TikTok influencers because they have followers and communities of potential supporters. As one former communications staffer described it, in the beginning, rapid-response, digital communications were separate from traditional communications.

> What that meant, right, was that typically the press secretary was more like the speech writer. And the communications director was setting overall strategy for the office, and also serving as on-the-record spokesperson. And then somebody whose title was something like "director of new media" or "deputy director of new media" was actually dealing with "online media." And really at the time, it fell into three buckets. One was Twitter. Two was blog, were blogs. And three were online-only reporters. (Interview 107)

[5] https://techpolicy.press/bots-in-congress-the-risks-and-benefits-of-emerging-ai-tools-in-the-legislative-branch/

Congressional staff were reaching out to the blogger community, and communications staff within offices were repurposing content for blog posts to spread their message and increase engagement. At one point, early in the transition to blogs, the online media reporters with credentials were from *Talking Points Memo* and the *Huffington Post* (Interview 107). For conservative media, the *Drudge Report* became the biggest megaphone for anything on the right, and the way *Drudge* found stories was through online media. To give a sense of the outsized role that bloggers could play, one blogger recalled a conference call around 2006 with the Republican candidates for Speaker that, as he described, didn't go well for former Speaker John Boehner's competition and is one of the reasons why Boehner rose to Republican leadership (Interview 135).

Digital Era: Convincing People Twitter Wasn't a Phase

Early on, doing digital looked a lot more like information technology support and systems administration. As one staffer described it, the person who ran the website, ran the digital newsletters, and managed email was the same person who made sure the computers worked (Interview 151). Many of these folks were hired as traditional communications staff but had an interest in computer science or technology, so they naturally shifted. And while digital is still gaining more prominence and respect within offices, early on people were being actively directed away from digital because it wasn't considered a serious path for staff within Congress. Senior staff were telling folks that "you didn't want to dirty yourself with that and get pigeonholed. 'You're better than that' was sort of the implication" (Interview 151). Among senior lawmakers and staff, there was a perceived risk "that it would make the organization less serious," but as one staffer quipped, "they ended up doing [that] by themselves anyways!" (Interview 118).

The push toward digital integration was often driven by the need to surpass opposing parties' digital efforts (Macdonald & Russell, 2024). After the institutional rules changed to allow for digital practices, Twitter and partisan media became prime outlets for political gamesmanship. If one side invested in digital promotion, the other side felt compelled to follow suit. If a Republican office was promoting a digital person, then Democratic staffers could go back to their boss and say, "Hey, this is what they are doing and we need to match or best that." So while the advancement of digital has largely been at the behest of partisan leadership, there is some diffusion across offices that pushed the role of digital staff further than it might have otherwise gone.

As one former staffer described, the backdrop for a lot of this transition was simply moving from traditional press norms to digital and email norms.

> Every Monday morning, I would send out an email to the, to the press back home. Every six months or so I would just do a quick survey . . . what we were doing that was helpful and what we might consider doing, so these Monday emails sort of evolved based on that feedback. And so the first thing I would do is just sort of highlight here are the big votes that we're gonna have this week. As the media continues to cut positions of local papers, it's harder and harder for them to cover, so a lot of them are just picking up wire stories about national news. But if they know that there's a vote coming, now they know that maybe we can grab a quote from your release and drop it into this wire story. Sometimes they would have a local angle that we weren't aware of, which not only helped us realize maybe this is something we should focus on more, but maybe we want to make a floor speech about this, because now we're aware of this local angle that we weren't before. (Interview 14)

And then social media changed everything—abruptly: "It was baptism by fire. I mean you go in, it's fast paced. And that was even in 2007. But you've just got to dive in and learn and adjust on the fly. And it's exciting and incredibly fast paced. It only got faster."[6]

Early notions of social media benefits centered on increased access to constituents. Reports by the Congressional Research Service detailed how, in 2011, members were using social media to connect with their audiences back home. Social networking services were expected to enhance the ability of lawmakers to "fulfill their representational duties" by providing greater opportunities for communication between members and individual constituents with limited additional costs.[7] But the realization that social media "was not real life" meant that offices were no longer just thinking about Twitter in terms of their local relationships. "The number one way they interface with constituents is less through social media, actually more through just responding to people who email in directly. I usually get between 2,000 and 3,000 messages a week, and a lot of people send form letters back to constituents" (Interview 140).

If you ask folks what kicked off the social media era in Congress, they all give different answers, but there are a few common refrains. Many associate it with the presidential campaign cycle and President Barack Obama's win, noting the changes in both Democratic and Republican networks that

[6] Tara Dijulio Oral History, https://www.senate.gov/about/oral-history/dijulio-tara-oral-history.htm.

[7] Congressional Research Service Report R43018, https://crsreports.congress.gov/product/pdf/R/R43018.

began around 2008. They talk about the digital game the candidate built, the announcements that went to people's new "smart" phones, and the fundraising that occurred online. While governing lacks the fundraising component, members of Congress also saw the ability to reach new and different audiences through digital means. Early on, the novelty of social media was that it provided the ability to engage directly with followers and curate content outside of the media, but quickly people realized that the great capacity of social media wasn't just answering constituent requests. The push for lawmakers and staff to move into the social media era came from both inside and outside the institution. The leaders of Google and Facebook wanted lawmakers to utilize their platforms and organized training and discussions around the concept of "new media." There was a collective effort from tech companies to be part of the conversation driving communications in Congress.

> Facebook brought Adam Connor in, in late 2007 when they launched Pages. They created a page for every member of Congress using their Wikipedia profile. And then they hired Adam to go around and get them to convert that, give them the admin keys, and to use it. So Adam was the first there, and then Adam Sharp was the first person for Twitter. He basically started around the same time. There was a period—about five or six years there—that between the two Adams, myself, and Andrew from Google, we could pretty much give each other's presentations. (Interview 147)

In addition to Facebook and Twitter working directly with staff in Congress to build out the digital operation, communication and press staffers were tasked with wading into the Twitter waters and figuring out how and when to bring their bosses along. If you've ever played the role of tech support for a senior family member, it is a familiar position that young communications staffers found themselves in.

> I remember being in the Senate Rotunda with a colleague, another communications staffer who was with another senator at the time. We were talking about Twitter. We both said, "this is a phase!" We were both asking, "do we have to get on Twitter? And get our bosses on Twitter?" And yes, the answer was quickly, "Yes!"[8]

This phenomenon is notable given that some senators, through this digital evolution, admitted to never sending a single email. In 2015, in a comment

[8] Senate Oral History Project, interview with Tara DiJulio, https://www.senate.gov/about/resources/pdf/dijulio-tara-oral-history.pdf.

foreshadowing the 2016 election, Lindsey Graham told Bloomberg News, "The next president of the United States needs to be good with people, not just technology." Twitter altered staff and lawmaker expectations about how fast the news cycle could move, meaning that communications staffers and reporters were constantly updating their priors about how to do their job. The days of calling a reporter to correct an error in a story were gone, because even if the story changed on the website, the news was already diffused through Twitter.

> With social media, that story is just spreading like wildfire and you cannot rein that in as quickly. You'll get more retweets now on a story that might have inaccuracies or a quote that is inaccurate or whatever it may be. And not as many retweets on the correction, of course. So that really changed how strategic communications was done in the Senate.[9]

Social media and the way the news cycle has changed have also altered the way communication offices meet one of their most basic demands—clips. Clips are usually done by lower-level press staffers. They include all mentions of the lawmaker in news outlets ranging from local weeklies to national papers. Clips used to be compiled into a physical package that would be given to a lawmaker and senior staff, but with technology shifts, that process has evolved to be email based or done digitally. As one former Senate staffer described, it wasn't just being done differently; rather, the process norms fundamentally changed.

> We went from faxing press releases, cutting out clips, to everything electronically—everyone communicating through social media—and it's just so much of monitoring not just the news but the pulse of the people back home. It changed everything, it really did. And it also changed how you manage expectations for your senator. Are they getting too focused on the comments they are seeing on social media? Are you making sure that you're keeping the big picture? The speed in which a communications job changed from 2006 or 2007 when I started, to when I exited is just incredible.[10]

The deluge of information on social media and the need for rapid response laid the foundation for the crisis of communications that would come to pattern Congress, where viral content is king and there is a new set of digital tools

[9] DiJulio interview.
[10] DiJulio interview.

to vie for new audiences. Information was already abundant in Congress, but social media turned that firehose of news on full blast. "It got harder to cut through the noise, too. There's so many ways to get your news. How do you cut through the noise and make sure your message is heard? That was hard, too, that became more of a challenge."[11]

The expectations for news dissemination escalated with news consumption such that, while legislative work on the Hill is rarely a nine-to-five job, the clock for communications became unending. Staffers had to grapple with the potential demands of the job versus the reality that there are only 24 hours in a day.

> It became 24/7. You're never off the clock when you're in communications in the Senate now. And that's hard. It's also an adrenaline rush. I would be emailing reporters, 10:00, 11:00 at night. If you have breaking news in the middle of the night, especially foreign policy issues, before, you could wait to roll out the statement the next day. Now, you better have your statement up on Twitter. I mean it is, it's 24/7.[12]

Digital Goes from "How Much?" to "How Well?"

As the norms of social media shifted from unknown potential to experimenting with more robust digital tools, the risks of doing social media poorly began to grow. In 2012, the expectations for what a member could or should say on Twitter were still minimal. Reporters and those tracking lawmakers didn't take anything on Twitter too seriously because for many offices, it was simply seen as an extension of the work they were doing elsewhere. Got a press release? Put it up on Twitter! But those days quickly faded as Twitter became a primary resource for information about the institution, the policy agenda, and the political headwinds swirling about the Capitol. And that information was more accessible and received more quickly on Twitter than an email that went to the graveyard of a reporter's email inbox.

Digital had finally asserted itself as a presence on the Hill, but quickly the question became less about whether to do it and more about the right way to engage. Early suggestions—and easy metrics that can still be a trap for many offices—were that all engagement was good and taking traditional content and amplifying it on social media was preferred. Over time, this simplistic

[11] DiJulio interview.
[12] DiJulio interview.

attitude gave way to arguments that the nuance of digital, the differentiated audiences, and the demand for authenticity were necessary considerations for effective digital. The two primary platforms for Congress—Twitter and Facebook—were coming into focus, but staff had the new task of educating those around them about the differences across the two platforms because what worked on Facebook was not going to work on Twitter. When a principal asked, "Why isn't there any engagement?" on a post, staffers faced the challenge of explaining why digital is often an art rather than a science.

> Twitter is, like, the megaphone. So if you really just got to get a message out to a lot of people real quickly, Twitter's the place to do that. Facebook's more like an organizing tool, I would say, where you can develop closer connections. Instagram is not as widely used, I would say it's also not, like, great for fundraising. It's, it's a secondary platform to Facebook and Twitter. And then tick tock is, of course, just, you know, painting the candidate in a fun, approachable way. I think that, like, tick tock can be used to show, you know, that politicians can be workhorses as well as show horses, or they have a fun-loving side. (Interview 68)

Staff improved the quality of digital content by having a clear picture about the audiences for each tool. National and global audiences plus younger people are more likely to be on Instagram, Twitter, or TikTok. Older Americans and a member's core supporters are more likely to use Facebook. Congressional staff adapted to having a whole digital toolbox to draw from when communicating their boss's priorities and preferences across multiple, overlapping audiences. Constituent messages were bolstered by e-newsletters and Facebook posts. Reporters and supporters were more likely to see tweets that packed a punch in 140, and subsequently 280, characters. The integration of more data about engagement and audience diversity, along with the fragmentation of public audiences in general, meant that digital complexity was part of the daily routines for communications staff on the Hill. Press staff couldn't afford to simply share a message across multiple platforms; rather, repurposing and repackaging information based on audience became the norm.

> We cross-pollinate a lot of our content between platforms. But some things that go on Twitter don't necessarily go on Facebook. Facebook, as you definitely know, is, like, much older. It also has a narrower partisan breakdown between Democrats, Republicans, and Independents, whereas Twitter is much more left leaning. So if

> we have something that's, you know, a bit more partisan, that we have on Twitter doesn't necessarily go on Facebook. (Interview 68)

And though the "left-leaning" nature of Twitter may no longer be realized in a Twitter/X and Elon Musk era, the realities of the audience and the needs of that audience shape how Congress engages across platforms. Communications staffers acknowledge that the risk of ignoring or misappropriating content for an audience can mean hefty electoral costs down the line (Interview 153).

Looking Ahead at Congressional Communication: Future Directions and Artificial Intelligence

The evolution of digital and social media in Congress has been a transformative journey, shifting from having a peripheral role to becoming an integral part of communication strategies. Initially, digital work was seen as akin to information technology support, focusing on website management, digital newsletters, and email management, but it has evolved into a modern digital institution that next faces the challenge of grappling with artificial intelligence (AI). In a 2023 executive order, President Joe Biden defined AI as "a machine-based system that can, for a given set of human-defined objectives, make predictions, recommendations, or decisions influencing real or virtual environments. Artificial intelligence systems use machine- and human-based inputs to perceive real and virtual environments; abstract such perceptions into models through analysis in an automated manner; and use model inference to formulate options for information or action" (15 U.S.C. 9401(3)).

In 2023 and 2024, Congress saw a sharp uptick in the number of AI-related activities on Capitol Hill, including the AI Forum in the Senate, hearings in both the House and Senate, and the Congressional Hackathon in September 2024 featuring AI-focused remarks from Speaker Kevin McCarthy and a video appearance by former House Majority Leader Steny Hoyer. Additionally, the Committee on House Administration is releasing reports through its new Modernization Subcommittee that highlight the House's efforts to facilitate responsible AI use. In a December task force report by House lawmakers, Democratic Leader Hakeem Jeffries noted, "The development and safe adoption of artificial intelligence holds great promise to make a positive difference in the lives of the American people. . . . At the same time, we must ensure that appropriate guardrails are in place to prevent bad actors from exploiting this transformative technology."[13]

The push toward digital is often driven by the need to best the digital efforts of opposing parties, but despite historical partisan impetus, the shared uncertainty surrounding AI is an unknown future that all offices have begun to experiment with. AI offers members of Congress various tools to improve communication with reporters, constituents, and special interest groups, but offices must also be mindful of the likelihood of error and lack of specificity.[14] AI can help lawmakers monitor and analyze news and social media to stay informed about current events and public sentiment. By using AI-powered media-monitoring tools, lawmakers can track mentions of their name, bills, or key issues, allowing them to respond quickly to media inquiries and shape their messaging accordingly. Additionally, AI can assist in drafting press releases, speeches, and social media posts. Natural language processing algorithms can help lawmakers create compelling content tailored to specific audiences, increasing engagement and impact. AI can also enhance communication with constituents by analyzing their feedback and preferences; however, offices and staff must be mindful to limit any confidential information shared across AI or large language models. By leveraging AI-powered messaging, lawmakers can gain insights into constituents' concerns and interests, enabling more personalized outreach and better representation. AI can also facilitate multilingual communication, helping lawmakers reach communities and audiences who speak different languages.

Platforms like Facebook and Twitter were instrumental in reshaping how lawmakers interacted with constituents and managed their public image, and AI is poised to do the same at some point. AI presents a wealth of opportunities for members of Congress to enhance their communication strategies, but there remain many uncertainties about the role of AI as a viable path forward for an office and how it is then integrated into that office's organization and daily practices. These are the same uncertainties members faced when grappling with the impact of television, the internet, and social media. Congress is already experimenting with AI tools like the Comparative Print Suite and has established the AI Working Group to test out new strategies for engagement. Learning from established strategies and standards in other government areas, members of Congress are leveraging AI to improve data hygiene and access to resources. Staff and lawmakers recognize the importance of AI,

[13] https://science.house.gov/2024/12/house-bipartisan-task-force-on-artificial-intelligence-delivers-report

[14] https://static1.squarespace.com/static/60450e1de0fb2a6f5771b1be/t/66ead6d8f9fa8313e5e89976/1726666457746/AI-Augmented_Operations.pdf

with administrators bringing in experts from the Government Accountability Office and other outside networks to assist policymakers. The need for transparent AI use cases and comprehensive governance documents will inevitably force Congress to address its internal issues by adopting AI, potentially reorganizing communication and constituent casework operations, and data processing capabilities.

4
Organizing a Press Office in Congress

The notion of what constitutes a "best" press office is akin to asking a room of 20 people their preferred way to drink coffee. No two answers are the same, and those are *strongly* held opinions from trial and error trying to find the perfect blend. The creative blend of communications within a congressional office is nothing short of complex, and so variable that most predictive models of organization and performance would struggle to predict outcomes or capture how communication is prioritized within an office.[1] Layered on top of that is a digital demand that shapes how information moves throughout the office, as well as the institution, and creates new avenues for messaging while also placing new demands on the limited attention and resources of the people trying to run a creative department on a shoestring budget. For nearly a decade, social media has not been a choice but rather a mandate, and the question isn't "how" but rather "how well" you do the job of meeting a diverse set of interests across an increasing number of platforms that all serve the goal of member or principal reputation building. The cost of being on Twitter, Facebook, and so forth is relatively low, but the manpower required to distribute content across more platforms and for different audiences is where many offices are constrained or stretched far too thin to really meet the digital demand and maintain the traditional press relationships that remain a vibrant part of the culture within Capitol Hill. The responsibility of communicating a political brand and ramping up digital outreach fuels the crisis of communication where offices can be overwhelmed by the information deluge if they are not prepared to meet the challenge of communicating within a rapidly changing media climate. As digital has grown its presence across the Hill, the demand for rapid response places communications in the hands of a 25-year-old staffer who is charged with being the voice of a member at least 20 years their senior, each with a unique perspective on how to manage a congressional office.

[1] This observation alone is why writing this chapter was the author's greatest hurdle.

Tweeting Scared. Annelise Russell, Oxford University Press. © Oxford University Press (2025).
DOI: 10.1093/9780197808344.003.0004

Today's communications teams, or one-man bands in many House offices, are more akin to a creative services or public affairs department than simply a press office because they are expected to provide an array of digital and traditional products. Most communications directors are tasked with the responsibilities of what we would otherwise term a "creative director," where their time is split managing a diverse portfolio of press inquiries, media relationships, digital productions, and communication strategies. For example, a communications director may be spending the morning reviewing media clips, approving content for Twitter, making edits to an upcoming speech, prepping press materials for a new bill, and fielding calls from reporters asking for a comment on the latest news of the day. As the media landscape has shifted and digital has become a fundamental aspect of what an office is expected to do, communications directors have taken on more duties and management responsibilities as they are tasked with not just providing information but also packaging and presenting that information. The rapid-response environment puts communication resource inequities on full display and incentivizes political conflict across the institution, but that digital demand also shapes the organization within an office, how content is produced and approved, who gets hired, and the role principals play in their own communication strategy.

Social media, and its accompanying photography, video, and graphics, isn't just affecting the public dialogue; rather, it is shaping the way information is shared within the institution and among the professionals who manage the day-to-day operations of Congress. Many staffers won't check their overflowing email inboxes for updates on the schedule, but they will see a tweet from a congressional reporter. Since 2012, Twitter has been shaping their daily discourse about politics, policies, and processes whether they are actively tracking updates on Twitter or not. Staff don't need to be digital directors to be affected by what's trending on Twitter, what a member said in the hallway, and how reporters are covering caucus lunches. The uncertainty and low-grade panic regarding Twitter after Elon Musk acquired it highlight just how central the digital advertising platform has become to the daily information exchange in Congress. If you need updates on the floor, want to know the latest in policy negotiations, or even just want to enjoy some political theater, you check social media, which is directly shaping the daily diet of information that staff have about the institution. The media storms that surround elected leaders like Alexandria Ocasio-Cortez or Joe Manchin began years before President Trump made Twitter his preferred policy tool (remember Representative Anthony Weiner's wiener scandal?), but they are amplified and punctuated by the rapid response of digital engagement. And behind that storm is a team of communications professionals trying to set and affect the way information moves throughout the institution with, in reality, little capacity to do so. In this chapter, I explain the fundamentals of communications shops, how they differ, and how digital gets integrated into the broader communications picture. I explain why the approvals process (i.e., the chain of command for approving content) is central to the communications culture, affecting the role and capacity of digital. Congressional Twitter is a unique political ecosystem that offers lawmakers outsized discretion with regard to their messages, but being effective on digital can be a Herculean task for a single staffer trying to connect with multiple constituencies on a daily basis.

The chapter uses data from semi-structured, anonymous interviews with current and former staffers and journalists covering Congress. These interviews give a behind-the-scenes perspective to understand how communications offices are organized, managed, and engaged in Congress.[2] Respondents detailed how offices are staffed, the approval process for content, how relationships with journalists are made, and how Twitter tests all of those things. These interviews present common themes and experiences about managing the information overload and the role of party and committee leadership who provide members with support to manage the process. The interviews also describe important differences in communication organization between the two chambers of Congress, explaining how resource differences and electoral insecurity often shape communication priorities. Members who aren't at risk of electoral defeat communicate differently and take different risks—similar to what we know about how elections shape their policymaking behavior and effectiveness (Barber & Schmidt, 2019). Creating a typology of members' communication is a fickle task because there are both intrachamber differences and cross-chamber norms. Democrat and Republican divides may appear intractable, but the constant opposition in Congress is always the other chamber. While offices are widely reported as understaffed across both chambers, the fiscal and personnel constraints are felt most strongly by the average House office, where a communications staff may be a single individual compared to three- to four-person teams on the Senate side. Senators typically juggle bigger constituencies (i.e., not Wyoming) and more press inquiries, but they don't have to vie for attention in the ways that a rank-and-file House member, particularly a junior lawmaker, does to get their name on the evening news.

[2] Additional information about the interviews, protocol, and individuals sampled is included in the methodological appendix.

I take a behind-the-scenes look at how press content is produced, from ideation to mass production, accounting for the various steps and pain points along the way. Lawmakers and their staff collaborate to systematically present themselves to a digital constituency, and the priorities of the principal (and sometimes the chief of staff or the communications director) shape the way an office organizes its press operation. I detail how some members are just trying to get in the game because they can't avoid it, while others are trying to change the game one tweet at a time.

From Spotlight-Averse Wonks to Primetime Darlings

The first thing to know about the "typical" press shop in Congress is that there isn't one. When building a press team, offices may consider how specific people best complement each other and the office's unique needs, but at other times the strategy is simply finding a reliable staffer. Briefly putting aside the institutional and resource differences across the House and Senate, most offices are considered little uniquely managed units with variable staffing hierarchies and processes. The typical conversation with a staffer about how they organize their office begins with the caveat "Well, every office is different, but in my office . . . ." Many folks refer to offices as individual small businesses, based on the autonomy that offices have in terms of processes and human resource practices; as one former staffer described, the decisions about how to situate communications within offices make every lawmaker a feudal lord to some degree.

> I always say that Hill offices are little fiefdoms. . . . For example, there's not an HR on Capitol Hill. Each individual office decides pay rates and policies and harassment policies, all these things. But I mean, they are all their own little worlds. So it's very hard often to say, "Oh, well, Hill offices do X . . . ." There's just so much variation there. (Interview 72)

But beyond a medieval characterization (although some days the frantic pace can lead to a fire-and-brimstone atmosphere), each office has its own operations and procedures. No two offices are the same, from the physical layout to the institutional processes they put in place. In some Senate office buildings, the press offices sit cloistered in a second-floor attic, while others sit in pods and some sort of haphazardly made space just to get through the day. Some lawmakers want communications personnel just outside their personal office door, whereas others prefer a "less is more" approach to getting involved in the communications operation. More junior members tend to embrace digital communications more readily (like Senators Jon Ossoff or Josh Hawley), but in the Senate, in particular, senior members (like Bernie Sanders and Chuck Grassley) have infamous digital reputations.

The organizational chart for communications can be just as wonky as the broader staffing choices, albeit there are fewer deviations from a standard communications director, buoyed by a variable number of support staff. As new members transition onto the Hill, common guidance internally and from outside organizations suggests a communications director is the first and primary position within a communications shop. The choices about how to support that leader vary by the priorities of the member, their electoral security, and the other staffing needs they are simultaneously meeting. You have some members who tend to fall more into a policy wonk category such that maybe they're not as concerned with a late-night spot on Fox News or Newsmax (Russell, 2021b). Member investment is a function of not only resources but also the personal priorities of your principal. Do they want to build a reputation nationally? How do they see themselves within Congress? Do they like a good political fight? Do they define their success in terms of how many times they end up on cable news versus how many times they end up in *Politico* versus how many times they end up in the local newspaper or on local TV? These determinations will affect not only the digital output and how much they invest but also the type of staff they bring on and what they really enable their staff to do. A congressional communicator may have the latest skills in digital photography, but if the member is only interested in writing op-eds for the local paper, those skills won't be used.

Among congressional staff, employment choices begin with a primary decision about whether to focus on communication or policy. Multiple congressional staffers described it such that there are two tracks in Congress, policy and communication, and the divide between the two is both "formal and real" (Interview 72). For some, it means they start as press interns and that will predetermine their next steps, or they will have to really work to switch over to the track best suited for their background and expertise. Most staffers, with minor exceptions of those earlier in their careers when the main hurdle is simply getting a job on the Hill, will remain in one of those tracks that would, for policy, lead them into a legislative director position or alternatively, for communication, into a communications director position. "The path dependency starts immediately. And it is very, very hard to get off of it. I think for that reason, there's some hesitancy to, like, touch the other rail" (Interview 72).

Picking a track does not make a staffer immune to the changing culture around them—many communications staffers sit next to policy folks in a tiny office. Policy staffers may be writing briefs that communications directors then reformat (or completely rewrite) into content that is consumable and advertisable. Policy staffers are still tracking Twitter or scrolling *Politico* to figure out the world around them. Policy and communications staffers don't always get along—similar to competitive siblings angling for a parent's attention—but the ideal scenario is an office where policy and communications staff can complement one another. What a good communications staffer lacks in policy depth they make up for in their breadth of policy knowledge that crisscrosses issues and makes them conversant in the wide array of topics that come across their desks. Despite the path dependence of the job, those staff who do it best often take advantage of opportunities to collaborate with fellow colleagues while learning the norms of those doing work outside of their own sphere. Most policy staffers acknowledge that they need a communications staffer if they want someone who knows about the legislation or policymaking activities going on within an office.

Typologies of Congressional Communications: House and Senate

When considering the types of congressional offices that exist, adding the types of communications that exist within those offices, and layering digital on top of that, the picture becomes increasingly complex. That variation in communications staffing is most noticeable across two dimensions: (1) the chamber and (2) resources within that chamber. For example, Senate communications are typically done by a team, ranging from three to eight people in the average office, whereas in the House usually only one or two people manage both traditional and digital press operations. I break down the typical communications structures within each chamber next, with variation by rank-and-file members and those in leadership, including those who chair committees (Figure 4.1). Within each of those categories, there is a spectrum of communication and digital investment that structures messaging for the member and their staff. Electoral considerations layer on top of these realities, shaping further what a lawmaker chooses to do with their time in office.

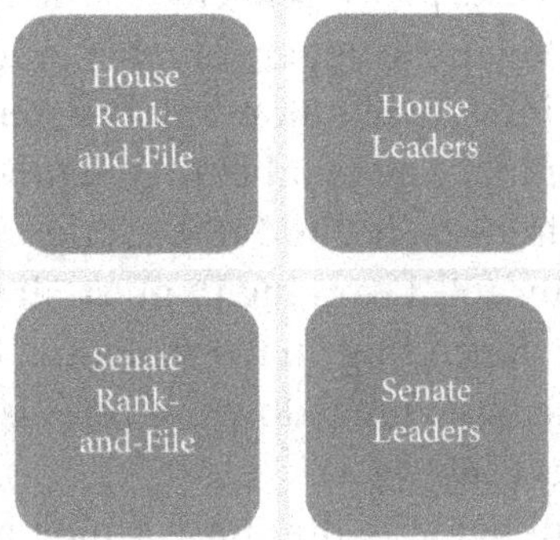

Figure 4.1 Chamber and resource dimensions for communication investment

Senate Communications Staff

In the Senate, there's more consistency when staffing a communications office—they have a lot more resources and the principals have longer terms, so investment is driven by longer electoral cycles and offices that typically have more institutional knowledge. Every office is unique, but each has at least three to four communications staffers, depending on whether their principal wants to be "out there" in terms of their engagement with digital and traditional media (Interview 7). In Senate offices, this basic rubric goes for both Republicans and Democrats; however, if you add roles like chair of the Senate Judiciary Committee, new resources and different staff drawn from committee responsibilities will be incorporated. Committee leaders are in a unique position to determine how they want to spread their resources across both the personal office and the committee office. Some lawmakers choose to keep their committee staff wholly separate from their personal office, while others blend the two press teams into, ostensibly, one larger operation. For example, Senator Brian Schatz, chair of the Senate Committee on Indian Affairs, posted this job advertisement in 2024:

> The Office of U.S. Senator Brian Schatz and the Senate Committee on Indian Affairs, Office of the Chairman, seeks a shared communications staff member for both offices. This position will be based in the Senator's personal office, and duties will be split between that office and the Senator's committee office in his role as Chairman.

The Senate is simply a more well-resourced chamber given that the average Senate office may have double the amount of employees that a House office has, and the budget surplus is reflected in the types of communications teams that are constructed in the upper chamber. Additionally, the Senate has a long track record of individual autonomy that reflects the diverse investments they make in staffing. The number of potential positions in the Senate communication arena is vast—in the 118th Congress there were more than 230 different job titles for folks working in press, digital, or media positions. The job titles will differ depending on the structure, hierarchy, and resources within an office, but the basic breakdown of roles is captured in nine of the most common positions (Table 4.1).

A communications director is the most senior and most common role within Senate offices, typically directing the strategy of an office, working closely with the chief of staff and legislative director, and managing a small team of other press and digital staff. A press secretary is the second most common role on a Senate communications team. This role tends to be fluid depending on the strengths of the communications director, how large the digital operation is (or if there is one), and their tenure. There is no standard job title for any of these positions because the hiring is specific to the

Table 4.1 Potential Senate Press Office Roles

1. Communications director—a senior staffer responsible for all office communications and determining the communications plan for an office. This person oversees press communications, builds relationships with reporters, and advises the member on interviews and crisis communications. This person oversees editing and approving content across digital and traditional products, working with the chief of staff and legislative director.
2. Deputy communications director—a more senior staffer, working with the communications director or other senior staff to determine a consistent communication message within the office. Some offices may not have a deputy as this role may overlap with that of a press secretary or digital director.
3. Digital director—a staffer who oversees all digital communications, often working under or alongside the communications director. A digital director has significant responsibility over a range of digital products, including social media, e-newsletters, photography, the website, data and microtargeting, graphics, and videos. This role typically ranks higher than a press assistant or junior communications staffer.
4. Press secretary—typically a staffer with some communications expertise, but not that of a communications director. The press secretary may serve a similar role to the communications director but typically works in conjunction with other communications staff and may focus on traditional media outputs like press releases or op-eds.
5. Local/state press secretary—similar role of a press secretary, with the focus being on local press, state media, regional radio, and state-based policy issues. This press secretary collaborates with the team but may reside in a district office to staff the member when they are not in DC and doing local media.

6. Speechwriter—the primary duties are writing formal remarks and statements for floor speeches and public events. The role can include assisting the communications team with media relations and strategy, plus drafting press releases, opinion pieces, or digital content. Offices expect a strong background in communications and an excellent writer; given that writing is not often an entry-level position, experience matters.
7. Digital manager—may often mirror or resemble a digital director, with the expectation that the staffer holds less experience or seniority within the communications team. The digital manager may oversee digital communications, working with the communications director, press secretary, or other assistants. The digital manager may have varying levels of responsibility over digital products, likely including social media, e-newsletters, photography and video content, the website, and some data analytics. This role ranks higher than a press assistant but can still be considered a junior communications staffer.
8. Press assistant—is likely responsible for monitoring media coverage and compiling daily clips, managing journalist and media lists, managing communication calendars, and other administrative duties as assigned by senior staff (typically the communications director). This role may include drafting communications materials across social, video, and print publications. This is an entry-level position.
9. Digital assistant—similar to a press assistant, the primary responsibilities include helping manage video, editing, and captioning; drafting social media content; assisting with the website; and helping produce newsletters. The typical assistant may have some experience writing for social media platforms. This is an entry-level position so experience with photography, videography, and editing is a plus but not required.
10. Less common: researcher, rapid response, videographer, photographer, senior advisor/strategist.

---

needs of the office and the expectations for that position are determined by the principal's priorities, in consultation with senior staff.

Senate Range of Alternatives

The typical Senate office—although even suggesting there is a typical office is a bit of stretch—takes those common positions abovc and formulates a team that matches the needs of an office and its principal. A senior senator with a 25-year legacy as the expert on defense policy, for example, is less likely to see the value in building up a large communications team, particularly when policy priorities are considered primary and he has already built up a reputation among his various constituencies. The option of forgoing communications isn't reasonable—just ask a policy staffer to set up a telephone town hall meeting and observe the fear in their eyes—but offices can choose where they want to dial it up or down. Most Senate offices fall into three categories—basic nuts and bolts, more digital investment, or robust creative suites—and the expectations for a communications team will differ across all three. Most principals set up these teams to match their expectations for communication prowess, yet even the most robust shops are always expected to do more with less than they would have in the private sector. The crisis cycle isn't alleviated in the Senate, because bigger press shops simply mean bigger expectations, and more staff also means more coordination and collaboration required for messaging.

Type 1: Nuts and Bolts: Democratic Senator Jack Reed

There is nothing flashy about how the senior senator from Rhode Island conducts himself in the Senate. Reed was elected to the Senate more than 30 years ago, before internet campaigning, digital media, and social media were ever a consideration. His reputation is based on his committee work—particularly in the armed services—and he has a record of bipartisan work with colleagues across the aisle on a bevy of military and defense issues. His office reflects those priorities, with only a couple of communications staffers and no explicit digital staffer in 2023. His communications director has been working in Congress for more than 20 years, with prior experience working as a professional staff member for then-Senator Joe Biden. Reed reflects an office that does the bare minimum with just a communications director/press secretary and a deputy. Many offices, even those without a large investment in communications, will add a third assistant to help with media mentions, clips, and drafting copy for statements.

> I would say the basic structure [in the Senate] is at least three people, like most people have the communications director, the press secretary, and some kind of research person. And oftentimes, there's a digital director, or, and sometimes the digital person is also the press assistant. (Interview 52)

Those senators who have little incentive to be in the national media or advance their agenda on salient or hot-button issues are the most likely to keep their communications staff at a low level. This staffing choice acknowledges that a senator cannot simply ignore the press or their reputation but rather sees communication as a supplement to other priorities that require greater investment.

> Within the Senate . . . there's a lot more resources to be used; they have longer terms. So we have, I would say that our team is reflective of most of the others in our offices, usually three to four communication staffers, again, just depending on how out there the senator seems to be on media. (Interview 7)

Type 2: More Digital Media Investment: Democratic Senator John Fetterman

Newly elected senators face the daunting challenge of staffing a Senate office out of thin air, but increasingly members are choosing to hire additional staff focused on digital media. Even for a junior senator without the benefit of added resources, the choices about how to invest in communications are paramount to building a successful Senate reputation. Senator Fetterman's campaign was defined by a strong digital game (Figure 4.2). His chief of staff had a press background—running communications for former Senate Majority Leader Harry Reid—and he also has a seasoned communications director, a digital director, a state press secretary, and a press/digital aide.

Figure 4.2 One of Senator John Fetterman's tweets from the 2022 campaign
Source: Twitter.

Fetterman's office is reflective of those that are trying to incorporate digital investment into their broader communications strategy and reputation-building efforts. Some offices are more equipped to build a team than others, but whether based on electoral incentives, personal preference, or simply adaptation to the media environment, these offices are likely to make specific investments in digital—relying less on outside support for their primary communication priorities or at least building a team to capitalize on what is offered by the caucus or conference.

A current Senate digital director explained what the typical staffing scenario looks like for an office that is able to make the added investment in communications, particularly digital media.

> The way our comm shop is divided—there are five of us. So you have the comms director who will be at the very top and they're responsible for obviously overseeing the entire strategy as well as managing everyone else in the department. We have a state press secretary, so they're responsible for handling state events as well as state press and pitching to local publications. You have myself, as a digital director, so I'm responsible for managing our digital projects, working across our department, as needed, whether it's, you know, clipping or getting video of the senator speeches, state events, and all of that. And then we have a speechwriter who writes all the remarks the boss gives as well as writing any op-eds or anything else. And then we have a press assistant who kind of helps each of us as needed and kind of works across the department. (Interview 144)

Even when not focusing as heavily on digital, many senators are still investing in communication by having either speechwriters or local press secretaries who can then focus on state issues or requests from back home. Those senators who have a state-based focus or local preference for communication invest in state-based press more readily. For example, in 2024, Senator Chris Van Hollen advertised for a state press secretary, listing the following responsibilities:

> closely monitoring local news; fielding reporter inquiries; planning, organizing, and staffing press events in state; taking photos and working with other team members to create social media on state events; developing relationships with reporters; drafting press releases and memos; and working collaboratively with the rest of the communications team and members of the Senator's policy and state teams.[3]

[3] https://www.senate.gov/employment/po/positions.htm

As one former press secretary described their office, sometimes the mix of folks includes state-based people, but sometimes additional positions are created simply based on the needs of the office and the member.

> My current [Senate] office is just a five-person team. So it's a comms director, the press secretary, and the local press secretary and a press assistant. But we also have a director/senior writer. So her position is very interesting, actually, because it's very, it's half comms and half legislative. So she edits all the letters that we get from constituent mail and like what the LCs (Legislative correspondents) and LAs (Legislative assistants), you know, respond to. She reviews and edits and everything. But she also obviously helps with fact checking and things that we need for releases or tweets, etc. So she is, like, really in the middle of everything. (Interview 52)

Type 3: Robust Creative Departments: Republican Senator Ted Cruz

Senators in leadership positions and with large populations and located a far distance from Congress (i.e., Texas or California) get more dollars to divide among their many priorities. Some senators just want to be left alone to do their committee work and would rather eat dirt than give interviews, while others invest in a robust team of media and communications professionals to support their priorities for presentation. One example of the latter is Texas Republican Ted Cruz, whom you might find scrolling through his own mentions in the middle of a Senate confirmation hearing (Figure 4.3). As a former candidate for the Republican presidential nomination, he has a national presence, a vast audience of more than 3.4 million followers on Twitter/X, and a robust team of communicators to manage the information flow within his office. As a principal, he values communications, and it is common for seven or eight communications staffers to be working within his office—compared to colleagues' teams of three to four press staffers just down the hallway. Senator Cruz invested in a director of speechwriting (not a common job within the Senate) and a rapid-response director to coordinate communications across multiple platforms (Interview 146).

In an office like Senator Cruz's, Twitter and social media are not just considered digital tools; rather, "they use it as a measure of success unto itself" (Interview 156). The priorities for Senator Cruz are not only the lawmaking but also what type of news coverage he gets, how much penetration he can get across media, and how his message is received by copartisans. The senator's

Figure 4.3 Picture of Senator Ted Cruz scrolling his mentions on Twitter during a hearing
Source: Twitter.

staff knows that advancing the communication agenda is a priority-central goal of the office. "I know with Senator Cruz, he's obsessed with how many retweets his tweets get, how much engagement you get. . . . And then they spend a bunch of time, like, on Twitter getting into fights with, like, their opponents" (Interview 156).

Digital incentives and the ability to send messages on Twitter have changed business in Congress to incentivize rapid responses, limiting time for detail-oriented policies that don't draw attention, and enabling connections to a new, digital constituency that may not reflect the geographic constituency back home (Russell, 2021a; Tromble, 2018). Senators with robust communication shops lean into those communication incentives to build their political reputation and make important connections to partisan media and partners on social media. The ability to quickly respond to the changing political agenda, across multiple digital platforms, puts these senators at an advantage that allows them to be the first to respond to news and likely have their name quoted in the newspaper the next day. For instance, in the wake of the 2022 *Dobbs* decision determining abortion access, Senator Cruz was featured in the lead article from *Roll Call* describing senators' responses.[4]

[4] https://rollcall.com/2022/05/03/draft-leak-a-shocking-change-for-typically-airtight-supreme-court/

House Communications Staff

Transitioning from a Senate office like Senator Ted Cruz's or Bernie Sanders's to one in the House with its associated budget constraints is essentially entering a new reality. These offices exist in relative proximity to one another, but they might as well operate in a completely different universe given what most are capable of and what they are expected to manage. As one staffer described, the biggest differences in congressional communications are an issue of bandwidth, most noticeably across chambers (Interview 187). There are fewer communications folks in a House office than in a Senate office, and there are more streamlined processes in a House office because of the smaller staff (Interview 28). On the low-press-capacity end of the spectrum are rank-and-file members who do not have the resources to devote to communications to rival those of committees or among party leadership. Most notably, in freshman members' offices, they are still trying to figure out how to buy pens and access their own Facebook accounts. Staff acknowledge that it's difficult to have a proactive communications operation that encompasses digital, constituent outreach, and traditional press with just one staffer—no matter how talented they may be. As one former staffer described, there is no such thing as an overarching message plan because there isn't the time to develop one, and much of what communications folks are doing is reacting to the news of the day or legislative developments (Interview 187). But the realities of managing multiple priorities with the limited dollars of the Member's Representational Allowance lead to a smaller press shop than what is (1) preferred and (2) the reality in the private sector.

House communications departments can be likened to a one-man band where they are expected to play the music as if they had a quartet, but inevitably the sound will be different given the tools and constraints. Most House offices, similar to the Senate, staff a communications director, but unlike Senate offices, that director may also be the press secretary, the digital director, and the speechwriter all rolled into one! House members want to be as visible as other lawmakers across the chamber, and there is an expectation that digital content should be polished and equal to the Senate standards across the building, but the reality is that some House offices don't even have the resources to invest in Adobe Photoshop. One staffer told the story of a friend who wanted to better her digital skills, so she attended staff training to improve her photo editing, but once she got back to the office she realized the software they had been learning had not been purchased by her member (Interview 142). House staff must bootstrap their way to communication success, making trade-offs and prioritizing their messages to keep up with

Table 4.2 Potential House Press Office Roles

1. Communications director (deputy chief of staff)—a senior staffer responsible for all office communications and determining the communications plan for an office. This person oversees press communications, builds relationships with reporters, advises the member on interviews, and oversees editing and approval of content across digital and traditional products. They may be expected to advance press events and staff the member as needed and will work in close collaboration with the chief of staff, district director, legislative director, and other staff as appropriate.
2. Digital director (digital manager/press secretary)—a staffer who oversees all digital communications, often working under the communications director. The digital director has significant responsibility over a range of digital products, including social media, e-newsletters, photography, the website, data and microtargeting, graphics, and videos. This role typically ranks higher than a press assistant or junior communications staffer.
3. Press secretary—typically a staffer with some communications expertise, but not that of a communications director. The press secretary may serve a similar role to the communications director but typically works in conjunction with other communications staff and may focus on traditional media outputs like press releases or op-eds.
4. Press secretary/legislative staff—on the House side, press and legislative duties, or constituent correspondence, may be combined into one role. Given limited resources, a press secretary may also have a small policy portfolio to also work on.
5. Press assistant—the most junior staff in terms of press responsibilities, principally to help create additional content and to assist the other communications staff. Duties include drafting press releases, statements, and other press materials. The press assistant may also be responsible for maintaining press lists, compiling and distributing daily press clips, media monitoring, and other tasks as assigned by senior staff.
6. Less common: deputy communications director, digital assistant, state press secretary, speechwriter.

the information exchange both on- and offline. Senate offices have a team to collaborate on broader strategy and juggle national press versus local press, speechwriting, digital distribution, and clips. In the House, that is all one job or the job of a senior staffer and an entry-level press assistant (Table 4.2).

House Range of Alternatives

The range of alternatives for staffing a House communications team is more limited than in a Senate office simply because there are fewer combinations of staff available at any given point. Within the House, there is a much more centralized structure of party-led messaging that influences both strategy and organization. House members are more likely to get a roadmap from party leadership for staffing and recommendations for communication capacity because more new members transition onto the Hill, at two-year intervals.

On the low end of the spectrum are rank-and-file members who do not have the resources to devote to communications to rival that of committees or party leadership. Most notably, freshman members' offices are still trying to figure out how to set up their correspondence management system. So they are expected to not only build up a basic office from scratch but also staff an effective communications and digital team and quickly establish a political reputation. But even for the members who have at least a couple of terms under their belts and don't feel the electoral pressure, it's still increasingly hard to do digital along with traditional communications, because they simply don't have the resources or the personnel priorities that align with stronger digital or messaging investment. How an office incorporates interns or digital fellows may affect their communication investment, but most offices either manage with a bare-bones staff or are blessed by having two to three folks working together on a small team. This is not to say that being a newly elected member means you can't have an effective digital strategy—relatively new members have captured the spotlight with digital. We've seen this with Republican Representative Marjorie Taylor Greene and her ability to use digital content to propel her into the news. She's notable for what she says online and how she uses digital tools to build her infamous political reputation. Some of these trends have changed over time as freshman members have come in knowing just how important digital media is and placed greater emphasis on their online image, but the resources still constrain what they are able to do despite this recognition (Interview 121).

Type 1: Doing a Lot with a Little: Republican Representative Frank Lucas

Republican Frank Lucas of Oklahoma has been in the House for more than 30 years, has had multiple committee chairmanships, and over the last dozen elections has averaged a 70-plus-point victory. The senior House member is very focused on his district in Oklahoma, is keenly aware of agricultural policy needs, and staffs a congressional communications shop with one communications staffer who largely manages the entirety of the press output. His "do a lot with a little" type of office is common in the House where even members who want to shine in the national spotlight staff their press shop with only a single staffer to manage multiple audiences—constituents back home, partisan supporters, issue-based groups, reporters, and so forth. Lucas's is just one of many offices that do a lot with a little in terms of the robust communication effort they manage. Even in the modern digital era, the standard of one person to manage communications remains a staple on the House side.

> Typically, what I've seen is that the comms person and a personal office tend to be a bit of a one-man band. They might be doing the statements, the social media, calling out pitching reporters, and setting up interviews from the members back in the district or remotely when in Washington. They are sort of a jack of all trades. (Interview 100)

Even when a member has an outside reputation that extends onto the national scene, these offices remain constrained by their resources, their priorities, and their staff's capacity to manage their profile. For example, former Speaker Nancy Pelosi—who remains one of the most in-demand members in terms of press and outside requests—had 17 communications staffers while she was Speaker; this was reduced to 2 staffers, a communications director and a press secretary, after she stepped down from leadership (Interview 192). She does not have the capacity or resources to even maintain a digital director going forward—fundamentally shaping how the former Speaker will be engaging the broader political community and signaling where the office will focus their attention. "Being a one-person job [in the House], you kind of just have to pick and choose. Digital, it's I think where my passion lies, but, like, at the end of the day, the speech tends to be more important than, like, the 280-character tweet" (Interview 123).

Communications directors in the House tend to be younger and paid less than their Senate counterparts, but the need for digital and traditional press to be managed by the same person in the House also necessitates a typically younger staffer with both those skills. Party leadership and their staff work with members to give their staff the tools they need to compete digitally, but the ability to execute those skills is conditioned simply by the workload and how the member wants to respond to politics and news of the day.

Type 2: Doing a Lot with a Little More

"We just have the two comms staffers within our office. So I'm press secretary and digital director, and then my immediate supervisor is our office communications director" (Interview 142). This is what luxury looks like for the average House office. Outside of leadership, those offices that have two or even three press staffers are putting more resources, on average, toward

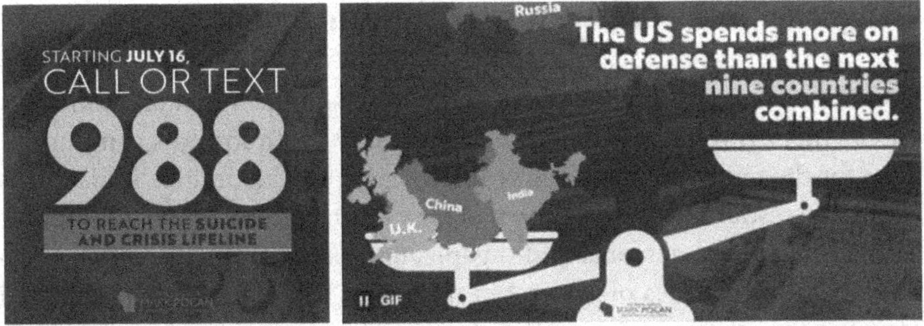

Figure 4.4 Examples of graphics from Representative Mark Pocan's communications team

communication. Splitting the duties of communication between folks allows them to engage with more audiences more often. One lawmaker whose office operates this way is Democratic Representative Mark Pocan, whose time in Congress almost perfectly mirrors the rise in digital over the last 10 years. In 2023, Pocan introduced legislation to amend House rules to require that cameras show the full House chamber during legislative business—further leaning into digital technology and the power of cameras to tell the story of Congress. His office uses their graphics prowess to vie for some of the best digital representation within their caucus (Figure 4.4).

Dividing up the tasks for digital is not the only advantage of having multiple staffers managing communications in a House office. For many folks, being able to delegate tasks across paid, owned (socials), and earned media (press) is critical to doing each effectively. An office with multiple people managing press is better positioned to get their boss on cable news or pitch ideas to bookers looking for quick hits on drive-time radio. "For our member who was really focused on media, and wanting to talk to media and wanting to be in the headlines, it's definitely a priority for our office to have two folks working on that" (Interview 106). But just like the Senate, the range of what an office chooses to do comes down to the priorities of the principal. Even when there are more people to share the load of those priorities, it means juggling multiple tasks. Each office curates a specific number of positions, but the demands of each position are widely different, and what it means to do each job is likely different. As one House staffer described, being the deputy communications director also means managing digital. That balance of having to manage both digital and traditional press would likely never happen on the Senate side (Interview 110).

Congressional Leadership Communications

Outside of rank-and-file members, there are also offices that are unlike any other—managing additional resources and tasked with strategic communications for the entire conference or caucus. Party and committee leaders have additional resources by the nature that they also have leadership and committee staff that blend personal and organizational staff at the discretion of the principal. The realities of leadership resources, while nuanced by chamber, are a similar experience across the House and Senate in terms of the relative messaging power a leader has relative to the other lawmakers in their caucus.

> When I worked for Schumer, the organization there was completely different, and it was massive [relative to a rank-and-file office]. It was, like, 23 to 25 communication staffers, and it was, like, a comms director, director of strategic communications, research director, deputy research director and, like, research assistants, three press assistants, because we were monitoring the news, pretty much all day, at all times. (Interview 52)

Party leaders run weekly messaging meetings with all communications staffers, and leadership offices coordinate messages between the House, Senate, and White House, if applicable. Digital investment and training are managed by leadership offices, which have the resources and incentives to improve the overall message strategy for the entire party. On the House side, Representative Steny Hoyer's office managed a digital fellows program for 12 years that provided a pipeline of digital talent that could mitigate some of the future digital staffing needs for other Democratic offices.

The effect that leadership and resources have on digital output is further explored in Chapter 5, but it's important to describe here just how different a leadership office is compared to what we commonly see in Congress. These offices are better equipped because they have more resources. Their members, compared to the average House member especially, have much higher profiles and are always in high demand by reporters and media regardless of the news topic. Anytime you think about those who have greater capacity in terms of resources, you also have to account for the fact that they have a greater demand on their attention. If Congress is scrambling to make a decision, the power of leaders to harness policymaking power means they also garner the most attention and press inquiries. And so they juggle an unlimited number of press requests and are constantly being followed by reporters in the halls of Congress. A typical House member is much less likely to be expected to comment on every issue versus a Senate member, but that same mantra doesn't hold for House leaders. They are expected to have a comment on any development and what it means from their perspective, what it means for their state, and what it means for their party. It's a much different supply of resources as well as division of priorities.

Communications professionals within leadership offices guide the entire caucus or conference in terms of communication or messaging. Leadership offices play a central role in growing the brand not only of the leaders themselves but also of the party more generally and in thinking about how they coordinate messaging. Leadership communications staff run weekly messaging meetings for both parties across both chambers to discuss messaging for the week, how leaders think they should talking about issues, and what sample text for those issues or legislation might look like. Members' staff receive talking points and different examples of messaging across platforms, providing a toolbox for the members to either (1) supplement their work or (2) know where the leadership is going to be driving the conference. A House leadership communications advisor may get four to six emails per week from other communications staffers asking for additional press materials or advice on how to respond to a potential problem (Interview 183).

> The Republican conference is sort of viewed as a messaging clearinghouse, I guess, on the Republican side, and similar on the Democratic side, and so they are the ones typically who are generating sample graphics—and that could be for something as simple as marking a holiday or it could be for something that's more complex. (Interview 100)

On the Senate side, there are institutional mechanisms in place for some of the support that lawmakers regularly need. Unlike House offices, Senate offices don't need talking points as often, but they do need the resources and staff support to manage the increasing digital output by members (particularly those lawmakers of the first two office types who can't supply their own creative team like Senator Cruz). The Senate Democratic Media Center is one example of leadership-driven communication capacity, or a communication subsidy, that allows for that routinized support. Across both chambers, a lot of informal networking goes on, yet every office to a certain extent will need some sort of guidance, assistance, or collaboration at some point. In an institution where members are increasingly expected to rise to the level of an Alexandria Ocasio-Cortez, Jim Jordan, or Chuck Schumer in terms of what they're able to produce, members will continue to turn to leadership to support those efforts. And that digital production drives engagement as well as the party and the broader political message that leadership has invested in.

Much of what Congress does in terms of digital technology would scare the pants off of Silicon Valley because the legislative branch is not a digitally advanced institution. But compared to the other members within the institution, leadership has extensive resources, has dozens of staff, and is able to harness communication technology in ways that allow them to go in depth on issues while also elevating the voices within their own conference.

Reporter Relationships: Targeting Earned Media

Media and press relationships with House versus Senate members are notably different given that a senator can draw a gaggle of reporters on the way to the bathroom while a House member, outside of leadership or a handful of notable members, is likely to go unnoticed. Across the House and Senate, there is a different culture that affects both the ways that members and their staff reach out to reporters and the ways that reporters expect to engage with an office. "No one's texting with Pelosi," but there is a more accessible culture on the House compared to the Senate side (Interview 50). The competition and swarm of reporters surrounding a single senator can make it difficult for policy reporters trying to find out about budget projections to get a comment, while House members are far easier to find for and more eager to comment. Every congressional session, the US Senate press gallery allocates about 1,500 press credentials to journalists. A photo of that gaggle from a blog post by a Senate communications director highlights just how chaotic comments from a single senator can become.[5]

> On big news days, a single senator, especially like Joe Manchin, is going to be swarmed by so many people that you don't get the chance to really pull them aside and have a back and forth. In the House, depending on the member, you can say, "Hey, do you have a few minutes to talk to me during votes?" and they're probably not going to be swarmed unless you're trying to get a question from Pelosi at her press conference. (Interview 57)

Because House offices have a shorter call list, the trick, then, becomes using their resources to draw the attention of reporters, producers, and bookers who can elevate their voice in ways that a press release would never do. Senate offices are often high enough in demand, as they are expected to have an opinion on nearly every policy topic, that similar attention-getting tactics are not required.

[5] https://www.linkedin.com/pulse/unwritten-rules-covering-congress-matthew-felling/

The mechanisms for engaging with reporters have ebbed and flowed with changes in technology, changes in the media climate, and expectations for news at a moment's notice, but many of the basics continue to shape the way communications staffers and reporters interact. A text message between a journalist and a staffer is the primary mechanism for getting a quick comment or checking on the status of an issue. A direct message on Twitter for a digital-first staffer is another way reporters connect with sources—albeit the future of Twitter relationships remains a bit in flux after 2022.

In 2017, a Senate staffer posted what he considered the "Unwritten Rules of Covering Congress," or rather, what he expected from his interactions with the press.[6] This short list by a practitioner with more than a dozen years of experience gives a small window into the reality of what it means for a member of Congress to interact with the press, what those interactions can look like when walking from their office to the Capitol, and how press staff think about these interactions.

1. Leave the obstructionism to the lawmakers: If you are in a hallway or corridor, don't stand in the way of the senator. Walk alongside as they get from point A to point B.
2. Be nice, even if the situation gets rocky. The Senate is a professional environment like any office, so be firm and assertive but stop short of being hostile. It works both ways too. Senators have long memories, and the folks that thread the needle between aggressive and respectful get tugged into longer conversations.
3. Don't hold an elevator open to keep an interview with a senator going; be mindful of their time.
4. If you are one of the TV reporters doing a live shot and you catch a senator's attention, be sure to state at the outset that your camera feed is hot.
5. Many of these lawmakers are not as spry as they once were (who among us is?), so give the older members of Congress a bit more room to operate and walk. As one reporter told the *Washington Post*, "we are one tripped Senator away from disaster."[7]
6. Don't forget the communications directors and their teams. It may surprise some, but they're not just there to give unsolicited feedback on

[6] Matthew Felling, "The Unwritten Rules of Covering Congress," https://www.linkedin.com/pulse/unwritten-rules-covering-congress-matthew-felling/.

[7] https://www.washingtonpost.com/lifestyle/style/inside-the-heaving-jostling-capitol-media-mob-we-are-one-tripped-senator-away-from-disaster/2017/06/06/8197da7c-4ae8-11e7-a186-60c031eab644_story.html?utm_term=.d994c1e3e471

coverage! Some are more helpful than others, yes, but they know their senator's schedule and availability.

Approvals: A (Painful?) Process for Producing Content

For a communications director, managing the approvals process is likened to running air traffic control; they must determine who needs to be looped into a message and who are the relevant staffers needed to ensure message accuracy and clarity. This process determines who needs to review a press release, a tweet, or a newsletter before it becomes public record; however, understanding the approval chain can be bewildering, as there is no standard procedure. The chain varies, requiring consideration of factors such as the relevance of legislative staffers and the need for input from senior staff, like the chief of staff, or lawmakers. "The most confusing part of what we do for basically anyone new is to figure out what the approval chain is for any given thing that needs to be approved. And the reason for that is because there is no standard chain" (Interview 129).

The approvals process is vital for a successful communications operation because a well-structured chain can prevent headaches and mitigate risks from errors. Conversely, a lengthy chain can halt an office's responsiveness, particularly in the digital age, where delays of just a few hours can make a message irrelevant. Common questions driving approval chains include "Do we need to go to the relevant legislative staffer? Does it also need to go to the relevant outreach staffer in the state? Does it also need to be seen by the legislative director or the chief of staff or the senator, or the state director?" (Interview 129). Decisions on how to approve messaging are key to an office's successful communications operation because having the right chain in place can mitigate headaches and risk that could arise from simple mistakes. On the other hand, a lengthy approval chain can bring an office to a screeching halt in a digital information world where three hours for approvals means you have missed your window of opportunity to be relevant on an issue or be a central voice in a political debate. "You hear nightmare stories about offices who are just completely paralyzed because their approvals process takes hours and hours to do" (Interview 27).

The approvals process across the House and Senate, just like the organization of an office, is a unique reflection of how much a principal wants to be involved in reviewing their own press materials, the level of trust between a member and their staff, and the number of staff able to participate in the process. For a typical House office, the communications director may draft a press release for review and the congresswoman might sign off on it, but other members can be far more removed from the process unless there is an urgent or sensitive matter that requires additional scrutiny on messaging (Interview 26). The relative engagement of the member depends on both the trust between a member and their staff and the style of engagement a member prefers on a daily basis. Some senior staff develop long-term trust with a lawmaker and that, in turn, shapes the approval chain's length. "There are probably some cases where you have a comms person who's very senior, or who's been around a long time, and they can maybe skip some of those steps just because there's such a level of trust between the member and the staff" (Interview 27).

For digital content specifically, the approval chain may differ according to content and platform, particularly when you have different staffers managing digital separately from traditional communications. How an office writes content for Facebook is different than how it does so for Twitter, and those platform differences require different engagement by the member and senior staff. For example, press release language may need to be approved by a House member, but this may not be true for social media content because those accounts are managed by staff.

Some approvals for digital can be streamlined by using preapproved content and reformatting it for social content. A decade ago, members were simply linking to preapproved press releases on Twitter, and while that trend has mostly evaporated given elevated digital standards, there is still a push to make the most of office-generated content by presenting it in different or unique ways across digital platforms. Particularly for those offices where the principal has a longer record in Congress and where there is naturally a record of more content to pull from, these types of approvals and quick responses are made easier over time. "By second or third year, a lot of the things we were saying were not necessarily new, because they're things she had commented on in the past. So a lot of that I could very easily pull from her previous comments for current stuff we are actively drafting and structuring" (Interview 26).

The approval process can become a nightmare, especially in the Senate, for digital-first staff who want to drive the conversation forward but don't have the latitude or personal discretion to do so on Twitter. Senate offices benefit from the ability to share communication responsibilities among many staffers, but the trade-off is that more people may have to weigh in on a piece of writing before it's ready to go out. Some offices require five or six people to give press materials at least a passing glance, and doing that efficiently isn't always realistic.

> It was a very arduous approval process, and I did not have any discretion. So that meant I was getting sign-off from a comms [staff] member, the leg member, and the senator themselves. And you know, that could even be more complicated by a committee member or an additional legislative member. So that would often end up being a two-, three-, four-step process, especially when the member themselves is involved—that can really be difficult to navigate. (Interview 157)

The impetus for a multichain approval process is the expectation that anything that comes out of the office is coming, officially, from the lawmakers themselves. Staff work to develop "the voice" of the member, drafting statements that reflect their priorities and personalities. Digital products, which were initially considered less serious, are now official statements like traditional press content and often require approvals via a similar process.

> It is a is a very rigorous approval statement for anything that supposedly coming from the senator. . . . I run it by the policy people who handle whatever issue it is. And from there we send it to what we call "senior staff"—chief of staff, the legislative director or state director, for the local feel. Once they've approved it or offered any changes, then it goes directly to the senator. Anything that's in his voice, he likes to approve it. (Interview 13)

Sometimes the exception to the approval process is social media content, given the fast-paced nature of the platform, which often moves more rapidly than any approval chain could. As one staffer described, they have more discretion on Twitter when there is something they like or that they think might be a good tweet, even if it is a little bit risky (Interview 13). Social media managers like Hootsuite can provide offices with options for routine approvals for social media content, where posts can be drafted and automatically sent through the approval chain. In offices where digital communications aren't as high a priority, communications staffers are often trusted to use the right language on social media, and that comes with inherent approval.

For senators who care more about their digital footprint, even if they are not running the account, they may propose or draft content, which can then add a new layer to the approval process. "If we have a big hearing, and we're going to tweet out something after the hearing, it's like an opinion, [the senator] will have eyes on it too" (Interview 128).

For policy-centered offices, where the focus is more on legislation and issue-oriented messaging, the relevant policy staffers would be heavily involved in the approval process, sometimes not just approving content but also writing and providing content that communications staff could then use for social media and traditional coverage (Interview 33).

Organization Communications around a Crisis

"There's probably not that much of a difference between crisis comms and digital communication now. I mean, you're not always dealing with the 'crisis,' but everything is, at least in someone's mind, urgent and, like, requires a response right away" (Interview 156).

Crisis is a common feature of communication in Congress and is why many former staffers and political communicators have taken on crisis management positions. Because key types of crises are reputational and political, in Congress, these are regular features of the daily dialogue that covers column inches and furrows the brows of communications staffers. Crises don't have to be traumatic, and they may very well be self-inflicted. While much of this book warns against the crisis of communication in Congress, that culture is also one that can positively drive a communications shop forward.

In 1994, *The Simpsons* (season 6, episode 11, "Fear of Flying") aptly identified the upside to a crisis:

- LISA: Look on the bright side, Dad. Did you know that the Chinese use the same word[8] for "crisis" as they do for "opportunity"?
- HOMER: Yes. "Crisitunity"! You're right.

This quote is inaccurate regarding the Chinese language and is meant as a joke, but the underlying idea holds true in congressional communication—crises can create opportunities for those who are both wise and cautious enough to seize them (Oga-Baldwin, 2024). Not everything that goes wrong is ripe for engagement opportunities, but using that crisis culture to engage audiences, raise brand awareness, and target specific audiences has become a staple for a congressional communications shop. For example, an office could think of a constituent survey email as both a crisis and an opportunity by quickly presenting the audience with a problem that will attract them to open the email and respond to the survey. Lawmakers can use that crisis-like problem to drive responses, because many people want to share their opinions on

[8] https://en.wiktionary.org/wiki/%E5%8D%B1%E6%A9%9F

big issues—and members can use the moment to solicit information for their member.

In 2014, Ike Brannon, a fellow with the Cato Institute, was describing the current culture in politics and concluded his thoughts by saying, "It would be a shame if we were to let this crisis go to waste." People are hyperaware of reputational blunders in Congress, which can be used as political threats and as fodder for conflict-centered news stories and unending form letters from constituents. During a crisis, there is often heightened public attention and interest in the actions and statements of elected officials. This increased attention provides Congress with a unique opportunity to effectively communicate its response to the perceived crisis, convey important information to the public, and demonstrate leadership and accountability. Additionally, a crisis often requires quick and decisive action, which can benefit an office that can respond quickly and effectively to challenging situations. By rapidly responding during a crisis, members of Congress can demonstrate their relevance by standing out amid the many members aiming to have their voices be the ones telling the story on MSNBC or Fox News.

A crisis culture can provide Congress an opportunity to engage with the public by soliciting feedback, addressing concerns, and providing reassurance. This can help build trust and credibility and strengthen the relationship between a member of Congress and their audiences. A crisis presents numerous challenges and does little for the actual capacity of the institution to function over the long term, but it also presents offices with an opportunity to communicate effectively, demonstrate leadership, and build trust with the public.

5
Crisis Implications
Asymmetric Resources and Constrained Capacity

> *It is still sort of an elite population whose communication tend to rise to the surface on [Twitter]. (Interview 109)*

When it comes to technological or organizational change, Congress is often a top-down institution playing a game of whack-a-mole. The institution is not known for anticipating new ideas or problems, so when a crisis emerges or the cultural calculus changes, Congress responds and does so in a way that requires the least amount of coordination and institutional disruption. Party leaders have resource advantages and creative capacity, so adaptation regularly stems from leadership rather than broad consensus or unified problem recognition because that's simply the quickest way to address a perceived crisis. Congress is an institution full of boundedly rational actors—policymakers who can satisfy rather than maximize their needs and wants. "Good enough" is a phrase that applies to the way Congress responds to emergent ideas, whether those are policy changes or digital innovations like Twitter.

For example, consider the institutional trajectory of the House of Representatives' emergency management operation, more officially known as the Office of Emergency Planning, Preparedness, and Operations. The Sergeant of Arms Emergency Management Division has been the organizational home for the office since February 2010. The office handles emergency planning for House members, their staff, and the Capitol, often highlighted by coordination during new member transitions and events like the State of the Union. But this lesser-known congressional office began its tenure as a unit within the Speaker's office. In the wake of 9/11 and the threat of bioterror, the office was established in January 2002 with direct oversight by the Speaker in consultation with the minority leader. For eight years, the continuity of operations in the House was managed within the confines of a party leader office rather than a separate institutional home. Congressional response to emergent threats has been described as at a "hurried pace" to preserve the continuity of operations. But even when national security isn't the primary

Tweeting Scared. Annelise Russell, Oxford University Press. © Oxford University Press (2025).
DOI: 10.1093/9780197808344.003.0005

focus and the crisis is one of communication rather than terror, the need for continuity often stems from rapid response within a leadership office.

Digital trajectories in Congress follow a similar path. Competitive members who want to find new ways to engage with the press and public drive innovations, but underlying those incentives is an institutional force of leadership with the capacity to shape both communications operations and the resulting output. Party leaders are the resource advantage personified. Leaders are largely unsuccessful at telling lawmakers what to talk about or even how to talk about an issue; however, they shape the digital narrative coming out of Congress by wielding the support and resources necessary to maintain an effective communications operation. Just as leaders provide lawmakers with policy information—taking advantage of asymmetric information—so too they provide the necessary tools and resources for effective digital communication that amplifies a political brand and policy narrative. Offices invest thousands of dollars in Facebook ads, email newsletter programs, telephone townhalls, and targeted outreach. Twitter itself may be cheap—theoretically—but creating a comprehensive digital operation that is both effective and efficient requires an investment that goes beyond just an iPhone and a social media–savvy college graduate.

Members of Congress and their staff turn to party and committee leaders to manage and filter the overload of information coming in and out of Congress because the media storm is often more than a 26-year-old digital staffer can manage alone. Twitter has only amplified the information avalanche as staff attempt to filter out the necessary information of the day, engage on topics of importance, and predict what information can wait for another day. Digital communication in Congress has developed as a crisis of communication where offices increasingly acknowledge the power of rapid response but do so with uncertainty about the long-term gains. The growing incentives for digital, paired with the potential for a bigger spotlight, necessitate coordination and external support by party leaders because the demand for digital tools outweighs what many offices can supply. The crisis of communication cycle continues because offices are perpetually preparing for digital disruptions, managing the threat by reaching out for external support and communication coordination. The implication of that demand is unequal power structures between leaders and rank-and-file members, fueling asymmetric institutional power and capacity.

In this chapter, I explain to what degree lawmaker resource advantages shape two fundamental aspects of digital behavior in Congress: (1) how lawmakers manage their communications operation and (2) how they message to connect with a digital constituency. The challenge to understanding the impact of disparate resources across Congress is the effect it has both behind the scenes and on offices' digital presentation. The scope of what lawmakers are expected to do digitally is expansive, and the incentive to "do it all" shapes both organization and the final messaging products. Lawmakers use digital tools to buttress their reputation, making investments in staff and prioritizing communications that meet their political goals. Interviews with congressional staff and reporters suggest that the resources an office has indicate its investment in digital. When an office can't afford to purchase Adobe's Creative Suite, that signals more than just how a lawmaker thinks about photo editing and suggests that an office is going to turn elsewhere to meet its digital demand. Additionally, offices able to invest in communications manage their priorities and self-present differently on Twitter. What lawmakers say on Twitter reflects their diverse priorities—ranging from climate change policy to political pot shots. I detail the impact of resources on digital communications using multiple datasets of tweets across the House and Senate to examine patterns in lawmakers' digital agendas and how their rhetorical agendas online connect to institutional norms and resource constraints. I illustrate how the political content in lawmakers' official tweets is patterned by resources and associated leadership advantages. Each lawmaker makes unique choices regarding their digital strategy, but a content analysis of their rhetorical agendas on Twitter suggests this pattern is not completely idiosyncratic.

This mixed-methods approach illustrates how these resource advantages shape lawmakers' investment in communication capacity and contribute to the cycle of crisis communication. Resources matter for curating digital reputations, but even Twitter's low communication costs can't overcome the resource asymmetries between rank-and-file members and party leaders that define legislative behavior. Lawmakers see the potential to influence the narratives coming out of Congress with their digital investment, but that influence over the supply of information is conditional on both the office's digital strategy and the resources accessible to break through the political noise.

How Resources Matter for Digital

The notion that Twitter could be the great equalizer in political power is akin to the American dream that we "pull ourselves up by our bootstraps"—the perception is powerful but largely far-fetched as most lawmakers don't have the resources to make that messaging independence a reality. Members cannot rival the digital engagement of Representative Alexandria Ocasio-Cortez with just a cell phone and some good ideas. In 2010, members could get away with just linking to a press release on Twitter to build a digital presence, but in 2023, they are expected to have eye-catching graphics, professional videos, and edited photos that mirror the quality of a public relations firm. Most of Congress simply can't meet that expectation, due to lack of either resources or expertise—which often go together. Party leaders extend their asymmetric advantage beyond just policymaking by providing the graphics, videos, and social media content necessary for digital reputation building. Twitter and Facebook were originally lauded for their ability to disrupt traditional media norms, and while they have altered the information environment in Congress, the political structures that support that exchange remain intact. The incentive to be a digital powerhouse while also maintaining other office functions ultimately constrains staff capacity and perpetuates a crisis of communication. Digital norms have made the average member of Congress more resource and party dependent in terms of both policy and messaging. Communication hierarchies are maintained by political, committee, and caucus leaders who can invest in their own communication capacity while also providing what I refer to as a "communication subsidy" to resource-dependent members. In the House, this comes in the form of toolkits, talking points, and templates for graphics. In the Senate, it's not about the content but rather the coordination, staging, and logistical support from the caucus (Interview 187).

Even among Senate offices that typically have more autonomy from leadership, some lawmakers are better positioned to expend the necessary resources for digital engagement. In the Senate, where large state populations bolster an office budget, some lawmakers have the capacity to make bigger investments in communication. Texas Republican Ted Cruz can take advantage of an office budget bolstered by a large, distant constituency in Texas and uses those resources to nab the spotlight on Twitter, cable news, or his own podcast.[1] He is able to build his national reputation with a comparatively large communications staff of seven or eight staffers, including a communications coordinator to direct rapid response (Interview 146). Conversely, Virginia Democratic Senator Tim Kaine has traditionally staffed a smaller press team that rarely enters the political fray on Twitter; for many years he left the responsibility of Twitter content to campaign staff (Interview 52). Comparing the two lawmakers, Senator Cruz has more than three million followers on his government-run Twitter account, while Senator Kaine's Senate account,

[1] https://www.independent.co.uk/news/world/americas/us-politics/ted-cruz-ketanji-brown-jackson-twitter-b2043898.html

which wasn't active until August 2022, has just a few thousand followers. Even Senator Kaine's individual account, that of a former vice presidential candidate, has fewer than one million followers. Cruz and Kaine are two senators with very different priorities, and those priorities shape the digital investment they make and how they publicly present in a Twitter-driven information environment.

The autonomy to set and promote an agenda online is constrained by office budgets and political capital. More specifically, budgets influence the digital priorities across offices because the money that staff have to spend on communication will incentivize different behaviors and limit possibilities. For example, an office that has allocated $500 to digital equipment is differently positioned than an office that has $5,000 to spend. Even taking into account the House Member's Representational Allowance increases in 2022, the budget is always a constant push and pull. An office with a smaller digital budget may be using an iPhone as its primary tool for capturing content, while another office may be able to spend $2,000 on a nice Canon or Sony camera. An office with more resources may be spending more money on photo editing software, while others have to rely on alternative, cost-cutting software that limits what they can offer presentation-wise. These investments are not just about producing industry-quality digital content; they are central to the broader communication strategy because a well-placed graphic can become the basis for a floor chart or a graphic on MSNBC (Interview 187). Strategic communication in Congress, ideally, considers digital as a way to amplify a message and build connections across more traditional media outputs that some senior members, who may be digitally hesitant, more readily understand as a value-add.

Resource asymmetries are not a novelty in Congress—policymaking has been increasingly the purview of party leaders who maintain information inequities relative to rank-and-file members. Members of Congress make strategic choices constrained by resources, and those resource-driven incentives influence how they access the political agenda, the scope of their influence, and how information moves throughout the institution (Curry, 2015; Sinclair, 2016). Congressional rules, structures, and norms affect legislative outcomes by directing the distribution of power and resources (Anzia & Jackman, 2013; Schickler, 2005; Wawro & Schickler, 2007). Members pick their battles in prioritizing and devoting attention to issues, splitting time and staff between policy and representation (Furnas et al., 2021; Hall, 1998; LaPira et al., 2020; Russell, 2021b). This is compounded by lawmakers who have more resources, such as staff and time, being less reliant on others for information (Anderson et al., 2020).

This book broadens the application of asymmetric resources to include digital decision-making, explaining how institutional constraints link up with digital representation in terms of both communication strategy and digital outputs. Those same policy information inequities are tied to digital reputation building, leaving some members unable to be sufficient content producers in an increasingly digital environment. The problem of too few resources is a constant across both chambers, albeit felt even more strongly in the House where communications are the responsibility of just one or two staffers who must compete for digital influence and attention. These resources directly and indirectly shape both their legislative behavior and their relationship with party leadership in the chamber (Anderson et al., 2020; Curry, 2015). How those resources are managed shapes agenda setting within the chamber, intra-institutional relationships between members, and legislative activities that senators use to build reputations during their time in office.

Defining "Communication Subsidy" in Congress

Legislators and their staff form what Salisbury and Shepsle (1981) call a legislative "enterprise"—also referred to as a small business, dictatorship, and political fiefdom—and the collective mission is to advance the principal's goals. Congressional communication is driven by the need to sell a member's political brand, and staff are largely responsible for the content that supports that brand. There are a handful of lawmakers who maintain their own Twitter accounts (e.g., Senators Brian Schatz and Chris Murphy), but even lawmakers who take part in the digital load still make investments in digital support. Senators may be sending their own tweets, but there is no senator making their own graphics or shooting their own video footage. Members rely on a team because priorities atrophy unless there is a plan to manage immediate needs while moving toward strategic goals. Many members of Congress do not even have the password to their own Twitter account because that is not the role they play on that team. But the enterprise of a congressional office remains limited in terms of its communication capacity as time, labor, and information filtering are all costly and scarce resources that require some level of external support to maintain a robust operation. The demand for digital is one reason the burnout rate is so high for communication and digital staff on the Hill. The price of promoting legislation and a political brand often exceeds the capacity of a single office and means staff look for messaging support

—what I term a "communication subsidy." This subsidy consists of the regular support that lawmakers and their staff receive from party leaders, committee staff, and the caucus that guides messaging, supports digital training, and targets the needs of communications staff. The emphasis on professionalized communications contrasted by the limited resources within each office facilitates leadership's influence through communication subsidies, distinct from their policymaking influence, based on their ability to provide information to congressional offices that aids their digital communication efforts.

The notion of lawmakers seeking external support for their lawmaking activities is nothing new, as members have sought out what others term a "legislative subsidy"—a source of costly policy and political information that supports legislative efforts (Hall & Deardorff, 2006). Like lobbyist support that aims to assist lawmakers in seeking similar objectives, party leaders support lawmakers' digital efforts that reinforce a common political effort. Party leaders cannot force members to stay on message—it would be a fruitless exercise because members are not only politically diverse but also fiercely stubborn—but they do aim to provide the means for lawmakers to reinforce political messages that meet the collective needs of the party and its status within the institution. A "large, large role" is how one staffer described the role that leadership and the caucus play in providing guidance and graphics for offices to incorporate into their communications operation. Language gets "trickled down" from leadership such that talking points are provided and then members can adapt that content as necessary for their own priorities and audience (Interview 115). "We get daily emails, almost like hourly emails, from the Speaker's office about talking points, or what's happening on the floor, or what's coming up, or just a transcript of the speaker's messaging . . . so tons of content" (Interview 87).

From a logistical standpoint, parties maintain communications websites where staff can log in and find talking points from leadership as well as potential communication pitfalls to avoid (Interview 115). For example, during the impeachment of President Trump, House Democrats were given explicit guidance from Speaker Pelosi's office on words the office wanted them to use on a daily and weekly basis (Interview 115). Party leaders become a central hub for members who need sample messaging, ideas for navigating political pitfalls, and graphics that fuel a unified message (Interview 183). For example, the presence of the caucus in digital messaging is easily felt during holidays, when members rely on external graphics rather than devoting scarce time to more routine messaging. In 2022, dozens of Democratic offices used

Figure 5.1 House Democrats Easter 2022 graphic
Source: Twitter.

House Democrats' branded digital messaging to celebrate the Easter holiday (Figure 5.1).

Leaders can provide communication assistance to members with constrained budgets, and lawmakers can support their own digital efforts while also supporting the party's political agenda. In many ways, the framework for a digital and communication strategy is a function of constrained budgets in addition to preferences. As one staffer described (Interview 118), the mission of the conference chair's office was to provide a communication subsidy that ensured offices had templates for messaging that could help sell agenda items. The staffer noted that the office worked to counsel members on how to use social media—which was often needed by younger staff—and to provide training, videos, and content that they could share.

Leaders within the party and at the top of committees are not aiming to change legislators' policy preferences but rather to give them the tools to engage in digital agenda setting with resources that set the agenda for how an issue will be discussed. Leadership often provides the support but then amplifies individual members on the backend, making sure members get ample attention when pushing a digital message or political agenda (Interview 118). Those with the resources for robust communications can subsidize the necessary digital resources for members within their caucus who lack the capacity otherwise. Some members never use the materials that leaders share, whereas others are especially dependent on those materials, but the regular maintenance of communication support suggests leadership has a fundamental and accepted role in how messaging is considered and the issues that will shape the messaging calendar for an office.

The literature on communication investment in Congress is relatively nonexistent, and the impact of digital on congressional capacity has largely gone unexplored. At the same time, the impact of digital communication within Congress has only increased and been amplified by politicians seeking to affect the political agenda. As digital norms rapidly shift along with technological innovations, there will perpetually be uncertainty about the future of digital incentives for lawmakers. But one certainty is that regardless of the platform or mechanism, seeking new tools for communication is not an anomaly, and the support for such engagement will only continue to grow as members position themselves to communicate in a digitally connected political ecosystem.

Resource-Driven Organization and Management

The contemporary Congress relies on digital to amplify political agendas and share information across many media venues, which can then be filtered and consumed by individual offices, committees, and staff. All lawmakers' offices use Twitter as a mechanism for tracking information and producing tailored content for reputation building, but an office's digital discretion is bound by the costs of information, available resources, and lawmaker priorities (Gandy, 1982). Twitter is not a costless activity, and neither is the communication infrastructure necessary to support a robust digital and traditional press operation. Lawmakers have their own priorities and preferences that shape the digital discernment within an office—they aren't going to spend human or political capital focusing on issues or debates that do not support their representational goals (Hall & Deardorff, 2006; Salisbury & Shepsle, 1981). Offices must decide where communication, and digital specifically, fits into the broader set of governing priorities. In addition to member-specific preferences, the institutional limits placed on offices shape how lawmakers engage in the digital political ecosystem. Resources vary in predictable yet unequal ways, both within and across chambers, to affect not only choices about policy but also how to communicate and what to talk about.

Budgets and the allocation of resources across an office impact not only the style of lawmaker behavior but also the digital choices an office can opt into. Resource asymmetries shape digital representation, leading to variable patterns of communication organization within offices, uptake of digital material from party leaders, and differing styles of digital engagement across members. Not all legislators prioritize communications the same way, both for electoral and for policymaking reasons (Russell, 2021a), but that communication is also tied to institutional constraints. For example, in the House, the Speaker's office has 17 communications staffers to advance the leader's and the caucus's agenda, but a rank-and-file member is considered well staffed with two people managing communications.

I argue that resource asymmetries pattern how offices organize their communications operation and invest in digital production. Members weigh the incentives for investing in communication as an office decides how to define a lawmaker's own success within Congress. To examine variations in that reputation-building behavior and understand the behind-the-scenes choices associated with the more visible digital inputs, I conducted a series of interviews with communications professionals in and around Congress. Interviews with communications and digital staff, policy staff, and the congressional press corps illuminate variable communication strategies across the Hill, the rising role of digital in those practices, and a communication subsidy that leaders provide to coordinate digital outreach. Respondents were asked to discuss their professional practices, communication coordination, and the challenges of digital communication in Congress.

The most common refrain among respondents was that to understand congressional communication norms, as well as digital practices, you must consider each office's individualized norms. Staffers describe each office as its own enterprise, and to be able to maintain those operations, each office decides how it wants to prioritize digital and traditional communications. Some offices place an emphasis on digital engagement—their senator would argue that the job is "half applied history and half political communication," while in other offices it wasn't uncommon for communications to be an afterthought (Interview 145). The growing role of digital is acknowledged by all, but how to take advantage of it and what that looks like daily is variable. One office may consider sufficient digital engagement to be at least one tweet per day, while others are churning out seven or eight tweets, with another four or five from the principal (Interview 133). The priorities for digital are directly tied to the investment—as President Biden once quipped, "Show me your budget and I'll tell you what you value." And digital isn't cheap. The budget is a big problem for communications staff because most likely won't get the incredibly expensive, difficult-to-obtain software and equipment they need (Interview 95). Some offices, particularly frontline members and those in competitive races, are encouraged to spend more money on Facebook ads and franked mail, which can quickly limit their additional capacity to execute an effective communications operation. "Capacity was a huge deal. If I had more capacity, it would have been easier" (Interview 143).

The need for greater communication capacity tied to limited budgets is one reason rank-and-file offices seek out a variety of support sources, most often from leadership, caucuses, and committees. Each of those entities is designed to play some organizational or collective role in policymaking, but collaborative communication is an equal part of the mission. The caucus or conference regularly plays a role in disseminating message strategy, coordinating with party and committee leadership. Staff recognize that those coordinated communication resources—the basis of my conceptualization of a "communication subsidy"—play an important role in shaping how and when lawmakers engage to build a reputation online. Those offices that don't invest in communications or that lack the ability to do so can't build the same online strategy unless they receive support in seeking out resources to meet the digital demand. As one former communications director described, the incentive for reaching out is simply a lack of manpower within an office to create content that meets the 24/7 demand for engagement. "Resources weigh very heavily on how you're going to respond, and they can definitely be limiting as well. If you don't have it, you don't have the manpower or the technology. You just can't do as much" (Interview 56).

To mitigate resource constraints, instead of further investment across offices, Congress manages communication needs through leadership office support and those with the resources to make and distribute communications content. As new members are entering the Hill with more native digital skills, the relationship between leadership and offices has changed in terms of what they need on a day-to-day basis, but the support structure has continued throughout the modern era of digital and web-driven communication in Congress. In 2010, leadership offices were holding meetings with press secretaries to simply encourage them to be on Twitter—much to the amusement of staffers at the time who thought Twitter was ridiculous (Interview 151). Five years later, Republican leadership had five digital staffers working at the Capitol doing digital training around the clock, Monday through Friday. Democrats established a six-week digital academy through the Progressive Caucus, and later caucus leadership, to train junior staffers to be effective communicators in an increasingly digital-driven institution.

Beyond training staffers and encouraging more collaboration across communication platforms, leaders' offices also play a central role in supporting members' outreach by coordinating with cable news programs and facilitating radio spots. Leaders maintain and reinforce their communication asymmetry by offering up cable news opportunities to members. A staffer in Speaker Pelosi's office served as a filter for bookers from network news stations—MSNBC, FOX, and CNN. When producers or bookers reached out, she would tell members and staff "you should do this" (Interview 143). Among congressional Republicans, where talk radio is a higher priority, leadership would set up "radio row" in the basement of the Capitol through which communications staff could bring their members (Interview 103). In the Senate, bigger budgets also mean more digital communication support, but it is still coordinated by parties. For example, the Senate Democratic Media Center provides a ticket system for offices to request graphics, training, photo, and video assistance, but that support is run by the majority leader. Some offices, like that of Senator Bernie Sanders, make the choice to invest in videographers, but a dedicated team of photo and video editors remains a rarity in personal offices in 2023. As one communications director described it, having a digital content creator who can manage video editing and production on their own means you are "blessed" in terms of what you can do with your press operation (Interview 129). These offices can be nimble with their digital content without relying on external support. While House offices raised the Member's Representational Allowance in 2022, giving offices more latitude for investing in digital, the reality remains that there is great competition for digital staff and resources need to be maximized for effective social media.

Not all tweets are created equal, and a professionalized digital communications shop requires investing in staff who can discern how to manage the influx of information and filter out the political riffraff from the news of the day. Part of this judgment comes from doing the job, which requires investing in staff that have that experience. Resource advantages in communication also stem from staffing priorities, the choice to manage dual policy and communications pressures, and the ability to control the narrative by responding to events in real time online. Party leaders, like Republican Senator Mitch McConnell, are able to maximize the professionalization of their digital outreach because the press team is easily double or triple that of an average office and tends to have less turnover. For example, Senator McConnell retained his primary communications advisor during the digital shift in Congress for more than a decade. That longevity means consistent messaging, trust between a principal and staff, and long-term relationships with reporters covering Congress. Many staffers and journalists attribute a leader's professionalization to the resources they can dedicate to communications to manage the information deluge. On the House side, former Majority Leader Steny Hoyer developed a team of digital fellows who were producing graphics, running live-streams, and learning to create digital content across multiple platforms. The difference often comes down to the available dollars to pay for a team of press staffers versus a "one-man-band" press team and a lack of institutional support from leadership or the caucus (Smith & Russell, 2022). One journalist noted the "discipline" applied to communications in more professionalized offices, using the example of Senator Chuck Schumer, who shifted from being indiscriminate in his press access—the guy who never turned away from a TV camera—in his early years in the House to carefully calculating the risks and consequences of his policy-directed communications in Senate leadership. With Schumer's rise to the top spot in the Senate came a doubling-down of digital investment across the caucus and support of digital and traditional media through the Senate Democratic Media Center.

Another example of resource advantages across offices is the balance lawmakers strike between policy and communications staffing. Multiple staff members interviewed emphasized how that balance shapes the priorities that then get revealed in public-facing communications. Former communications staffers gave examples of members who are known publicly for viral videos but within Congress for high turnover and junior staff in leadership roles. One example of this is the reputation of former Democratic Representative Katie Porter, whose white-board persona is seen as an example of policy prowess but actually reflects her messaging bona fides. This type of trade-off in policy staff is constrained by both the resources available to relatively junior members and choices about how to spend those resources. Across the respondents, there was a sense that lawmakers can afford to forgo a policymaking reputation if their digital policy presentation is effective. A few members have been explicit about their decision to forego developing policy staff and instead focus on political or communication priorities; for example, *Roll Call* reported in 2012 that Senator Ron Johnson was dropping his legislative staff in a pivot toward messaging.[2]

The growth of digital means new opportunities to coordinate messaging, new venues for new constituencies, and greater decision-making about how to be creative with a political brand. But with the potential advantages of digital comes the reality that Congress struggles to keep pace with technological change. Offices seek remedies for coordination problems, inefficiencies, and increased digital demand—which for now are solved by whatever digital subsidy that leaders, caucuses, and committees can provide. The Congressional Data Coalition describes Congress's digital capacity as "far behind what it

[2] *Roll Call*, https://rollcall.com/2012/04/12/in-pivot-to-messaging-ron-johnson-looks-to-purge-staff/.

needs to keep up with emerging technology trends,"[3] and the reality is that limited capacity is fueled by the resource asymmetries for communication within the institution.

Resources Shape Digital Outputs

Congress now shares information online in 280-character snippets where policy, politics, and constituent outreach account for the majority of members' digital output (Hemphill et al., 2021; Russell, 2021a). Congress has transitioned from an institution struggling to convince lawmakers to take digital seriously to one where a common goal is more digital, more engagement, and more content production. The costs associated with digital production shape behind-the-scenes behavior by congressional staff and their principals, but those costs are also tied to an office's digital output. A lawmaker's priorities and capacity to promote those priorities are revealed through the choices they make online about what to talk about and when. For example, a freshman House member with a shoestring budget still trying to define their political brand will communicate differently than a Senate leader with a team of communications professionals managing the conference agenda. Partisanship, ideology, and elections explain a lot about lawmakers' self-presentation (Gulati, 2004; Niven & Zilber, 2001; Russell, 2021a), but the resources an office has influence its digital outreach. Resource asymmetries and institutional resources constrain what an office can do in terms of digital strategy, and the realities of those asymmetries affect lawmakers' rhetorical agendas on Twitter.

Resource and Chamber Differences in Policy Communication

Communicating as a House member means playing an almost entirely different ballgame than the folks in the Senate, as detailed in Chapter 4. The Senate and its individual members have long been viewed as being more enterprising and individually impactful when it comes to the legislative process, and those same assumptions extend to reputation building on Twitter, where senators are expected to do and say more. On any given day, the average senator has to be ready to answer questions about any issue moving through the policy process, but a House member is more likely to be questioned only on the

[3] https://congressionaldata.org/

few issues related to their committees or expertise. Most research on congressional messaging focuses on one chamber or makes general assumptions across both, but chamber nuance and the associated resources suggest important differences in lawmakers' digital agenda setting. By examining tweets by both House and Senate official accounts during 2017, I show distinct chamber differences in online self-presentation. The typical senator tweets more frequently, prioritizes policy more often, and curates a more diverse policy agenda online.[4] These differences in digital engagement are tied to both the resources that lawmakers have and the broader expectations for engagement that reflect differing levels of congressional capacity across the two chambers. The presentation choices that lawmakers make are particular to their legislative environments.

On a per-member basis, the Senate has higher capacity in terms of resources and personnel (Brudnick, 2024). A Senate press shop is two to three times larger than a House press team. The Senate has more than a two-to-one advantage in personnel per member, across all major positions. Recently, the number of communications professionals has increased as a function of representation staff (Crosson et al., 2021), but senators have more money to spend per office and average a higher number of communications staffers (Brudnick, 2019). These additional resources paired with the nationalized, partisan environment in the Senate mean that engaging with a broad-based digital constituency on Twitter fits the incentives of the platform and the institution.

Research suggests that all politicians are increasingly messaging on national policy debates (Abramowitz & Webster, 2016; Sievert & McKee, 2019), but senators have added opportunity to capitalize on policy discussions. Matthews (1960) noted that being a member of the Senate facilitates a national reputation. Senators' resources and electoral incentives mean they can develop a national policymaking reputation and use that in their self-presentation (Sievert & McKee, 2019). Senators must engage in digital representation with a more diverse policy agenda because of their incentives for policy expertise and placement across multiple committees/subcommittees. Members of the Senate average a higher number of committee assignments and employ more policy staff (Reynolds, 2021).

To test the expectation of institutional differences in digital outputs, I use data from Hemphill et al. (2021) that codes all tweets of the official accounts of members of the 115th Congress by topic, totaling ~1.47 million tweets. To

[4] A version of this subsection was previously published: Smith, S, & Russell, A. (2022). Different chambers, divergent rhetoric: Institutional differences and policy representation on social media. *American Political Research*, *50*(6), 792–797.

Table 5.1 Descriptive Statistics for Twitter Activity in the 115th Congress, by Chamber

	All	Senate	House
Number of tweets	2,835.6 (2–9,458)	4,053.2 (243–8,941)	2,544.8 (2–9,458)
Overall topic diversity index	0.27 (0.9–1)	0.23 (0.09–0.40)	0.29 (0.10–1)
Policy diversity	0.11 (0.07–0.53)	0.11 (0.07–0.20)	0.12 (0.07–0.53)
Tenure	15.5 years (2–54)	20.4 years (2–48)	14.3 years (2–54)
Female	20.6%	20.8%	20.6%
Republican	54.2%	52.5%	54.6%
Party leader	9.2%	19.8%	6.7%
Committee leader	8.8%	22.8%	5.4%
	$N = 524$	$N = 101$	$N = 423$

measure differences in policy-specific digital presentation, the tweets were coded first to identify any mention of public policy and second, using the Comparative Agendas Project schema, to categorize tweets with mentions of policy into 20 categories (Hemphill et al., 2021).[5]

Senators, in general, tweet more than House members, and nearly all the counts by policy area by chamber are statistically different in favor of greater policy comment by senators (Table 5.1). The picture is similarly nuanced when considering the share of attention (i.e., the share of a legislator's tweets devoted to a given topic) as senators spent a higher share of tweets on policy across different issues and across chambers.

Senators are more likely to tweet about policy topics and general government operations. They are more likely to prioritize social topics, including health, social welfare, and housing. They also are more likely to produce tweets relating to the physical environment and energy. The implications of these chamber differences suggest that the institutional differences, including resources and digital support, are associated with lawmakers' presentation and digital output for reputation building (Figure 5.2).

To further test chamber and resource differences, an ordinary least squares regression reports the relationship between the number of tweets per member of Congress and individual and institutional factors. The total number of policy tweets overall is the dependent variable, and each column reports results for either the Senate chamber indicator, personnel expenditures, or

[5] The coding is derived from manually labeled data by Russell (2018) to train a logistic regression classifier, finding that a bag-of-words vectorization and logistic regression achieved the best performance in correctly identifying policy tweets.

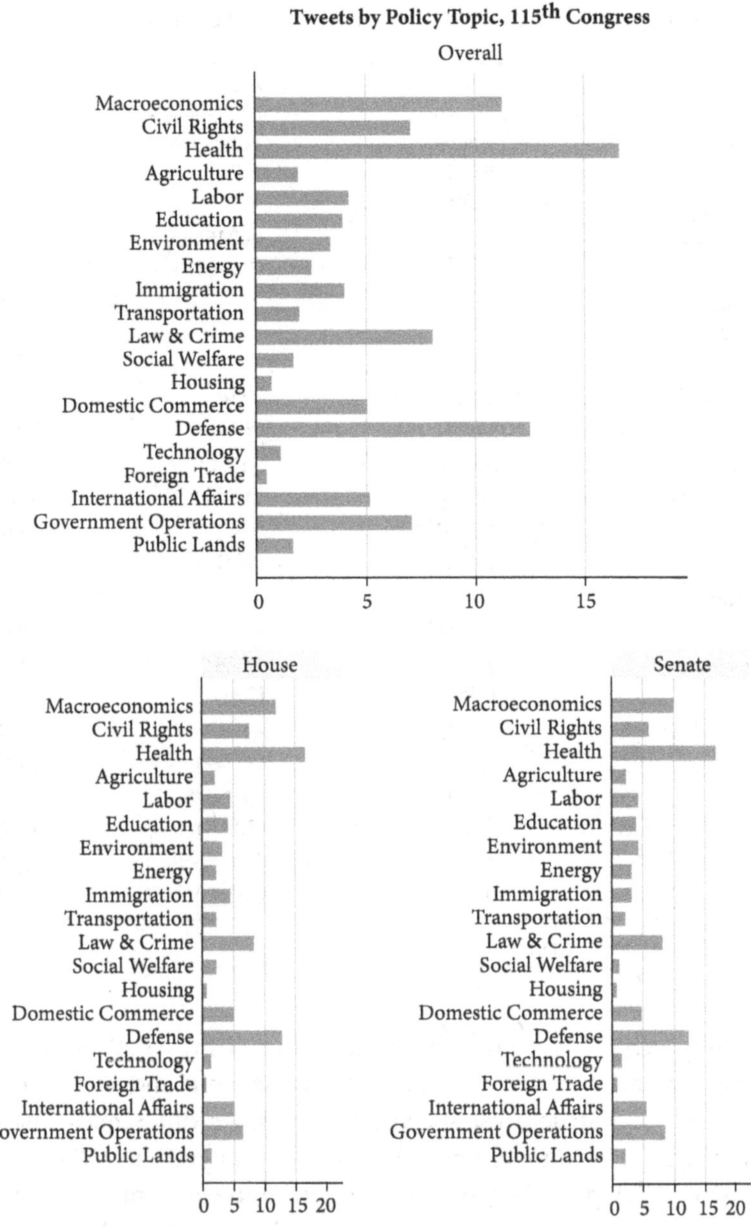

Figure 5.2 Tweets by policy topic during the 115th Congress, House and Senate

jurisdiction population as the main variable of interest. There is a high degree of collinearity between these variables; this is unsurprising given that member office budgets are, in part, a function of the constituency served. The results support the expectation that senators tweet more and that tweeting is associated with greater capacity and a greater population served (Table 5.2).

Table 5.2 Policy-Related Twitter Activity for Members of Congress

	(1)	(2)	(3)
	Policy tweets	Policy tweets	Policy tweets
Senate	936.7***		
	(130.9)		
Personnel spending		0004578***	
		(00005957)	
Jurisdiction population			00008672***
			(00001379)
Tenure	13.44**	12.91**	16.26***
	(4.68)	(4.5)	(4.817)
Electoral security	−12.59*	−12.48*	−15.09*
	(6.153)	(5.954)	(6.325)
Female	377.9***	359.7***	365***
	(107.7)	(105.5)	(109.9)
Republican	−487***	−466.3***	−514.8***
	(85.73)	(84.28)	(89.23)
Party leader	322.2	267.5	296.5
	(197.7)	(197)	(207.3)
Committee leader	−174.9	−141.8	93.4
	(126.9)	(123.4)	(143.9)
Constant	1,971***	1,649***	2,092***
	(343.3)	(329.8)	(360)
Observations	519	515	515
R^2	0.332	0.358	0.300

*p < 0.05, **p < 0.01, ***p < 0.001.

The results suggest that how we understand self-presentation in the Twitter environment is defined by not only partisanship and media norms but also institutional structures, specifically chamber differences, that extend to nonlegislative actions online. Members of Congress use Twitter to promote their policy priorities, but given the resource advantages, institutional incentives, and electoral context of a senator, how a senator builds that reputation is notably different than a House member. Senators are more vocal on Twitter, particularly about policy issues, and the institutional and resource advantages of senators are associated with these communication differences. Different political and institutional hierarchies shape digital presentation across chambers and constrain how lawmakers build a political reputation on Twitter.

Resource Differences in Partisan Politics on Twitter

The resources that pattern congressional organization also pattern lawmakers' expressed policy and political priorities. As one communications professional outside Congress noted, "We would try to supplement their work as much as possible because they don't have the budgets necessary to adequately understand every issue that their boss, that member of Congress is going to need to be speaking on. . . . Those offices are so underfunded it's a travesty" (Interview 109). The centralization of power and resource inequities (Crosson et al., 2021; Curry, 2015) that embolden some lawmakers' policymaking power extend to their self-presentation.

To further assess the association between resources and communication outputs, I categorize senators' digital communication into two dimensions—partisan content and policy information.[6] Each tweet can contain—or not contain—either dimension, where partisan tweets address their party's successes or the other party's failures and policy tweets include mentions of an issue. This produces a four-part categorization for each communication, where tweets contain none of either dimension (valence tweets), policy-only tweets, partisan-only tweets, and both policy and partisan tweets. A valence tweet, like a birthday message or picture of a senator at a town hall, doesn't require input from a policy director or looping in of the senator for a carefully crafted statement. Policy and political tweets that could draw outsized attention or political opposition are more costly because they take time and investment. These tweets require more eyes to approve content and more time to consider the language and phrasing. This categorization of tweets allows me to assess potential resource- or capacity-related associations in senators' Twitter output.

I expect that the resource advantages linked to member communications will lead to systematic patterns. First, given party leaders' additional funding for staff and digital investment, these resources should mean party leaders have a distinct digital communications strategy. Party leaders have centralized nearly all party office–appropriated spending within the Legislative Branch Appropriations Act (Howard & Owens, 2022; Lee, 2008). This leads to expectations that additional resources for these party leaders will shape behavior that assists the broader membership, and the communications staff

[6] A version of this subsection was previously written for and presented at the Center for Effective Lawmaking Conference in Nashville, Tennessee. Russell, A., & Howard, N. (2021). *Constrained communications? Choices in congressional representation.* Center for Effective Lawmaking Conference.

within a leadership office are often working to provide party messaging support across the entire caucus.[7] Coupled with the need to relay policy successes and partisan fights for their respective parties, these resources mean party leaders should have distinct digital communications. These leaders have the knowledge and capability through selected staff (Montgomery & Nyhan, 2017) to disseminate information to interested audiences and thus should push both policy and partisan types of communication content onto Twitter.

In addition to party leaders, committee leaders have relative resource advantages that stem from chairmanship allocations. These funds provide committees with additional staff to oversee the executive branch, bureaucratic agencies, and courts—as well as conduct sessions to manage legislative development. Thus, the committee chair receives outsized benefits of staff allocations for this role, in addition to the staff allocation for their personal office. Given the directly stated nature of committee jurisdictions, committee chairs should communicate with their digital constituencies about policy work. That is, these senators are uniquely situated to develop a policy-specific agenda on Twitter. While these same senators may face pressures to communicate partisan messages to attain—and maintain—their position, this is mitigated by the strong presumption of seniority as a determining factor in chair selection.[8] Therefore, I expect committee chairs to communicate much more about policy content than any other member.

Finally, the Senators' Official Personnel and Office Expense Account (SOPOEA) provides certain members, regardless of leadership status, with more resources to produce digital content. The SOPOEA allocation is directly tied to administrative allowances based on state population, office expenses, and their distance from Washington, DC (Brudnick, 2020). Resource-advantaged senators here are those whose home states are a greater distance from Washington, DC and whose states have higher populations. These members, though they have more constituents—and therefore more interests—to manage and a greater distance to travel to be visible to constituents, can push out more content due to their increased staff. As one Senate staffer noted, a senator from California—a large state with more extensive matching resources—could invest in communications in ways that a senator from North Dakota could not (Interview 81). This means that the communications issued by these senators should accomplish more than those of senators without such capital, who have the ability to travel home more often and face a smaller electorate. Those members should prioritize local or direct ties

[7] Personal communication with congressional staff.

[8] The senior-most majority party committee member who has not been selected as a chair for another committee or timed out of their eligibility is most often appointed.

to a constituency, as they are both closer to their constituents and lack the resources to communicate about public policy or offer meaningful contributions to national partisan debates. Members with a longer distance to their states or higher populations should use Twitter to accomplish a more diverse range of goals, as they use social media as an additional constituent interaction tool on all fronts. Thus, I expect all forms of communication across these categories to be more likely for these senators.

Together, these expectations suggest that senators are constrained by the costs of generating nonvalence communication. These resources consist primarily of the money given to a member's office to hire staff who provide policy- and partisan-related communications. Senators are not provided equal access to these resources, as some members have more and others have less access. This allows resource-rich members to expend considerably more resources on communication strategies and effective messaging compared to senators with limited capacity and, in turn, self-presentation constraints.

Model and Results

I expect that the way senators shape their messaging online is influenced by the resource imbalances that guide how they prioritize their communication strategies. To examine this, I analyze their Twitter activity over three years—2013, 2015, and 2017—using data collected from their official accounts via the Twitter API, which adds up to over 286,000 tweets. These years capture a key period when Congress was transitioning into a Twitter-focused information environment. Plus, the first year of each congressional session tends to see a spike in Twitter activity (Russell, 2021b). I intentionally chose nonelection years to avoid the messiness of electoral distractions for at least a third of the senators.

I break down my expectations for how senators prioritize their tweets across three big areas: policy, party politics, and more general valence issues (see Russell & Howard, 2021). Tweets about public policy or legislation are labeled as "policy rhetoric." On the partisan side, I include any tweet mentioning political parties or their leaders, like "Republican leader." Everything else—whether local matters, shoutouts to constituents, or holiday wishes—falls under valence issues. So, the framework for the coding captures the types of tweets senators put out, categorized into one of four groups: (1) valence communication, which is the baseline I use in the models below; (2) policy communication; (3) partisan communication; and (4) a mix of both policy and partisan communication.

I measure each senator's unique characteristics, factoring in a series of variables to capture both individual limitations and the resources they have from the institution. I focus on resource advantages tied to things like whether a senator holds a leadership position in their party, the size of their state's population, and how far their state is from DC. Population and state size play a big role in shaping a senator's budget, and they're key to understanding the resource differences between members. As one former communications director put it bluntly when describing her large staff, the office budget is directly proportional to the state size (Interview 146). I also include dichotomous measures of committee leadership, candidacy in the next election cycle, party affiliation, gender, and racial minority. Political incentives are measured by senators' ideological extremity from the median, percentage vote share in their previous election, seat security in the presidential election, and the similar party affiliation of their same state-colleague. I also include standard measures of congressional session, seniority, and continuous age, and legislative effectiveness scores are borrowed from Volden and Wiseman (2014).

I estimate a multinomial logit model to test the expectations about the institution-linked constraints on digital reputation building. The coefficients relate lawmakers' individual characteristics to their preference for policy, politics, or valence issues, and the standard errors are clustered by member.[9] Table 5.3 presents the results in three parts, with the first column focusing on policy tweets, the second on partisan tweets, and the third on tweets that have both partisan and policy content. As each part is a different outcome within the same multinomial logistic regression, all results relate to the effect that an increase in the covariate has on the probability a tweet falls within a dependent variable category relative to valence issues. As you can see in Table 5.3, when a party leader sends a tweet, it has a nuanced impact on what that tweet is about. The results generally back up the idea that party leaders are more likely to combine partisan and policy content in their tweets. Interestingly, there's even more focus on partisan messaging than I expected, with a noticeable increase in tweets that are purely partisan. On the policy side, though, being a party leader doesn't seem to have any significant effect on the likelihood of tweeting about policy compared to valence issues. Previous

[9] This model structure is common practice, with a nonordered dependent variable and explanatory variables that are attributes of individuals, in our case US senators. To account for potential downward-biased standard errors (Mortensen, 2012) and produce unbiased standard errors, we conduct the model with clustered standard errors (Williams, 2000). Re-estimation is also conducted with traditional standard errors with consistent results.

Table 5.3 Regression Analysis of Senators' Tweets by Content Type

Variables	*Tweet Content Type*		
	Policy	Partisan	Policy and Partisan
Party leader	−0.0768	0.350*	0.446*
	(0.103)	(0.150)	(0.155)
Population	0.00778	0.0184	0.0189*
	(0.00663)	(0.00956)	(0.00833)
Distance	0.125*	0.191*	0.188*
	(0.0479)	(0.0771)	(0.0853)
Committee leader	0.0282	0.0676	0.241
	(0.0864)	(0.226)	(0.214)
Republican	−0.318	−0.000711	0.681
	(0.331)	(0.428)	(0.457)
Extremity	0.305	1.303*	2.405*
	(0.468)	(0.576)	(0.585)
Republican * Extremity	−0.0987	−0.234	−1.344
	(0.845)	(0.936)	(0.951)
Same party delegation	−0.0698	0.516*	0.337*
	(0.0874)	(0.188)	(0.156)
Candidate	0.0827	0.231	0.134
	(0.0818)	(0.169)	(0.183)
Vote share	0.00115	0.00429	−0.000455
	(0.00492)	(0.00728)	(0.00811)
Legislative Effectiveness Score (LES)	−0.0385	−0.153	−0.147
	(0.0509)	(0.0840)	(0.0846)
Seniority	0.00563	0.0104	0.0131
	(0.00820)	(0.0128)	(0.0107)
Senator demographics	YES	YES	YES
Senator activity	YES	YES	YES
Congress fixed effects	YES	YES	YES
Observations			279,133
Log likelihood			−281,319

*p < 0.05, **p < 0.01, ***p < 0.001.

research (Lipinski, 2001) shows that party leaders work hard to get their partisan messages out there, and that trend seems to hold true on Twitter as well.

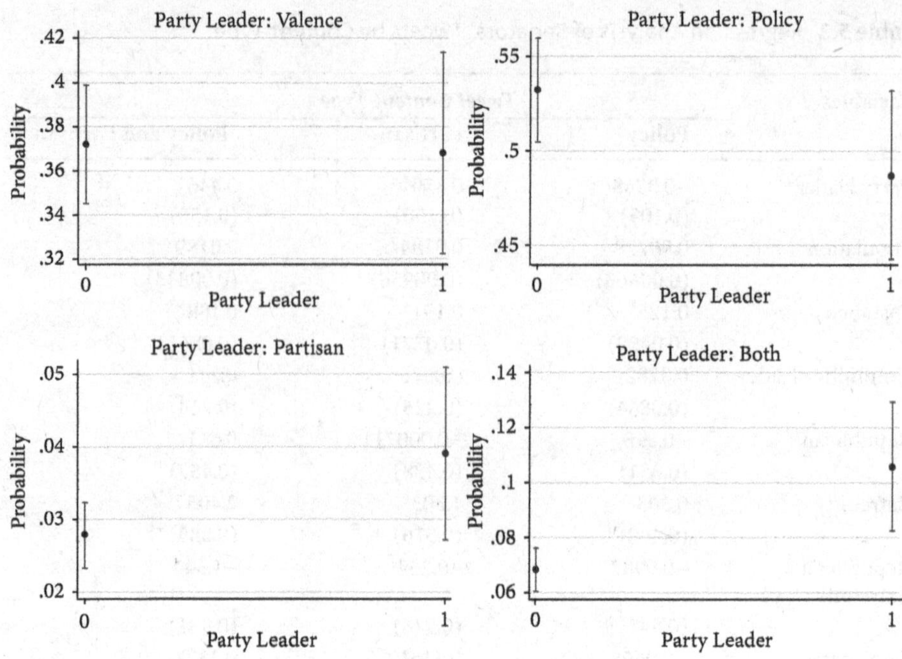

Figure 5.3 Predicted tweet content for Senate party leaders

To help better understand these party leader results, Figure 5.3 presents the predicted probability of a party leader's tweet falling within a category across the dependent variable's four categories. Leadership status doesn't seem to have any clear impact on whether a tweet contains valence content. As shown in the first column of Table 5.3, there's a slight negative effect of party leadership on policy content, but it's not statistically significant (check out the northeast quadrant). However, the lower half of Figure 5.3 tells a different story. The southeast quadrant shows that tweets from party leaders are about 45% more likely to be focused on partisan content compared to those from nonleaders, and they're 54% more likely to include a mix of both policy and party content. This is again statistically significant, demonstrating the effect that the motivations for partisan rhetoric and increased institutional resources have on senators' social media communication.

Additionally, I find support for the political incentives expectation as the results suggest that increases in state population do increase the likelihood of tweets containing content similar to that of party leaders. Figure 5.4 expands upon this, with predicted probability of tweet content across the range of state populations. The results present a relatively flat probability of policy content

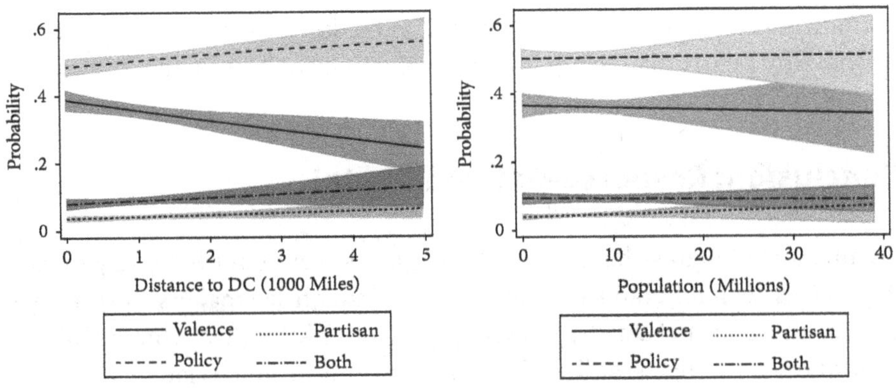

Figure 5.4 Predicted probability of tweet content by state distance and population

tweets for all populations, consistent with Table 5.3. However, I observe a rise from near zero for partisan content for those senators with the lowest population states to slightly above 2% for those with the highest. The same is true for tweets containing both policy and partisan content, only the increase is more dramatic across the range of state populations than partisan content alone.

Table 5.3 and Figure 5.4 also show the effect of additional resources due to increasing distance from Washington, DC. Valence content tweets decline as distance from Washington, DC increases, fitting with the results in Table 5.3. Additionally, there is a statistically and substantively significant increase in the probability that a tweet contains policy content across the range of distance, beginning with a slightly less than 60% probability and ending with nearly 70%.

The one big surprise is that committee leadership doesn't seem to impact how senators present their personal brand on Twitter. Whether a senator leads a committee doesn't influence how they engage with policy or partisan topics, and it's not linked to seniority or policy expertise either. One possible explanation is that committee leaders may separate their personal and committee responsibilities in nuanced ways, which shapes their decisions about how to present themselves online. We know that some senators divide their communications between their committee and personal office in very defined ways, while others take a more holistic approach.

Overall, it's clear that resource advantages do affect how senators present themselves on Twitter, but the impact varies. The results aren't just different based on the type of content; they also depend on the source of resources. For example, distance from Washington, DC is the key driver for policy-focused tweets, while party leadership influences partisan-only content.

Conclusion: Resource-Related Digital

Members of Congress have more choices than ever about how they present themselves to public and elite audiences. Though lawmakers have unparalleled discretion to set their own agenda on Twitter, the content of that reputation building is still tied to the institution and relative resources. Both the dynamic nature of office management and the role that resources play in influencing those digital outputs are linked to resource and budget constraints. The interviews and quantitative analyses suggest that those who make the investment in communications and have the capital to do so engage in a distinctly different self-presentation on Twitter—leveraging their resources and different capacity for digital investment. Not every lawmaker wants to define themselves by their digital prowess, but the options available to staff and the ability to engage with a digital constituency are tied to the way an office is organized and the priorities of the principal. Digital doesn't just come out of thin air but rather requires a broader communication strategy that reflects time and careful consideration—something those offices with greater capacity are better positioned to manage.

In the Senate, having extra resources—especially for party leaders—tends to lead to more focus on party politics. The content senators put out online is pretty consistent across different roles. While Congress could benefit from more funding and capacity overall, the current power structures show that simply throwing more money at the problem doesn't lead to more policy focus. Instead, those with communication resources use them to stand out with partisan messaging. Party leaders and senators with bigger budgets often lean on partisan politics to shape their style of representation, channeling their professional communication teams toward political goals. Ideologically extreme senators and those from the same party as their state's other senator also use more partisan rhetoric on Twitter, connecting this style to the most polarized lawmakers.

Normalization theories of social media adoption suggest that existing power structures shape the flow of information online, and those power structures extend offline to how digital and communication priorities are managed within Congress (Gainous et al., 2018; Lasorsa et al., 2012). Digital investment is tied to capacity in terms of the dollars an office is willing and able to invest—influencing both the content and management of congressional communication. The network of Twitter promised the potential of new audiences and new voices, but the reality of constrained resources and attention within congressional communication shops leads many lawmakers to approach social media as just another tool rather than a nuanced value-add that rises above the limitations of the institution.

6
Crisis Implications
Partisan Pressures and Political Incentives for Digital

Twitter is a happy home for pissed-off politics, and there are no ethical or institutional guardrails high enough in Congress to prevent lawmakers from using the platform for eye-catching partisan attacks. Unlike the franking rules, which force lawmakers to be a bit more tactful when taking on political opponents in their official mail, Twitter is an opportunity to land wild political punches in quick succession. The majority of what gets shared on congressional Twitter has no obvious partisan cue (Russell, 2021a), but the content that gets shared and is likely to end up on the evening news is often political, negative, and anger induced. For example, within an hour of *Politico*'s story about the leaked Supreme Court document previewing the overturn of *Roe v. Wade*, senators were already turning to familiar partisan rhetoric to make sense of a story that had no precedent and scant information on its source. Republican Rick Scott blamed "radical Democrats," while Josh Hawley remarked about the Left's "assault" on the Supreme Court. Democrats like Elizabeth Warren lambasted the court for its "extremist" and "far-right views," and Chris Van Hollen assigned blame to the "Trump SCOTUS nominees." Within a couple hours, the leak engulfed the rhetorical agenda of Congress, with most members adjusting their messaging to address the leak and pushing regularly scheduled content for another day, when their policy or political priorities wouldn't get lost in the digital crossfire (Figure 6.1).

Everyday politics via journalists' reporting paint a negative picture of Congress (Soroka & McAdams, 2015), and Twitter is compounding that picture by amplifying the partisan and attacking rhetoric that draws attention and propels lawmakers onto cable news. "The bigger asshole they are on cable, the more they raise money, the less they have to pay attention [to the institution]" (Interview 155). Lawmakers and their staff make strategic choices about how to build a political reputation, and increasingly those choices play out on Twitter, which reporters, cable TV producers, and copartisans monitor for new information. Twitter and digital tools are not the causal mechanism behind the partisan divide in Congress; if Twitter disappeared tomorrow,

Tweeting Scared. Annelise Russell, Oxford University Press. © Oxford University Press (2025).
DOI: 10.1093/9780197808344.003.0006

Figure 6.1 Examples of Senate tweets responding to the Supreme Court decision on abortion
Source: Twitter.

the political blame game would surely find a new home, because the persistent digital evolution continues to push Congress to adapt its practices for stoking political division. Sure, 3 a.m. tweets by President Trump didn't help matters and added unprecedented fuel to the fire, but the incentives to wade into the political fray online existed before and after Trump cemented himself as "Tweeter in chief."[1] The biggest changes in congressional communication stem from the escalating pace of information and out-party voices who look for digital outlets to maintain a voice of sustained opposition.

Congressional policymaking is only getting more complex as the breadth of what government can do has increased (Jones et al., 2019), but paired with that complexity is a crisis of rapid information and constant engagement that leaves even less room for nuance. To meet that demand for information and appeal to a conflict-driven digital audience, lawmakers and their staff are using Twitter and digital tools to vent their frustrations, drive the emotional narrative, and cast their partisan opposition as politically criminal. The resources for digital communication are then controlled by partisan leaders who supply members with support and training but do so in a way that promotes the party brand, its message, and its members. Building digital capacity in Congress means going through the party or looking beyond the institution for expertise from communication skills honed during political campaigns. Digital investment wasn't always a partisan game—many communications staffers worked in a bipartisan fashion to accommodate digital changes—but the potential to gain an advantage over political opposition reversed the trend and further polarized digital operations.

[1] https://www.seattletimes.com/opinion/tweeter-in-chief/

The implications of party-driven digital engagement mean political frustrations become fodder for congressional Twitter. Over the last decade, Twitter has been an outlet for additional partisan attacks, increased angry rhetoric, and attention-seeking political signaling. Twitter is an appealing venue for increasing that political engagement as anger and negativity spread quickly across a network of users and divisive rhetoric is likely to land you a hit on cable news. Twitter has the power to amplify a lawmaker's political brand in ways that were unimaginable 30 years ago, even while Gingrich was playing charades with satellite news trucks. In this chapter, I explain how and why Twitter has contributed to a prevalence of angry, negative rhetoric that is both perpetuated by communications staff and covered by journalists. Using interviews with communications professionals on the Hill, I explain the rise of Twitter as a tool for political publicity and how taking advantage of this communication crisis culture has perpetuated a style of reputation building on social media that fuels conflict and partisan divisiveness. I show how the partisan divide in Washington, in addition to electoral security, is linked to representatives' angry communications online. Press staff are increasingly part of the digital content creation process, which supplies journalists and activists with divisive rhetoric that shapes the reported narrative about Congress. Members of Congress continue to test their political limits—seeing how far one can go on Twitter, who is fair game, and what lines they can't cross. The need to maintain a digital presence is met by regularly turning to Twitter to call out political opposition and reinforce partisan narratives, leaving the institution and the professionals within it grappling with disappearing folkways amid emerging digital trends.

Did It Have to Be This Way?

Civic relationships have been monetized and weaponized on Twitter, but it didn't have to be this way (Interview 155). Congress is a body made up of over 500 different opinions, and the trick is figuring out how to make sure your ideas are the ones covered by *Politico* or your preferred news outlet. Lawmakers play an active role in setting the agenda for how we think about Congress, and communications are always about lawmakers seeking new opportunities to define the terms of debate. Communications give lawmakers the ability to present themselves and their agenda to a preferred audience—variable across the many communications options they have at their disposal. Lawmakers who want to be quoted by *The Daily Caller* or *The Hill* are making sure they have a rapid-response plan for Twitter. Lawmakers who need to build support at home spend a lot of time on newsletters and shooting video of their service in the district. Robust communications don't necessarily mean minute-by-minute responses on Twitter, but that fast-paced information environment is the backdrop for the choices that those in Congress make about what to say and when.

The need to be visible and present is a bipartisan pressure that goes beyond partisan preference and gets at the root of what it means to be an active member of Congress with a political future to maintain. Building up message capacity to thrive within a digital environment was a collective desire across the institution and one that Congress initially faced as a united front rather than as a caucus or conference. As one former staffer described, she was almost surprised at how partisan communications have become; she noted that in the early days of digital investment and online messaging, the key to success was a collective push to rewrite the internal rules of Congress to allow for online engagement. "None of the institutional rules provided for the changing media landscape . . . and so we started to have ideas and realized the blockers of our ideas were not the members of Congress but were actually the rules of the House and Senate" (Interview 173).

Breaking down the rules and changing the way the institution regulated communication required a bipartisan effort. Franking rules that regulated the presentation of newsletters were being used to govern webpages such that analog assessments about what was an acceptable use of taxpayer funds were applied to the design of member homepages. An example of former Senator Ted Kennedy's webpage from 2001 highlights the early ways a webpage was used and its limited visual content, which changed just eight years later in the wake of his passing (Figure 6.2). Early webpages were only landing pages for information but developed into visual presentations that offered the necessary information for constituents.

Another early constraint on digital that was unrelated to partisanship or politics was the process for press credentialing in Congress, which limited the access of bloggers, who were opening up new venues for lawmaker engagement. Members across the political spectrum wanted that access to bloggers, who had a unique voice and provided an untapped resource for member engagement. In the hierarchy of needs, the institutional capacity for building out digital far outweighed the political incentives to best partisan opposition because everyone was trying to make the most of the opportunities the internet provided. Staff from both parties would get together monthly to talk about institutional barriers they were coming up against, whether that be pushback from the Franking Commission or limitations on credentialing from the

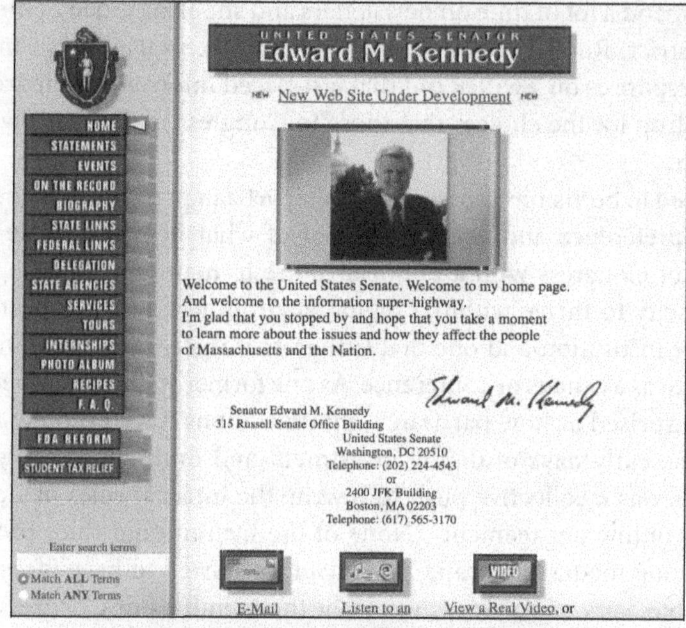

Figure 6.2 Images of former Senator Edward Kennedy's official website
Source: Senate website.

Senate Radio/TV Gallery (Interview 173). As one former communications director described, the community of staffers who believed digital was the future was a fairly small circle, but they worked across party lines so they could make the most of this digital future for their bosses. Staff had a shared interest in retrofitting Congress for digital engagement and the technology was changing rapidly, so collaborating with partners across the aisle made sense for communications staffers wanting to move the institution forward. The broader goal was using digital for transparency beyond any political gains, and that united staff in a bipartisan fashion to meet the digital demands of their members. "It was very collegial. We both want to communicate with the American people—we have different audiences, sometimes we have the same audiences—but no matter what we all want tools that are being denied to us in arcane ways" (Interview 173).

Within a couple years, however, the mission was no longer building a digital infrastructure and the influx of new voices working on "new media" shifted the conversation from collective transparency to political control (Interview 173). As the media and audiences fragmented along partisan divides, those divides came to shape the way folks thought about digital. The early advocacy for retrofitting Congress to meet the digital demand in a bipartisan fashion gave way to catering to digital communities that incentivized conflict, quick response times, and insider information about the divides within the institution. The influence of new staff who never shared the bipartisan pain points of digital, the growing power of money within elections, and the role of digital in those campaigns seeped into Congress's approach to the problem of digital investment. The climate was changing, and with that change came technology that enabled political rhetoric to grow across digital communities in ways that excited a new generation of members and staff.

News Media Incentives for Going Viral

> *The loudest voices on social media, on either side, are the ones that are going to generate the most virality.* (Interview 175)

Water rights across the Rocky Mountains aren't going to send cable news into a frenzy—much to the disappointment of the policy staffer who spent weeks on a legislative proposal to address the problem. Viral communication is like a flash flood that surges unexpectedly and rapidly, impacts large communities, and is difficult to control. What goes viral and when is also a little like pornography—"you know it when you see it"—and many staffers are continuously surprised by the information that goes unnoticed and the comments that engulf a news cycle. Producing digital content is a speculative endeavor, meaning that "you dig 10 holes in the hope that one produces a well" (Interview 103).

One incentive to go viral comes from journalists' preference for conflict and division because they provide the fodder for stories that generate more clicks and increased revenue. Journalism has embraced Twitter-friendly content (Crilley & Gillespie, 2019) and experimented with "clickbait" (Denisova, 2023). A social media–driven environment emphasizes ephemera, visual cues, clickbait reporting, and a shift toward video that matches algorithms that increase viewership (Denisova, 2023). News outlets want to tap into conflict because it drives their audience, and "the more polarizing you are on social media, the better chance you are going to have to go viral" (Interview 175). Research shows that in the wake of the Supreme Court leak previewing the overturning of *Roe v. Wade*, the lawmakers who responded first on Twitter were likely to be quoted in the news in the early coverage of the leak (Connor & Russell, 2024). Republican Senator Josh Hawley was the first senator to respond to the document leak, with his office issuing multiple tweets within 24 hours to show support for the potential decision, blame political opponents for the leak, and call for ethics investigations. His prompt and sustained response on Twitter led to him being featured in the lead photo and quote in *Roll Call*'s news coverage of the leak the following day (Figure 6.3).

The cycle of viral information leading to more content and more responses can drive a communications staffer to the brink of exhaustion and is what perpetuates the crisis communication cycle. Many people acknowledge that social media hasn't improved the transparency of information and that the speed at which content is produced actually counters many of the benefits of accessibility that digital tools offer. "There's a lot of cases to be made

| POLICY

Draft leak a 'shocking change' for typically airtight Supreme Court

Chief Justice John G. Roberts Jr. insisted the work of the court will not be affected, but senators and former clerks aren't so sure

Figure 6.3 *Roll Call*'s news following the leaked draft opinion, featuring Senator Hawley
Source: Roll Call.

that [Twitter] just made things worse. I think the country is more polarized, the news is more polarized. Journalism is widely distrusted, and journalists are widely despised. . . . [Twitter] sort of accelerated the pace of delivery of the news while removing the context that makes those moves digestible" (Interview 20).

Social media is not the right place for nuance; for example, a reporter might simply ask, "Do you think Donald Trump should be impeached?" A lawmaker's response is constrained by the fact that whatever they say—or don't say—is inevitably going to show up on Twitter. As one former staffer described, if you respond, you've ceded the premise of the question and you've lost control of the message, but if you don't respond, there is a threat that the *New York Times* reports that your member is avoiding the question or is not taking the question seriously (Interview 175). This is one reason most members, in the wake of big events or breaking news, issue a statement and post that statement on Twitter—to limit further questions about their response or reaction. For example, after the Senate's February 2020 impeachment vote, Senator Mitt Romney posted his reaction on Twitter (Figure 6.4).

As the media has fractured and partisan or biased news outlets have become more prominent in Congress, the digital norms for information sharing have changed. As one former journalist noted, there are many more subchannels you can tap into depending on how narrow you want the audience to be, whereas before there were only three or four (Interview 90). That mindset is the reason one communications staffer commented that he would rather give a scoop to Fox News or *The Daily Caller*—because they speak directly to their preferred audience—rather than waste that story on *The Washington Post* (Interview 184). Online political communities tend to have stronger partisan attachments than the average citizen, so incentivizing digital engagement on Twitter or Truth Social means prioritizing communication with copartisans. One former staffer argued that while Twitter didn't cause the partisan divides, there is a further widening between partisan political communities online that politicians are incentivized to be a part of. "I think you can make a strong case that a lot of the polarization has occurred based on self-selection of media, and social media is a big part of that when an algorithm is driving you toward reinforcing your worldview" (Interview 31).

Journalists and the news media are not just passive observers reporting on what they see or bystanders in the partisan digital divide. As one staffer described, "A lot of Capitol Hill reporters, I personally feel, have become on Twitter a little bit more editorial and a little less, sort of, 'just the facts, man.' And that changes the dynamic a little bit" (Interview 167). The notion of

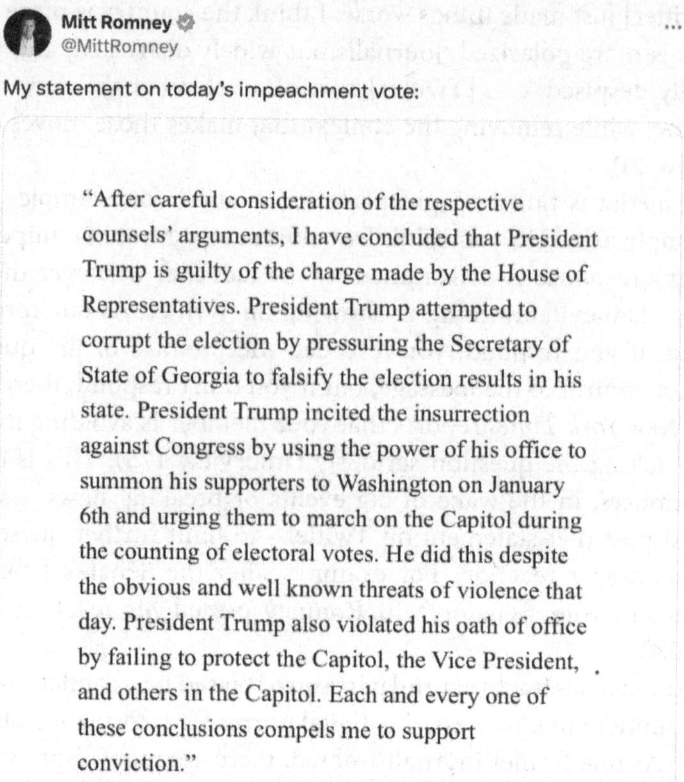

My statement on today's impeachment vote:

"After careful consideration of the respective counsels' arguments, I have concluded that President Trump is guilty of the charge made by the House of Representatives. President Trump attempted to corrupt the election by pressuring the Secretary of State of Georgia to falsify the election results in his state. President Trump incited the insurrection against Congress by using the power of his office to summon his supporters to Washington on January 6th and urging them to march on the Capitol during the counting of electoral votes. He did this despite the obvious and well known threats of violence that day. President Trump also violated his oath of office by failing to protect the Capitol, the Vice President, and others in the Capitol. Each and every one of these conclusions compels me to support conviction."

Figure 6.4 Republican Senator Mitt Romney's statement on the Trump impeachment vote in February 2020
Source: Twitter.

reporters actively engaging in the policy process is not a new phenomenon—for example, former Speaker Tip O'Neill had a gaggle of reporters he worked with regularly—but the access magnifies the role of those press folks on the Hill and gives way to them having voices with virtually no filters or limits.

Institutional Incentives for Twitter

Another source of incentives for viral content—and the partisan messaging that often accompanies it—is the pressure from party leaders themselves. "At this point, I feel like the parties are just predators feeding on the institution. At every level, the parties have turned members into telemarketers for their donors" (Interview 155). From 2013, when every senator was finally on Twitter, to recent years, where people remain on Twitter out of habit, staffers note the shift in how increasingly partisan the institution is becoming with each session, such that leadership positions are naturally more partisan, buffeted by more partisan party messaging by leaders (Interview 7). An errant tweet or a poorly timed comment in the Senate tunnel can send a leadership office into rapid response, but they continue to push lawmakers and their staff to be present, active, and popular across digital platforms. For example, to celebrate the anniversary of the Affordable Care Act, the House Democratic Policy and Communications Committee shared with all caucus members a toolkit of social media posts, graphics, and preferred language to talk about the impact of the act, Republicans' opposition to it, and the political wins related to its passage. Because the resources available on the Hill often don't allow good-quality digital work to be produced, party leaders, committees, and those with resources supplement office needs and foster digital dependencies.

One example of this party-induced engagement is the competition within the House of Representatives that both parties hosted for their members. In 2010, House Republicans announced a three-round media competition for their members, where points were won for adding new followers on Twitter, Facebook, and YouTube.[2] The competition was styled after the NCAA March Madness tournament—taking a popular game and turning it into digital political sport. For the Democrats, former Majority Leader Steny Hoyer hosted an all-star competition to increase the number of digital followers and grow the audience for Democratic members. Hoyer ran this program for 13 years, posting gains in the number of members on a leadership board so that office could compete for bragging rights.

Some members really took those party-induced incentives to heart—building into their operations new norms for digital engagement and taking these incentives to new levels. "[Marjorie Taylor Greene] gets so much media by being a Neolithic bomb thrower that she doesn't even need to pay attention to the curation rules of the institution" (Interview 155). For example, a tip was submitted to the "Dear White Staffers" Instagram account in 2022 that Democratic Representative Raja Krishnamoorthi was instructing interns to follow 1,000 people interacting with political posts each weekday. On Friday, his office would use an unfollow bot to unfollow all nonverified accounts. The tipster surmised that Krishnamoorthi is in the Top 40 in the House on Twitter simply because of this strategy for an oversized digital presence.

Members of Congress are incentivized by party leaders to use their digital messaging as a signal boost to rocket them onto evening cable news, partisan

[2] https://politicalticker.blogs.cnn.com/2010/04/20/house-republicans-compete-in-new-media-challenge/

radio, or podcasts. As one former staffer explained the incentives, explicitly: "You increasingly have lawmakers, I would argue, at both sides who, who care less about legislating and more about, like, becoming social media stars that, that get them on cable news at night" (Interview 59). Bold and bombastic statements, similar to those tweeted by Donald Trump or Bernie Sanders, ensure new opportunities for those voices on Fox News and Newsmax, using Twitter to amplify the message and reach new audiences. While Twitter is often thought of as having a different audience than that of cable news, in many ways it can become a launching pad to reach other voters indirectly and in a less costly manner than using paid media on the campaign side.

Digital Partisan Divisions: Minority-Driven Messaging

Tweets have changed business in Congress to incentivize rapid responses, limiting time for detail-oriented policies and incentivizing political connections with a digital constituency (Tromble, 2018). Twitter has become the most salient and accessible venue for members to blast political opponents and champion their own party. Congressional reputation building is complex—spanning policy, constituent concerns, crisis response, and holiday greetings—but politics is arguably one of the most visible and viral aspects of that digital branding. Most members maintain an active Twitter account to use as part of their official messaging in office, and the threat of Twitter as a political weapon existed long before President Donald Trump expanded its political possibilities. The rhetoric coming from members of Congress is sometimes akin to a battle of both fists and wits. In 2017, Delaware Representative John Larson warned that angry political rhetoric can have a spillover effect with dangerous consequences (i.e., January 6th), which is particularly relevant for messages shared on the far-reaching platforms of social media. Twitter is an efficient and accessible vehicle for politicians' anger and can fuel partisanship and political resentment. High-arousal emotions like anger spread more rapidly through a network like Twitter (Berger & Milkman, 2013) and facilitate mobilization for change (Jamieson et al., 2018), making it a powerful tool for viral engagement. In addition to the viral nature of angry emotions, the "strong action tendencies" associated with anger suggest that individuals are less likely to seek out information while existing beliefs are reinforced (McKuen et al., 2010; Valentino et al., 2008).

Members of Congress use this angry rhetoric to frame their political brand for a digital audience, and staff confirm that politically provocative tweets are more likely to go viral, but some members are cued to use that anger within the hyperpolarized Congress. Previous studies on congressional communications argue that minority party lawmakers within Congress are better positioned to use strategic communication and communicate their partisan priorities more frequently (Groeling, 2010; Kousser, 2019; Maltzman & Sigelman, 1996; Morris, 2001). As minority lawmakers are limited in their ability to control the institutional message or agenda, they turn to nonlegislative means to convey their frustration and opposition to the status quo. The underlying implication is that with Twitter, minority lawmakers have the opportunity and incentive to reinforce partisan attitudes, building a reputation as the angry opposition to the status quo. This underscores why understanding the variation in Congress members' emotional appeals on popular social media platforms is vital to explain the far-reaching spread of digital norms within Congress.

Additionally, those in the minority are not just angry—they are using their political opposition as punching bags in order to build a digital reputation. The normalization of Twitter as a platform for lawmakers' public agendas offers an opportunity to assess institutional influences on lawmakers' partisan appeals. Prior research highlights the asymmetric patterns of partisan rhetoric such that lawmakers from the out-party in the White House are more likely to mention party politics on social media (Russell, 2018). Both parties use their position on Twitter to call out presidential opposition, and that effect has only gotten worse over time. Twitter has become a vehicle for projecting partisan communication, and the cycle of crisis communication means that those trends become magnified over time.

Angry Content on Twitter

Angry rhetoric can be tied to partisan appeals as minority party members adopt different emotions in their messaging to reflect a digital constituency that increasingly shares a similar ideology (Hacker & Pierson, 2006; Mann & Ornstein, 2016; McCarty et al., 2016; Skocpol & Williamson, 2016). Angry tweets are a conduit for partisanship because they play a central role in facilitating political information—providing an echo chamber of cues that support specific views and ignoring incongruent political information (Suhay & Erisen, 2018). An important dimension to understanding emotional political messaging is the lawmakers themselves as a source of that anger, specifically considering how members and staff representing political opposition rely on angry rhetoric to circulate their agenda for a digital constituency. "Because of polarization, having the right people angry at you builds your relationship with your core supporters" (Interview 140). And even when a lawmaker isn't trying to ignite frustration in people, leaning into and constructing tweets around people's outrage is one of the fastest ways to generate clicks and draw a lot of attention (Interview 186).

When elected representatives perpetuate angry emotions in systematic ways, this has implications beyond just the social fabric of Congress. Research from campaigns suggests that there is an electoral-driven motivation for heightened levels of anxiety- and fear-inducing rhetoric to mobilize voters (e.g., Brader, 2006); emotive rhetoric, however, may also be wielded to increase engagement after an election, especially when anger inducing. Members at political odds with the sitting president are more likely to turn to Twitter to make partisan appeals (Russell, 2021) and, in turn, make angry appeals to build their political reputation online. I expect that and subsequently illustrate how lawmakers who are not in line with the interests of the White House are more likely to turn to Twitter to advance their agenda and voice partisan opposition.[3]

In reviewing the tweets from all official accounts of House members from 2013 to 2018, one can see the rise in the number of tweets over time (Figure 6.5). The figure illustrates that while there has been an undeniable increase in each Congress in the amount of member tweets posted—with the 115th Congress (2017–2018) recording the highest numbers—members of Congress are overall still consistently tweeting thousands of times per month.

Figure 6.6 plots over time the monthly average percentage of tweets with angry words for all members in the 113th to 115th Congress; from 2013 to 2017 the average ranged between 10% and 20%, and then it increased to about 30% in 2018. While most legislators' tweets do not contain angry rhetoric, public perception of escalating conflict and anger coming out of Congress is likely attributed to the greater virality and overall impact of the growing portion of tweets that do contain angry rhetoric, highlighting the importance of understanding the conditions under which members of Congress get angry on Twitter. Figure 6.6 pointedly illustrates a large increase in angry rhetoric during the campaign year leading up to the 2018 midterm election. In what some referred to as an "anger election," 2018 marked a sharp increase in angry appeals to constituents. This increase in angry words echoes research that finds heightened use of angry rhetoric by congressional candidates appealing to voters on Twitter during the same time period (Gervais et al., 2020). Across party and electoral constraints, angry rhetoric was more frequently used by candidates compared to measures of anxious or sad rhetoric (Figure 6.6).

[3] Excerpts from this chapter are part of previously published research at *Political Research Quarterly* and a working paper with Whitney Hua titled "Tweeting Red."

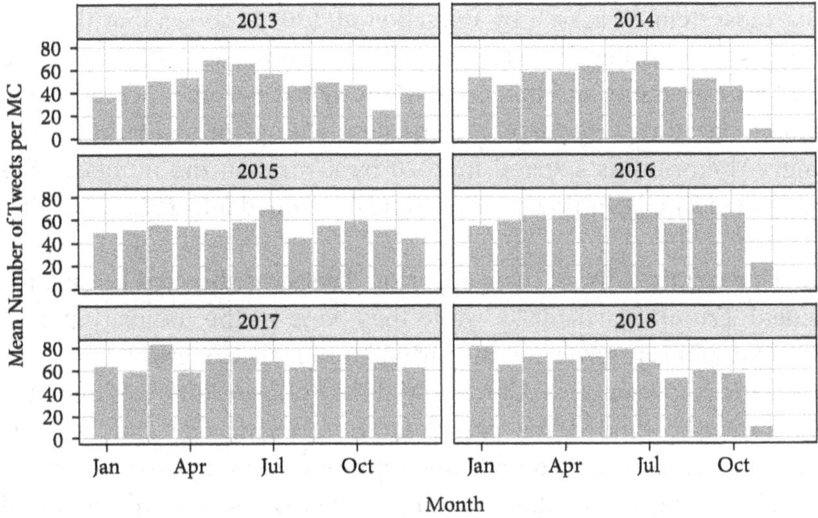

Figure 6.5 Monthly average number of tweets per member of Congress (MC) (113th to 115th Congress)

Source: Tweeting Red: Angry emotional appeals in Congress (with Whitney Hua and Maggie Macdonald). Presented at the APSA Conference 2020.

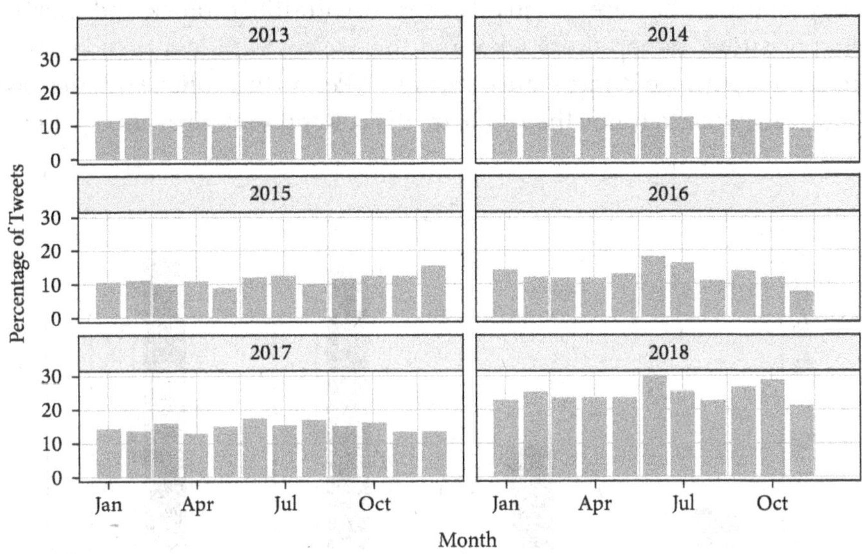

Figure 6.6 Monthly percentage of tweets with angry rhetoric (113th to 115th Congress)

Source: Tweeting Red: Angry emotional appeals in Congress (with Whitney Hua and Maggie Macdonald). Presented at the APSA Conference 2020.

Angry rhetoric has been a staple of campaigns for many election cycles (Evans et al., 2022; Russell et al., 2023), but it is also present in the ways that lawmakers engage with digital audiences in the Twitter-driven congressional media ecosystem. Research by Russell et al. (2023) shows that the number of angry tweets issued by male and female candidates has changed across the last four elections and that angry rhetoric has become increasingly more common over time (Figure 6.7). Consistent with prior research, the growth of angry rhetoric was spurred in 2020 by a surge in the number of angry words issued by all candidates. This trend continued into 2022 (Russell et al., 2023).

For Democrats, a lot of their anger on Twitter is directed toward former President Trump, particularly while they were in the minority party in a unified Republican government during the 115th Congress. For example, Democratic Representative Carolyn Maloney of New York was one of many Democrats who chided the president for his language and behavior in response to crises (Figure 6.8). While representatives in the out-party of the White House may frequently direct their angry tweets toward the president, as this example exemplifies, they also generally rely on angry rhetoric to challenge their disadvantaged position of power and criticize the opposing party in power (Russell, 2021). Looking beyond just Democrats, members of Congress often use Twitter to lay blame on politicians or institutions for policy failures. They are not just frustrated with the gridlock and therefore being negative; rather, those who find themselves with less agenda control and at odds with the White House are more likely to be explicit with the angry rhetoric they use to frame their time in office. Representatives' angry rhetoric

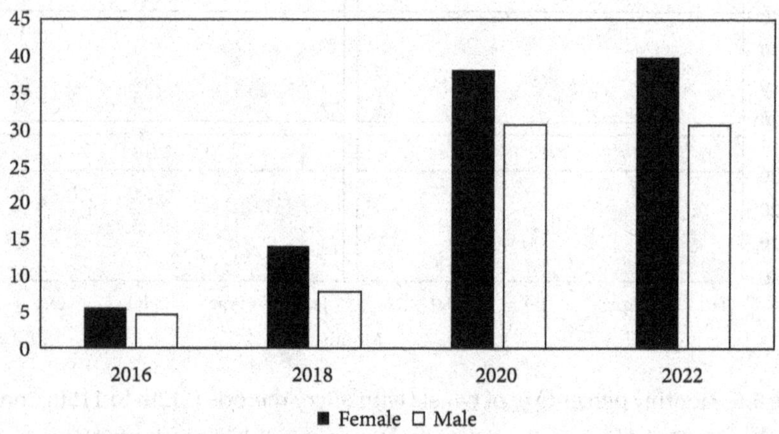

Figure 6.7 Number of angry words featured in tweets in the two months before Election Day, by year and candidate gender

Source: Russell, A., Evans, H. K., & Gervais, B. (2024). Not ready to make nice: Congressional candidates' emotional appeals on Twitter. *Social Science Quarterly*, *105*, 1848–1856. https://doi.org/10.1111/ssqu.13439

Figure 6.8 Example tweets from US House members that include angry rhetoric

Source: Twitter.

is linked to partisan institutional dynamics, expanding on work by Groeling (2010) that argues that majority party status and presidential politics impact the tenor of media in Congress.

Partisan Implications of Conflict- and Anger-Driven Digital Environments

Members of Congress are increasingly turning to social media to connect with their digital constituencies, and the negative tone of these connections on Twitter suggests that anger and outrage are incentivized for digital communication. Lawmakers are incentivized by party leadership, journalists' norms for conflict, and partisan communications online to lean into angry rhetoric that is likely to quickly spread across a digital network. While many point to President Donald Trump's fiery rhetoric on Twitter as a catalyst for angry responses by lawmakers and the culture of leading via tweets, the origins of the partisan digital climate and the incentives for conflict predate Trump. The president took advantage of a fire that was already smoldering. Adversarial relationships with the White House began before Trump's online barbs with Democrats, and research shows that digital politicking means calling out political opposition and using that as a powerful tool when you are a lawmaker without agenda control or political power within the institution. During the Obama presidency, House Republicans used these tactics and relied on angry rhetoric in their online messaging to activate voters, amplify their political narratives, and sweep the 2010 midterms.

Twitter isn't the problem; rather, it feeds the need of congressional communicators to shape their message, tap into the emotions of digital communities, and use their power online to entice reporters with quick nuggets that fill news holes minute by minute. Prior explanations of digital performance that focus on chamber partisan dynamics and electoral constraints are not wrong in their assumptions, but incentives for going digital in Congress extend beyond the ballot box. Angry, emotional appeals are part of the reputation-building discourse of elected members of Congress, and this chapter highlights the importance of also incorporating explanations of institutional power and media incentives into our expectations of lawmakers' communication strategies. Understanding the variation in members' social media appeal and the underlying motivation is crucial for explaining the spread of angry politics and their role in reinforcing partisan public opinion that goes beyond the walls of Congress.

The digital age has intensified the conflict-driven nature of political communication, particularly on platforms like Twitter. As one interviewee pointed out, "Capitol Hill reporters and other sort of pundits on Twitter, in the digital world, they just constantly have a negative view of everything. They think everything's always failing. It's always a conflict, right? It's a kind of, it's like a theme, 'everything's terrible, because conflict sells'" (Interview

167). This perception underscores the media's role in amplifying negativity and conflict, which in turn shapes public perception and political discourse. The relentless focus on conflict can create an environment where sensationalism overshadows substantive discussion, further polarizing the electorate and entrenching partisan divides. In the current political landscape, there are diminishing incentives for lawmakers to moderate their messages. Political communication is increasingly tailored to a specific subset of constituents, often at the expense of broader district engagement. Communications professionals now focus on targeting the small percentage of "movable" voters, often ignoring the majority of their district, or they abandon the notion of persuasion altogether, aiming instead to motivate their likely supporters to turn out. This shift allows for ideology-driven rhetoric and more partisan policy language, as lawmakers become disengaged from communicating with the political opposition within their districts. Consequently, the political discourse becomes more polarized, reflecting a strategic choice to prioritize base mobilization over cross-party dialogue.

The toll of this anger-fueled political environment is most acutely felt by those on the front lines—lawmakers and their staff, journalists, and active social media users who engage with political content. The continuous cycle of mudslinging and the back and forth between opposing sides takes a significant emotional and psychological toll. This constant exposure to hostility and vitriol can lead to burnout, disillusionment, and a general sense of fatigue among those who are actively engaged in the political arena.

Dealing with the repercussions of such a toxic environment requires acknowledging the impact it has on individuals and creating spaces for support and respite. One interviewee emphasized the need for understanding and support in the face of online harassment:

> You're going to get extremely nasty comments directed at you. And they might hit below the belt, or they might be, like, called a "baby murderer" on Twitter. . . . So I think, acknowledging that that's going to happen, and just creating space for people to have conversations about that, to be able to talk about the toll that it takes on them, if you can, if you're fortunate enough to, like, be able to give people a break. (Interview 109)

Recognizing the human cost of political engagement on digital platforms is crucial for fostering a more supportive and sustainable environment for those involved in the political process. Providing avenues for individuals to discuss their experiences and take necessary breaks can help mitigate the negative impacts of an increasingly hostile and polarized digital landscape.

Congress is an institution that relies heavily on "unwritten folkways" as central features of its daily operations. Election-minded and ambitious lawmakers traditionally abide by established rules that facilitate continuity and cooperation, but digital enables Congress to weather fractious political storms while simultaneously stoking political divisions. Prior research illustrates the critical role of civility in the actual relationships between lawmakers and how they communicate with each other (Burgat & Russell, in press). Policymaking and the business of marketing that policy are based on relationships, and those relationships can be tested in a climate that challenges collegiality and prizes conflict online. The manner in which lawmakers interact, talk online, and present themselves to their constituents has significant consequences not only for the institution's health but also for the prospects of legislation and compromise. The rise of bombastic rhetoric presents unyielding challenges to the folkways of Congress where the incentives for certain behaviors adapt to a digital logic.

As lawmakers pursue communication that leans into conflict and confrontation, Congress suffers (Alexander, 2021). The increasing prevalence of conflictual, personal, and dehumanizing rhetoric, especially when Congress has little capacity to curb it, normalizes such rhetoric and creates a culture of communication that reinforces it. Staffers and lawmakers alike are socialized into this conflict-driven environment, and leaders reinforce that culture by rewarding digital performance and providing lawmakers with incentives to double-down on it. Twitter and other digital platforms exacerbate this trend by incentivizing sensationalism and negativity. The impact of this digital environment is acutely felt by those on the front lines of politics, who are subjected to relentless hostility and vitriol. Recognizing the cost of such engagement is crucial for understanding the future of the digitally driven political environment.

Concluding Thoughts

Twitter has undeniably changed the way Congress communicates, with lawmakers and staffers using the platform to make bold, partisan statements that grab attention and fuel political conflicts. Unlike the more restrained and regulated official communications, Twitter offers a stage for quick, eye-catching attacks. This freedom has led to a surge in negative and angry rhetoric, which often dominates the news cycle and shapes public perception of Congress. The negative portrayal of Congress in everyday news is intensified by angry exchanges on Twitter. Lawmakers and their staff strategically use the platform to build their political brands, knowing that aggressive tweets will be more noticed by reporters and TV producers. The more sensational the tweet, the more likely it is to be picked up by the media, raising the lawmaker's profile but also contributing to a more divided and combative political climate.

The trend of using Twitter for partisan attacks is not solely a result of the platform itself but a reflection of broader changes in congressional communications. The fast-paced nature of digital information requires lawmakers to constantly engage with their audience, often through emotionally charged content. This has led to a communication crisis where nuance is lost and the loudest, most divisive voices gain the most attention. Party leaders have harnessed this trend by providing resources and training to their members, encouraging them to use digital tools to promote the party's message and attack the opposition. This partisan support has further polarized congressional communications, making bipartisan cooperation in digital strategies almost nonexistent.

The rise of Twitter as a tool for political publicity has significant implications for Congress. Angry and negative rhetoric spreads quickly on the platform, often making it to cable news and shaping the public's view of lawmakers. This cycle of conflict-driven communication feeds into the broader partisan divide in Washington, with representatives using Twitter to reinforce their political positions and rally their base. Interviews with congressional communications staff reveal how integral Twitter has become in shaping political narratives. These staffers play a crucial role in crafting the messages that lawmakers post, ensuring that their tweets are designed to provoke reactions and gain media coverage. This reliance on Twitter for political engagement underscores the challenges Congress faces in adapting to the digital age. Twitter has transformed congressional communications into a battleground of partisan rhetoric. Lawmakers use the platform to make bold statements, attack opponents, and build their political brands, contributing to a more divided and conflict-driven political environment. This chapter has shown how the use of Twitter in Congress has perpetuated a style of communication that prioritizes anger and divisiveness, reflecting and reinforcing the broader partisan divide in American politics.

7 The Future and Implications of a Digital Congress

In late 2022, after the sale of Twitter to Elon Musk, more questions without answers swirled in the halls of Congress about what this meant for digital and political communication norms. Musk threatened to bring back former President Donald Trump after his suspension in January 2021 and proposed sweeping changes, including staff turnover, removing content moderation policies, and rethinking the app's advertising model. Democrats were quick to scrutinize Musk and his oversight of misinformation (or lack thereof) on the platform, while Republicans began their defense of Twitter, its owner, and any threats to national security.[1] The sale of Twitter threw it into the middle of a partisan battle and shifted it from being a daily given to a daily choice despite steeping controversy. It's been more than a decade since Twitter became central to the daily diet of information in Congress, where reporters, staffers, producers, and activists come together to trade information and follow the day's news by waiting for tweets rather than just headlines. Folks in Congress accepted that Twitter and other advertising platforms could be used for governance and for many years we didn't think anything of it beyond "how can we do this" and then "how can we do this well?" But that certainty decreased when the rules of the game changed and the digital expectations around Twitter and other platforms became less defined. Congress had figured out who its audience was on Twitter, but now staff and journalists began to wonder how that audience would change. Even the most junior press staffers knew digital wasn't going anywhere, but still, in what direction was it heading? As many staffers would confirm, the uncertainty around social media and the once-consistent norms around digital—at least for the last decade—faced a new shift that was larger than any of the newest staffers doing communication and digital had ever faced. In December of 2022, one staffer told *Roll Call*, "The Twitter situation is at a point where . . . many of us are starting to think about what would take its place, if it either was technically nonfunctional or

[1] https://www.nbcnews.com/politics/politics-news/democrats-criticize-elon-musk-suspending-journalists-covering-twitter-rcna62047

Tweeting Scared. Annelise Russell, Oxford University Press. © Oxford University Press (2025).
DOI: 10.1093/9780197808344.003.0007

if it became too problematic to stay on."[2] The game of watching and waiting persisted—and continues years later. Congress has fully evolved into a digital communication environment, and the uncertainty around the central platform for information sharing reveals just how much staff and lawmakers rely on Twitter and other digital tools.

The game of "what would come next" if Twitter/X were to become defunct has become a constant hypothetical among staffers and technologists, who often look to regulators from the European Union for early warning signs about how governments manage new technology.[3] Some folks predicted the end of Twitter and continued to do so on a weekly basis despite no viable alternative with staying power and immediate uptake. Lawmakers claimed a spot on Mastodon, BlueSky, Post, and eventually Threads, but the waiting game was a bit like the uncertainty experienced by middle-schoolers at a Friday night dance. Everyone is looking for a dance partner and we all know the songs, but nobody is ready to step up and lead anyone onto the dance floor for fear of leaving friends for an uncertain digital dance that nobody really knows how to do.

Even for those who don't necessarily see an end for Twitter, the platform and what is to be expected on it have shifted over time as lawmakers and institutions adapt to new digital norms where bots are increasingly common, misinformation is widespread, and outrage is just the icing on the cake. As people waited for a journalist exodus from Twitter that never came, the congressional digital ecosystem tied to the platform remained central to dialogue but was no longer taken for granted. "It's hard to think about what a post-Twitter environment would look like for a political world where it has become so dependent on it," said one staffer in an interview with *Roll Call*.[4]

And that digital dependency—not just on Twitter, but rather digital communications as a whole—is the reason press shops on the Hill are central to congressional capacity yet undervalued. Beyond what an office will invest in social media production, House offices are paying hundreds of thousands of dollars to connect with online and geographic constituencies, but the staff managing those budgets and facilitating those relationships are often only making $50,000 a year. The institution continues to incentivize creative communications without a compensatory investment or a roadmap for what the future of digital Congress should or could look like. Party leadership

[2] Saska, J. (2022). https://rollcall.com/2022/12/07/congress-sticks-with-twitter-for-now/

[3] https://www.pbs.org/newshour/world/eu-investigates-x-over-potential-violations-of-social-media-law

[4] https://rollcall.com/2022/12/07/congress-sticks-with-twitter-for-now/

attempts to fill some of the void in terms of how to navigate digital advertising and online engagement, but oversized demand—plus the changing technology—contributes to the crisis of communication.

This book offers a new approach that suggests communication in Congress is a crisis—a failure of the institution to invest in technology and information dissemination that would enable Congress to more effectively communicate. And when Congress is ill-equipped to communicate in a political environment that thrives on rapid information sharing, the institution is setting itself up for a race to the bottom. The necessary tools exist for any lawmaker to be an effective communicator and maintain a robust press shop, but the information is moving faster than ever, and the institution lacks the capacity to manage that flow of information or use it in ways that improve the effectiveness of the institution. Staff, reporters, and press professionals drive the daily operations of Congress in terms of information sharing, constantly adapting to meet the rapid pace of news and information because there is no other alternative. In 2023, *The Washington Post* wrote an article about political reporter Jake Sherman—founder of *Punchbowl News*—describing his work as "feeding Official Washington's bottomless appetite for fresh intel, hot drama and chewy news nuggets from Congress."[5] In Congress, news and mistakes are both features of a fast-paced news cycle where something is always happening and even inaccurate statements are forgotten because new information gets its own 15 minutes of fame. And there is power in having the information a few minutes before everyone else.

For many folks managing communications and digital within Congress, the logistics of daily engagement look a lot like an emergency response given the constant readiness and 24-hour nature of the job. A calendar that looks clear on Wednesday could completely fall apart by Friday, and the information that reorients those schedules is a product of the digital communication environment where leaks are prized, conflict wins, and scandal means opportunity. Congress has developed into a disaster response operation that prepares for and puts out political fires, but like a volunteer fire department, it lacks some of the basic investment to do so in ways that don't come close to what would be expected in the private sector.

Congress is dependent on the digital tools that both spark and resolve conflict. Conversations with current and former congressional communication professionals underscore just how high the expectations for Twitter and digital media have become, yet the lack of true investment fuels the very

[5] https://www.washingtonpost.com/style/2023/10/30/jake-sherman-of-punchbowl-news-does-play-by-play-on-capitol-hill/

same power asymmetries we expected digital media to disrupt. The outsized demand for rapid, digital engagement benefits those offices and individuals who can make the investment in staff and technology to meet the demand. Those with outsized digital capacity can leverage their reputation online and get the first crack at the narrative coming out of Congress. Lawmakers like Alexandria Ocasio-Cortez, Ted Cruz, and Bernie Sanders have built reputations through their communication investment to harness native digital skills or prioritize office communications to foster a political brand that extends far beyond their constituents. But they are the exceptions to rule. These lawmakers set an unattainable standard for digital communication that many members of Congress cannot possibly reach because they don't have either the capacity, the resources, or the interest to prioritize communications. The power to affect the congressional agenda and facilitate rapid response has elevated digital and congressional communications in a way that ultimately constrains what little capacity lawmakers already had—telling them they can be media darlings on a shoestring budget is disingenuous and makes the average member of Congress resource dependent in terms of both policy and communication.

By examining the congressional communication crisis, we gain new insight into how digital communication became central to Congress, the logistics of daily engagement from a staff perspective, and the implications of using digital tools to build a political reputation. Lawmakers have fundamental goals—preferred policy, constituent service, and partisan politics—that communications can help them meet, but how they organize their agenda around these priorities is shaped by the institutional dynamics around communication and the investment in human capital to produce the desired results (Fenno, 1977). Some politicians see their interests served by spending time talking to reporters from *Politico*, while others are careful to avoid situations that make them headline news, but those strategies are connected to the institutional incentives for engagement and the power they have to direct their own digital press shop. Pressures from the institution, the party, and constituents affect how lawmakers communicate their priorities for representation.

The Secondary Crisis—An Identity Crisis

The crisis of communication in Congress is not just one of presentation resources—the central argument of this book—but also an identity crisis such that we don't consider communications central to the identity of Congress.

Among the academic community, our understanding of congressional behavior is largely limited to lawmaking and representation. Scholars consider the partisan polarization as an endemic feature of the institution, congressional committees are integral to the policy process, rules govern the legislative output (or not), and congressional leadership is a case study in political power (Curry & Lee, 2020; Poole & Rosenthal, 2011; Sinclair, 2016; Theriault, 2008). Much of what we deem the "study of Congress" is about the legislative or policy efforts within an office or the institution more broadly. For a researcher studying Congress, a prized interview is with the legislative director or chief of staff of a senior lawmaker on the Appropriations Committee. But legislative activity is only one of three critical components of a congressional office: (1) staffing lawmaking capacity while also building out (2) constituent services/operations and (3) the communications team.

Even if we consider policymaking the primary function of Congress, press and digital managers are a critical source of that policy information, and the ways in which we receive it are shaped by how they do their jobs and the tools available to them. Everything we know about Congress—the information we receive and the news that is packaged—touches the desk of the communications shop. Without a press staffer, releases don't go out, television spots don't get booked, and partisan press have nothing to quote. Communications professionals are the people in charge of managing the information exchange, and foundational to all action within Congress are the people sending and packaging the information. No member has the capacity to read every bill on the floor, but somebody is reading the information sent out by the committee communications staff to update members on legislation and talking points around the issues. Policy doesn't exist in a vacuum, no matter how hard leadership may wish it were so, because the political calculus and the presentation of policy reform are intimately tied to the legislative process. Party leaders are the most invested in communications—the power to set the political agenda with digital tools is one of the greatest assets leadership has developed over the last 30 years. Leadership offices, particularly on the minority side, have transitioned their teams away from a bloated policy team to balance their legislative priorities with the capacity to message and respond to the majority. An illustrative example from 2004 was when newly elected Majority Leader Nancy Pelosi reclaimed a Capitol office she had procured for her predecessor, Dick Gephardt, and chose to put her press team in prized Capitol real estate.[6]

Folks inside Congress and voters at home can't pretend the information just appears in their email inbox or they just happened to scroll past something

[6] https://rollcall.com/2004/01/09/pelosi-repossesses-office-from-gephardt/

on Facebook. Building subscriber lists and maintaining opt-ins for lawmaker messaging require coordination across systems and staff. The information environment is managed by communications professionals because policy folks are too busy and too involved in legislative issues to oversee both developing and distributing legislative ideas. Coming up with policy solutions and designing ways to package that information are separate skills that most staff—and even the most successful lawmakers—cannot pair together. Most members of Congress shouldn't even have the password to their own accounts because what they think makes for good content is rarely what works in reality. And lawmakers and policy folks lack the skills to effectively message on policy because, like academics, they don't necessarily appreciate brevity. For example, one senator wouldn't have any idea what was going on with his social media unless he scrolled through his Senate app, which aggregates all tweets. "They had, like, a new Senate app . . . where it shows, like, all the Senate members' tweets, and that's where he was seeing his tweets. He's like, 'Sometimes I'm surprised at how many tweets I write based off these events,' like as a joke, because he doesn't ever check his social media" (Interview 181).

Ask anyone in Congress and they will acknowledge that communications matter—some with glee and others with gloom—but there is an expectation that communications are a basic tenet of a functioning legislative institution. Nobody is operating without some type of communication manager carefully filtering the information coming into and going out of the office. Even most cash-strapped House offices realize that one person is not sufficient to manage both the logistics and strategy of congressional communication. This is why these member offices contract their digital advertising to outside vendors—they don't have the in-house capacity to produce ads for YouTube or run display ads on Meta. Communication comprehension, while an accepted necessity, largely remains understaffed and undervalued as press staff plead their case for $3,000 so they can send a text message to constituents. To manage the demand, offices double up on lower-level staff positions to assist in press efforts and constituent correspondence. For example, a lawmaker office may employ six policy staffers and retain a singular communications staffer, with a lower-level staffer managing clips as well as a ballooning email inbox. The resource allocation suggests a policymaking operation, but in an era of leadership-driven legislation, the burden of action is less lawmaking and more performance. Yet that performance is too often a one-man band or a small collective trying to manage the expectations for effective digital production. Good digital and good press don't necessarily get reflected in a count of media mentions or how many people watched a YouTube video. "A lot of political communications isn't about reaching everybody—it's about reaching the 1,

5, or 50 people that matter, or that will shape opinions" (Interview 132). But the lack of identity around Congress as a communications operation means that the nuances of messaging and expectations are not known to all, creating a disconnect between principals and staff and the realities of what is possible with a communications team of one or two people. The persistent digital uncertainty around Twitter, the unknown future of TikTok, and the realities of constant change further complicate the investment in communications when the goalposts are often changing and lawmakers can't easily quantify the gains.

Constituent Communication Won't Solve the Problem

One of the common solutions practitioners and academics prescribe to the polarization and nationalization of Congress is a restructuring of incentives such that constituent connections are prioritized and members of Congress are more often communicating with their district rather than a broader, ideological audience on Twitter. The lure of being a lightning rod on Twitter to then propel a lawmaker onto Fox News or Newsmax is powerful—and it's a much quicker path to name recognition than spending 10 years in Congress trying to get an immigration bill to the floor with the hope that leadership lets you take even a little credit for it. By reframing the incentive structure and shifting attention to the district rather than national media, lawmakers can, theoretically, give more attention to voters back home. Proponents of strengthening constituent connections argue that listening to voters enhances lawmaker knowledge and helps them make better decisions. Additionally, being open and transparent with constituents builds public trust and helps teach people about Congress's roles and functions.[7]

But the reality is that constituent communications are alive and well, and digital connections to voters back home are not the antidote to the crisis of communication. With all the power of *Politico*, CNN, or Joe Rogan's podcast, members of Congress have more opportunities to connect with constituents than ever before given the prevalence of voter data and the ability to target messages—text messages, Facebook ads, digital ads—among district households. Paid media, as opposed to journalist-driven earned media or owned media practices on Twitter, is an investment in constituent communication, but lawmakers have a lot of discretion when deciding who to talk

[7] https://www.iri.org/resources/iri-unveils-constituent-engagement-guide/

to. Spending money to engage constituents is a good idea—and fundamental to representation—but its execution in the modern Congress often falls short of the representation ideals we may imagine. Part of the congressional communication problem is the fact that most people know little about paid communication, let alone the difference between paid and earned media, and how offices spend those dollars. Twitter, as a means for government accounts, drives earned media given that members are using it to attract free media coverage from journalists, advocates, and the producers of much-watched cable programming. Earned media, or content, is simply information written about lawmakers or the office that they haven't paid for themselves, for example, getting a congressman on the 10 o'clock news to talk about the newly funded fire department or the opportunities for job creation. Earned media depends on an office producing content or generating newsworthy information that people are likely to engage with and share. Paid media, on the other hand, is essentially advertising. In Congress, paid media means paying to show ads or promotional content on social media, search engines, or websites. Lawmakers use paid advertising to build personal connections, increase name recognition, and ensure their messages are heard clearly and widely. This helps members reach the people they want to talk to, get more people to support them, and make the most out of their advertising dollars. Paid media is valuable because it provides direct channels to an audience, pushing one's political brand and driving the narrative. For as little as $0.06 per text, members can send information, surveys, and event advertisements directly to voters' phones. This method is both affordable and easy, making it a practical way to reach many people. Another powerful paid tool for lawmakers is tele–town halls. These are like large conference calls where lawmakers can speak to many voters at once, answer their questions, and create content that can be shared on social media. CTV and display advertising, as well as streaming ads, ensure that lawmakers' messages are seen by a wide audience on popular digital platforms. Digital advertising is central to paid content because Twitter- and Facebook-promoted content gives offices the ability to promote their lawmaker while strategically targeting the audience to boost visibility and foster the lawmaker's reputation. In many ways, these constituent-targeted communications simply build out the communications toolbox with more resources rather than redirecting attention to a limited audience or streamlining communications.

Paid media and the influence of constituent-focused targeted data aren't silver bullets for curbing partisan conflict, because that presentation is curated for a narrow audience of voters. Members of Congress get to choose who they want to target, and while franking rules prevent targeting by party, offices can still filter their advertising to likely voters, Trump supporters, and women over the age of 50. When there were fewer channels for communication—for example, when one had to hope that the local news picked up a story about a new bridge or a grant for the fire department—there was a moderating effect because the audience was less fragmented. Everyone was likely to hear about a project happening in their district. A lawmaker and their staff had to worry about alienating potential voters, motivating independents, and curating broad appeal because everyone was attuned to the same message. Now there are few, if any, incentives to moderate because the message is tailored to a subset of constituents depending on the message. Similar to Twitter, where hot takes and headline-grabbing quotes are likely to go viral, the constituent content that drives engagement consists of messages that target lawmakers' base of partisan support.

Communications professionals are either targeting the 10% of "movable" voters—ignoring much of their district—or dismissing the notion of persuasion entirely with the intent to motivate likely supporters to turn out. Ideology-driven rhetoric and more partisan policy language can occur because you are disengaged from communicating with political opposition within the district. When a Democratic member sends a text message to constituents inviting them to attend a town hall event that week, only moderate or liberal constituents are getting that invite. Even if they wanted to be in conversation with every potential voter, they don't have the budget to realistically communicate with that many people.

Congress struggles to support itself writ large, but digital communications do have some support outside the party-driven operation, both internally and externally. Externally, lawmakers have realized that Congress is not set up to facilitate campaign-level digital communications, either in the support for retaining high-caliber staff or in the intuitional knowledge necessary to navigate the ethics and procedures for engagement with constituents. Offices are acknowledging this heavy burden and using what few resources they have to outsource their constituent communications to third-party operations that can manage paid programs for the office. For example, a lawmaker may approach a digital vendor, saying, "I have $10,000 for a text message program. What can we do with that?" The franking rules around mail, messaging, and advertising can be tricky and cumbersome for a 23-year-old to navigate—let alone manage while trying to build up an earned media portfolio—so outsourcing constituent communication has become a necessary lifeline for offices that want to remain digital savvy but acknowledge the limits of their capacity. This type of communication subsidy—or rather communication outsourcing—is a function of the limited capacity within offices and the need to put their resources where they can be best used. For instance, one chief of staff confirmed that the primary responsibility of their communication director is engaging with reporters, managing earned media, and developing strategic messaging, but paid media is the purview of a press assistant and the external contracting they do for digital advertising because there is no leftover capacity for the communications director.

Like much of congressional reform, the route to better constituent communication is complex, and finding consensus and motivation for reform is a perpetual problem. Once you've given a lawmaker the capacity to manage their own communication operation—particularly in a political climate where many are distrustful of traditional media and journalists—few are willing to forgo that opportunity. One potential solution for incentivizing broader communication across communities is to limit how offices use voter data outside of a campaign. For many years, the most approximate data a lawmaker could get was at the zip code level, and that type of uncertainty or political diversity across a large swath of voters means lawmakers must be more cautious with their messaging. That messaging targets more voters within the district, rather than allowing them to narrowcast their message for a small percentage or to simply propel turnout. Lawmakers can still choose to moderate or not, but there would be less certainty of a hyperpartisan message resonating with a voter in the district. Alternatively, instead of limiting how they use the data, one could provide more resources so that lawmakers are less constrained in how they use the data and allocate more resources to those voters beyond the ones they "need" to engage with and reach out to build new connections.

The reality of members of Congress giving up information or a tool that has become ubiquitous with congressional communication is borderline ludicrous, underscoring just how pervasive digital tools have become to congressional functions. Members have rebuffed efforts to reform lobbying, essentially ignoring attempts to shape who gets to supply information to Congress, and digital reform faces similar opposition because it fundamentally shapes information distribution.

Building Internal Sources of Digital Support in the House

In early 2022, the chief administrator in the House of Representatives revealed a plan to establish a new House Digital Service (HDS) team that would be tasked with improving the technology solutions available to lawmakers. In her testimony before the House Modernization Committee,

Catherine Szpindor said, "Our intention is to leverage fellows from other agencies and the private sector—as appropriate—and expand the House Digital Service team over time."[8] The HDS was tasked with building digital solutions for the House and improving member challenges—many of which are communications related. In addition to solving offices' shared communication headaches, the HDS manages digital tools and coordinates with House offices. The Senate still lacks a similar counterpart, but the HDS offers one source of optimism about how the institution will manage the digital demand moving forward. For example, in 2023, the HDS launched Deconflict—a digital calendar tool to help committees schedule hearings and markups with fewer member conflicts.[9] It allows staff to view current events from other committees and determine if their committee members would have potential conflicts. In 2024, the support office launched Social Stats—a social media tracking tool that shows offices' trends across X (formerly Twitter), Instagram, and Facebook and compares them to averages in the House. The impetus for the tool stemmed from listening sessions with press and communications staff about how to help them do their jobs more effectively. Figure 7.1 shows one example of the types of projects and tools that staff conveyed to the HDS would be most helpful to their daily work.

As part of its digital efforts, the HDS established an advisory group to facilitate staff input on prioritizing the digital needs of Congress. Through the advisory group and HDS newsletters, surveys, and listening sessions, over 500 House staffers have provided feedback to prioritize and contextualize projects. During 2023, the HDS hosted nine events for congressional staff on technology topics and formed several focus groups to conduct user research. One of those groups focused specifically on artificial intelligence (AI) technology and the implementation of AI tools throughout the House. The group aimed to help offices understand and explore emerging AI technology, recruiting over 200 staffers who were interested in testing and evaluating new tools like OpenAI's ChatGPT.

Digital Politics amid Platform Uncertainty

Digital management means producing content and filtering information across many channels, diversifying your digital portfolio across numerous platforms. But inherent to any strategic political choice is uncertainty, and

[8] https://www.congress.gov/117/chrg/CHRG-117hhrg48606/generated/CHRG-117hhrg48606.htm

[9] https://www.linkedin.com/posts/house-digital-service_this-month-the-house-digital-service-at-activity-7052695348552593409-h16p/

Rank	Project	Category	Votes
1	Legislative branch staff directory	Administrative	12
2	Social Media Tracker	Communications	11
3	Tour request portal	Constituent Services	7
3	Anonymized constituent casework data dashboard	Constituent Services	7
4	SMS system	Communications	5
4	Flag orders tracking	Constituent Services	5
5	Collaborative/cloud-based legislative drafting and document management	Legislative	4
5	Audio file transcription	Constituent Services	4
5	Member connections and collaboration on legislative ideas	Legislative	4
5	PII capture during onboarding	Administrative	4
5	Leadership email list management	Administrative	4
6	Electronically adding bill cosponsors	Legislative	3
6	Electronic vote tallying for committee markups	Committee	3
6	Internal Committee Legislation Tracking System	Committee	3
7	Appropriations member office intake	Legislative	1
7	Service Academy nominations tracking	Constituent Services	1
7	Member feedback on committee operations	Committee	1
8	Public comment board for committees	Committee	0
8	Public comment board for personal offices	Communications	0

Figure 7.1 Staff feedback to poll by House Digital Services in 2023 regarding digital projects
Source: House Digital Services' LinkedIn.

amid some of the greatest digital fluctuations in at least five years, the choices about how to engage and with which audiences across platforms were made more difficult by this uncertainty. Musk bought Twitter in October 2022, and it wasn't clear what that would mean for the platform that had been a mainstay for Congress for over a decade. The answers to that question, daily, are a communications director or digital director's responsibility to provide clarity for the direction of the office. Ignoring the fact that the people making this decision are still young enough to pay a premium to rent a car, the uncertainty about what the role of Twitter is going to be is pervasive. A series of questions emerge (Table 7.1) with no clear or straightforward answers.

Much of Congress is currently playing a wait-and-see game to figure out where the leading voices turn for content and where they choose to produce. A number of high-profile journalists have adapted to multichannel platforming where they are visible regardless, but the long-term solution of being present everywhere is unlikely a viable strategy given that it requires individuals and organizations to extend their reach even further with no confidence that they will gain message visibility or actually meet their engagement goals like they previously did when Twitter was the primary platform.

Table 7.1 List of Common Questions about Digital Uncertainty and Communication in Congress

Question	Answer
1. Who is going to be the primary audience on Twitter?	**a)** In 2020, the Pew Research Center published a report that Congress was soaring to new heights on social media, but there seems to be a ceiling for digital in an Elon Musk X/Twitter world. Pew reported a significant increase in congressional activity on social media, particularly on Twitter. However, the digital landscape under Musk's ownership of Twitter (now rebranded as X) has experienced changes that may limit its growth. **b)** The culture of Twitter has likely changed in Congress, but the audience—reporter, and insider-driven—remains the same. Despite these changes, the primary audience on Twitter for Congress remains largely the same, consisting of reporters, political insiders, and engaged constituents. This audience is critical for Congress members to reach for policy dissemination and political messaging. **c)** When the journalists leave Twitter, Congress will likely follow, but that mass exodus has not happened to Threads or another platform. The presence of journalists on Twitter is a significant factor in why Congress members remain active on the platform. A mass migration of journalists to alternative platforms like Threads or BlueSky could prompt Congress members to follow, but such a shift has not yet occurred.
2. Will Twitter continue to be the primary platform for elite-to-elite institutional signaling?	Technology changes rapidly, and though Twitter/X seems to have staying power, there is never certainty that a platform will forever dominate a space as members and staff adapt their routines for new opportunities. While Twitter/X has demonstrated staying power and remains a key platform for elite-to-elite institutional signaling, the rapid evolution of technology and social media trends means that its dominance is not guaranteed. Congressional members and their staff are likely to adapt to new platforms if they present better opportunities for engagement and communication.

3. Will partisan perspectives of Elon Musk divide lawmakers' choice to remain on Twitter?	**a)** Partisan perspectives have already shifted how Democratic lawmakers think about Twitter, considering the platform as largely a means to an end rather than something they optimistically engage in. The ownership of Twitter by Elon Musk has influenced partisan perspectives, particularly among Democratic lawmakers, who view the platform more as a necessary tool than a space for enthusiastic engagement. **b)** Many Democratic staffers would be happy to post elsewhere, but the audience drives that decision. Despite their reservations, Democratic staffers continue to use Twitter because their key audience—journalists and political insiders—remains active there. The audience's preferences significantly impact the platform choices of lawmakers.
4. How will journalists respond to the changes, and will they move to other platforms?	They haven't—thus far. Despite changes to Twitter under Musk's ownership and the emergence of alternative platforms, journalists have largely remained on Twitter. This continued presence sustains the platform's relevance for congressional communication.
5. Will Threads and BlueSky offer viable alternatives to Twitter?	No. Currently, alternative platforms like Threads and BlueSky do not offer viable replacements for Twitter in the context of congressional communication and engagement with journalists and political insiders. Twitter's established user base and entrenched role in political discourse maintain its dominance.

In addition to concerns about where to target a message and the production of content is a concern about the filtering of information. Twitter is not just a platform for self-promotion; its simultaneous role as a filter of political and policy information is critical to the way Congress functions and the decision-making by lawmakers. Members of Congress are supplied with ample information, notwithstanding the new digital platforms popping up as potential replacements, and the need to filter that information has never been greater. One of the main advantages to engaging with the political disaster porn that is Twitter is the ability to figure out quickly what is going on, what is capturing the attention of journalists, and what is likely to dominate the agenda. Twitter was never truly a mechanism for constituent communication—at least in the traditional sense—but rather provided the pulse of the institution. The cost for filtering the information that Twitter provided has gone up because digital managers must monitor new platforms or at least can no longer trust the certainty of Twitter for flagging new issues or alerting them to potential opportunities for engagement. Crisis-driven communication remains, but the cost has gone up and further limited offices' capacity to engage when they were already struggling to monitor existing channels.

Limited Solutions to the Crisis Culture

According to the Public Relations Society of America, the first thing you do amid a crisis is control the situation to prevent further harm, but wrangling control of a crisis of communication that continually reignites is more than a single staffer or lawmaker can handle. One potential solution to this is to provide additional resources for the digital demand that is placed on congressional offices. A congressional office nearly always lacks the resources to do the research that provides the content for quality digital and often lacks the resources to even put that research into context. For example, simply asking a communications staffer how much Community Project Funding was directed to their district in the last year still requires a 15-minute search for the right numbers and the latest internal memo. If we are going to expect lawmakers to produce a series of content that rises to the level of private sector toolkits and creative direction, then we must better invest in that effort.

First, that investment is related to the overall budgeted amount an office must spend on both staff and equipment. Investing in staff allows Congress to manage its increasingly complex workload and sort through the information needed to make the policy and communication choices required. Offices can't keep good staff without offering competitive salaries, and even the most skilled employees cannot perform their jobs effectively without the right support (Brant, 2024). No amount of job satisfaction can outweigh the potential for much higher pay outside of Congress, even among a population of people who consistently value their roles as public servants. Over the past few decades, the pay for congressional staff has generally gone down, and at the same time, new technology has made connecting with voters easier, but it has also made these tasks more demanding (Dryzek, 2019). Despite a total inflation rate increase of 9.8% from 2013 to 2017, the Member's Representational Allowance has not always kept up. This means that even though costs have gone up, the House has not increased the budget for staffing and the realities of a digital Congress.[10] Paying staff fairly for the work they do and the long hours they work can help solve many of the underlying digital problems for both parties by supporting the people who manage the communication burden.

Second, the way resources are allocated within congressional offices is flawed. Many offices employ six legislative staffers for every one communications staffer. In today's world, where most policymaking occurs at the leadership and committee level, this resource allocation ignores the current reality of political communication. Minority members, in particular, rely heavily on messaging as their greatest power, since they can't control the institutional agenda. They can prepare policy solutions for when they regain the majority, but in the meantime, they need a robust messaging operation to counter political and policy narratives from their rivals. Effective communication is crucial for influencing public opinion, rallying support, and responding quickly to opponents. Investing in more communications staff and reallocating resources to prioritize messaging can help lawmakers be more effective in today's digital age. This includes hiring skilled social media managers, public relations experts, and digital content creators who can craft compelling messages and engage with constituents online. By recognizing the importance of communication and adjusting their staffing accordingly, congressional offices can better navigate the fast-paced, media-driven political landscape.

Twitter was never going to solve the problems of Congress, nor was it going to make things easier. Digital tools are not some magical solution that can replace outdated technologies like the fax machine and transform Congress into a more efficient institution. Congress continues to struggle with

[10] https://www.newamerica.org/political-reform/reports/congressional-brain-drain/long-term-trends-in-congresss-brain-drain/

adopting new technologies, and these challenges only make communication strategies more complex in a digital age. Some lawmakers understand the potential of digital platforms and are eager to be part of the digital transformation. They actively engage with their constituents on social media, using it as a powerful tool to share their messages, gather support, and respond to public concerns. However, many others lag behind, due to either a lack of understanding or resistance to change. This disparity means that while some members of Congress are effective digital communicators, others are not, creating an uneven landscape. To truly harness the power of digital communication, Congress as a whole needs to invest in technology training, hire skilled digital staff, and develop comprehensive strategies that integrate new tools with traditional methods. Only then can it become a more agile and responsive institution in the digital era.

Digital Demand in an Artificial Intelligence Future

Despite Congress routinely lagging in terms of technology, over the last few years it has put in place some federal laws on artificial intelligence (AI), either as standalone legislation or as AI-focused provisions in broader acts (CRS #R47644).[11] Examples of this work include passing the National Artificial Intelligence Initiative Act of 2020, establishing the American AI Initiative, and providing for AI development among federal agencies. Congress has also directed specific agencies to design AI-based programs and develop policies applicable across government. In the 117th Congress, at least 75 bills were introduced that either focused on AI and machine learning (ML) or had AI/ML-focused provisions (CRS #R47644).

But beyond AI as a policy tool, Congress is regularly thinking about how technology is integrated into its institutional practices and how technology supports congressional capacity in terms of lawmaking, communication, and constituent casework. Many of these efforts are highlighted by the Congressional Hackathon, a semiregular event hosted by congressional leadership to bring together staff, academics, practitioners, and technology professionals to consider new alternatives for technological implementation in the routines and norms of Congress. Early versions of the event, originally hosted in 2011, focused on basic applications of online technology and the digital footprint of offices, where many were still shuffling paper copies, social media was still novel, and fax machines were still in use through 2007. More recently,

[11] Harris, Laurie Harris (2023, August 4). https://www.congress.gov/crs-product/R47644

and now hosted in conjunction with the chief administrative officer, the event is being seen as an opportunity to highlight new technology challenges and troubleshoot problems. "It's a place where staffers and technological experts get together and brainstorm, completely beyond any silo of their individual affiliations,"[12] said former staffer Matt Lira in an interview with FedScoop. These hackathons are typically organized by congressional leaders and their staff to focus on leveraging technology to address specific challenges within the legislative branch. Recent themes have emphasized novel prototypes for data analysis, software applications, data visualizations, and other technological tools that make the most of the data Congress generates.

Use of open data and APIs provided by government agencies to build functional solutions.

From a communication standpoint, the Hackathon examines communication problems and how AI can be integrated into digital communication platforms, for example, to produce routine communications or newsletters for constituents. In 2023, the HDS purchased a number of AI licenses to allow a sample of offices to test AI technology within their individual systems, providing small laboratories of innovation that will likely shape how the institution addresses AI as a tool for managing the communication and legislative load within an office.

Conclusion

The landscape of congressional communication has undergone a seismic shift in the wake of Twitter's sale to Elon Musk, exemplifying the broader challenges and uncertainties that lawmakers and their staff face in navigating the digital era. The aftermath of this sale has not only thrown the platform into the center of partisan conflict but also disrupted the norms of digital communication within Congress. The repercussions of Musk's changes to Twitter's policies and structure underscore the institution's heavy reliance on digital tools for governance and information dissemination. As this chapter highlights, the once-predictable digital environment has become fraught with uncertainty, compelling congressional staff and journalists to rethink their strategies and consider potential alternatives. Despite the proliferation of platforms like Mastodon, BlueSky, Post, and Threads, none have emerged as a viable replacement for Twitter, leaving Congress in a perpetual state of

[12] M. Alder (2023)., https://fedscoop.com/congressional-hackathon-has-new-institutional-support/

watchfulness. This uncertainty underscores a fundamental truth: while digital communication is here to stay, its future is anything but clear while the crisis culture remains.

The dependency on Twitter and other digital tools reveals the precariousness of the congressional communication infrastructure. The institution's failure to adequately invest in technology and skilled personnel has created a communication crisis. Congressional offices, often operating with limited budgets and underpaid staff, struggle to keep pace with the rapid information flow and the demands of modern digital engagement. The disparity between the expectations placed on these offices and their actual capacity to meet those demands is stark.

High-profile lawmakers have demonstrated the power of investing in digital communication, using it to build robust political brands that extend beyond their constituencies, but their success is not the norm. Most members of Congress lack the resources, capacity, or interest to prioritize digital communication, and those with the means to invest in digital set a standard that is unattainable for many of their colleagues. The consequences of this imbalance are profound. The ability to effectively communicate and shape the narrative has become a key factor in political success, yet the institution's limited investment in the digital communication infrastructure hampers its overall effectiveness. The rapid pace of the digital news cycle, the constant threat of misinformation, and the need for perpetual readiness have turned congressional communication into a form of crisis management. Yet, unlike a well-funded fire department, Congress often operates more like a volunteer fire brigade, lacking the necessary resources and support to perform its role effectively.

This book underscores the critical need for Congress to reassess its approach to digital communication. By examining the evolution of communication practices, the daily logistics faced by staff, and the broader implications of digital engagement, we gain valuable insights into the institutional dynamics at play. Lawmakers' ability to achieve their fundamental goals—whether related to policy, constituent service, or partisan politics—is intricately linked to their communication strategies. Institutional pressures, party expectations, and constituent demands all shape how lawmakers prioritize and organize their communication efforts.

The digital communication crisis in Congress reflects a broader challenge: the need to align institutional capacity with the demands of the modern information environment. Only by investing in technology, human capital, and strategic communication practices can Congress hope to navigate the complexities of the digital age and effectively serve the American public.

Appendix

Qualitative Methods Notes and Design

This appendix offers detailed insights into the elite interview methods employed in this book about congressional communication. This appendix aims to offer further clarity on working with elite respondents and guide fellow legislative and communication scholars who may find these techniques useful for their own research.

Community Observation: Initial Access

My interviews with communications and legislative professionals form the core for this study, but in addition, the insights I offer stem from two experiences participating in and contributing to the information flows in Congress. These experiences provided me with necessary context, the opportunity to engage with my study participants, and the background to understand the dynamics my respondents described. Each of these experiences is detailed below. This participant observation research, while unintendedly so at the time, allowed me to access data through observation over a period of time that better enabled me to understand the culture and conversation of the community I have researched (Yanow, 2003). My experience included entry into private conversations and access to physical spaces that enable a more comprehensive lens by which to view the daily routines in Congress.

Digital Intern: National Journal

My first experience of participant observation stems from my role as an intern on the multimedia team for *National Journal*—working with folks at the magazine, *Congress Daily*, and the *Hotline*. I worked with the digital team in 2010, taking a semester off from college to work in Washington, DC, as a participant in the former Washington Center for Journalism and Politics. I applied to the program as a multimedia journalism student, eventually working with *National Journal* the same year they first fundamentally shifted their model toward a digital product. As an entry-level staff person, I was not involved in many of the decisions or behind-the-scenes discussions about congressional news coverage, but I was able to observe the changing news climate, the newsroom reorganization, the methods for congressional reporting, and the digital norms being integrated into the news-gathering process. For example, in November 2010, I was the staffer managing the digital overnight shift for the midterm elections—updating candidate profiles as the Tea Party candidates dominated headlines. During this experience, I worked with many of the respondents whom I would later interview for my elite interviews.

Legislative Action Team: Congressional Quarterly

My second experience was as a member of the legislative action team for *Congressional Quarterly/Roll Call* in the spring of 2012. This was my first job out of college, and I was essentially an intern working on lower-profile stories, copyediting different products, and tracking legislation. My first day in the office, I was handed Walter Oleszek's *Congressional Procedures and the Policy Process* and told to memorize it. My understanding of Congress and its procedures largely stems from this experience reading at my desk and then putting those principles into practice when I was covering committee action on the Hill. My role as a junior member of the team meant often observing those senior staff around me, following along on email threads, and tracking how stories were reported on a daily basis. My portfolio of work was often whatever was left over, and that gave me the opportunity to tackle multiple types of stories and issues and to work with lots of people across the newsroom. My daily schedule usually included a mix of committee hearings, occasional markups, tracking bills, email and phone communications, meetings with other reporters, reading, and research. Even in 2012, my work was dictated by digital norms—with my iPhone always at hand, I needed to be ready to answer emails, follow Twitter, or respond to messages from editors.

Both of my experiences were comprehensive and immersive, allowing me to participate in the daily routines and understand what it is like to be a professional on Capitol Hill. My immersive experiences pre-date my research on Congress, but it is worth noting how these roles shaped the way I understand the institution. I was never in a position to choose the types of experiences I was privy to—as a junior staff member you are often following orders—but with each opportunity the goal was to prove my value, contribute to the goal of the newsroom, and be a trusted member of my reporting team.

Continued Access and Immersion

I returned to Congress in 2022 as a researcher seeking immersion for my research as a Kluge Fellow at the Library of Congress. Access to the Capitol grounds during continued lockdown from COVID-19 regulations granted me the opportunity to exist in the physical space of the actors I was describing and researching. Interpretive researchers cannot detach themselves from the environment they are studying because they are intrinsically a part of it (Curry, 2015). My goal was to continue minimizing the difference between my understanding of Congress and that of my participants in the elite interviews I engaged in. There is an ongoing challenge to convince those subjects you engage with that you understand their perspective, their challenges, and the nature of their own reality. I was able to use this time at the Library of Congress, across the street from Senate and House office buildings, to update my priors and better understand the daily challenges faced by staff and reporters. I connected with the congressional community over our shared media experiences, congressional communication, and the realities of legislative politics in a polarized environment. I did not want my status as an "outsider" to alter the behavior of the people I was talking with and learning from. One approach I used was meeting people in locations that required badge access, thus communicating that I am part of the physical community that they existed in.

I built relationships and immersed myself as a staffer on the Hill during the waning days of a pandemic where the only people allowed in congressional offices were those who worked there and those escorted into the building. I gained a greater level of access than I would have before the pandemic given that the public and outsiders were few and far between—removing further layers between me and the communities I observed. This exposure led to better experiences and shared observations that only those of us who experienced the strange silence could understand. I developed an "ethnographic sensibility" of the congressional community and its participants. I interacted with members of Congress and their staffers as one of the professionals working in government, talking about processes and legislative politics, as well as the merits of the coffee shop in the Russell Senate office building. These experiences felt natural and enjoyable, and the professional social connections I made elevated the authenticity of my research. Full immersion and the development of these personal connections were crucial for my understanding of congressional actors. In interpretive research, distance from subjects and objectivity are neither realistic nor desirable (see Schwartz-Shea & Yanow, 2012), and my work interviewing my elite subjects would not have been possible without those personal connections. Many of the key insights in this book were only made possible through the connections I built during my immersive participant observation research.

Elite Interviews

Between February 2020 and March 2023, I conducted elite interviews with current and former staffers of Congress, reporters, digital media professionals, and campaign staff. To increase readers' confidence in the interview process and subsequent evidence (Bleich & Pekkanen, 2013), this section details the interviewees, the process of obtaining interviews, the interview procedures, and the methods I used for transcribing and analyzing the data.

The Respondents

To encourage participation and limit any risk to the interviewees, each interview was conducted with the promise that our conversation was "not for attribution" and all quoted material would be anonymous. Offering anonymity allowed interviewees to speak freely without fearing retribution or harm to their careers. I have made every effort to protect the identities of the respondents, but I do provide basic descriptions. Table A.1 provides key details, including their office's party affiliation, their gender, and their current status at the time of the interview.

The sample of respondents is intentionally diverse, though it leans Democratic, with 56% of the interviewees being Democrats or professionals working in Democratic offices. The group of 191 participants includes representation from both parties and various roles, including rank-and-file and leadership offices, campaign and advocacy organization staff, and journalists covering Congress both on site and remotely. Most interviewees have worked in multiple professional capacities, broadening the scope of the study to draw on their experiences from an even wider array of political environments and communication settings. The sample includes

Table A.1 Breaking Down the Respondents

Party	
Democrat	108
Republican	44
Nonpartisan	39
Role	
Policy	40
Communications	125
Media	26
Gender	
Women	84
Men	107

staff serving in at least 15 different types of roles within a congressional office, from chiefs of staff at the top of the office hierarchy and to interns who had just completed their short stint in Congress. Additionally, 60% of the interviewees were actively working in Congress at the time of the interview, while the rest had left Congress or were working in other politics-adjacent fields. As my interest was in the ways in which communication changed over time within the institution, I strategically sought out interviews with respondents who were no longer in Congress but could speak to prior norms or routines that current staff could not.

Recruiting Respondents

Expanding on the approach I referenced in Chapter 1, I approached interviewee selection with a snowball selection technique alongside contacting offices where I had a direct or indirect connection to a professional. Notably, the many individuals who were referred to me through the snowball method were significantly more inclined to agree to an interview. Many of my interviews were based on a shared contact or a shared commonality, highlighting the importance of "credentials." Each potential interviewee received a customized form email, similar to the example provided below:

> Mr. XXX,
>
> [Respondent] and I recently had a conversation about changing congressional media, and he suggested I get in contact with you. I am a public policy professor at the University of Kentucky and I am currently conducting research about the role communication and social media play in Congress. Given your experience, I would appreciate the opportunity to briefly discuss the topic with you in an interview. Any information we discuss would not be for attribution and solely for my academic research, and all records from the interview would be securely stored and accessible only by me. I understand that you have an exceedingly busy schedule and promise to not take up too much of your time. I would greatly appreciate it if you would be willing to speak with me sometime over the next month. I can be flexible on times and dates to match your schedule. I hope to hear from you soon. If you have any questions about the interview or interview process, I will be happy to answer them.
>
> Best,
>
> Annelise Russell

In successive emails, the structure of the email largely remained unchanged, with variations based on the name of the reference, the position of the contact, and any relationship I had with the potential respondent. If contacting individuals without a reference, I omitted the initial sentence and rather emphasized my role as a former reporter in Congress or a fellow at the Library of Congress. For each of the respondents I offered further details about the study's goals, how their response would be used, and the long arc of academic publication timelines. I also highlighted my university's Institutional Review Board policy and my adherence to it. I clarified any uncertainty about our shared understanding of "not for attribution" and assured them that if any specific details arose that revealed their identity, that information would not be included in my research.

Conducting Interviews

The interview protocol consisted of in-depth and semi-structured conversations, primarily consisting of open-ended questions that allowed the respondents to talk about the many facets of their time in Congress or in political communication. My aim was to structure the interactions such that I could uncover unforeseen insights that would yield new and fruitful information, while also ensuring enough structure for comparability across interviews and being mindful of the limited time to speak with some individuals. The most consistent aspect of the interview process was my standard introduction, where I addressed my goals and the process and provided further clarity on anonymity. After addressing any additional questions from the respondent, I started each interview with a similar set of initial questions, followed by flexible follow-up questions to explore diverse avenues. Each respondent was first asked to explain their current role and the progression of their career into that role. The intention behind this question was (1) to make sure I was correct on the experience of the professional while (2) also giving them an opportunity to become accustomed to talking about themselves and their experiences. Many respondents have never been asked this line of questioning about their jobs from an academic, so ensuring a comfortable and conversational rapport was paramount.

Interviews typically lasted between 20 and 40 minutes, but interviews ranged from as few as 10 minutes to a full hour or more. I conducted most interviews over Zoom or on the phone given that this project was initiated weeks before a global pandemic. In 2022, I added in-person interviews to the data set—working hard to maintain consistency and clarity between the different types of interactions. Each interview began with a brief project overview, as described above, assuring interviewees of the anonymity of their contributions and emphasizing that all discussions would be utilized solely for academic research. Many of the respondents' uncertainties were alleviated when I described the interviews as such: "Congress comms paint by numbers—where everyone gives their own unique experience to fill in the bigger picture." Interviewees were identified only in basic terms, such as current or former members of Congress or staffers, categorized, for example, by their role as a "Republican communications staffer." All interviews were recorded, both in person and remotely, to ensure fluidity in the conversation and avoid frenzied note taking. This tactic was especially important in person where the conversations with the respondents were necessary for the best-quality interview and trying to take notes would have detracted from the fluidity of conversation.

The structure of the interviews varied slightly depending on the interviewees' role. Congressional communication staffers were asked about their information-gathering processes, their approvals process for communications content, their relationships with reporters, and challenges experienced in producing digital content. Interviews with noncommunications professionals in Congress asked about the relationship between policy and communications staff, the Twitter-driven climate, the news media, and the changes that occurred during their tenure. Regardless of the type of interviewee, follow-up questions often led to more insightful discussions, as some respondents delved deeply into their norms and processes. Drawing from my experience as a reporter, I leveraged my familiarity with Capitol Hill jargon and the mindset of those employed in Congress to formulate questions and establish rapport. For example, when speaking about paid communications, being able to discuss "499" strategies designed to limit franking around elections was helpful to signal to my respondents that I was familiar enough with their environment to give a more detailed account. Different interviewees necessitated different approaches; some folks provided detailed responses up front, while others required targeted follow-up queries or discussions.

With each interview, particularly with those involving junior congressional staff, conversational, less formal interviews tended to yield the most rewarding insights as the interviewees felt most comfortable in a more casual setting. Among more senior officials, I began with greater deference to their position and status. Every interview offered slight variations that enriched the study, as each conversation illuminated unanticipated information and enhanced both the theoretical and empirical aspects of the project.

Transcription and Assessment

My process for transcribing and interpreting interview data adheres to the interpretive tradition, focusing on understanding the depth and context of what interviewees conveyed. To capture the full meaning of their responses, I recorded each conversation to remain invested in the moment with my respondent rather than trying to scribble notes as fast as possible. During my time as a reporter, I quickly learned that I was not capable of having a quality conversation while also taking notes as another was talking. These prior lessons were invaluable in my process, as every researcher finds their own method for data collection.

Upon collection, I tried to place each interview in the broader communication context, persistently reevaluating respondents' statements, considering previous discussions, and looking for consistent narratives in light of other interviews and emerging patterns. This iterative process involved constant reflection and reassessment to develop a comprehensive understanding of my data. My participant observation experiences further enriched my analysis, helping to contextualize the interviewees' words and uncover deeper meanings that would not have been significant without these prior experiences. The initial goal was to develop a thorough understanding of each interviewee's words and how they aligned with or challenged the framework of my theory, and to offer unprecedented information about the power of congressional communication. My transcription method reflected this goal. For recorded interviews over the phone or online, I used a notepad to capture additional features, such as tone, which are not evident in audio recordings. Each of the interviews was saved as a digital copy, anonymized, and transcribed via Otter.ai. This is the same software that reporters in the congressional press pool used to share information during the COVID-19 pandemic. Those transcripts were then cleaned by research assistants.

These interviews offer insights from influential staffers and reporters with extensive congressional experience and knowledge of the changing communication climate. Combined with evidence from participant observation and statistical data analyses, they provide a multifaceted and compelling basis for my conclusions.

Bibliography

Abramowitz, A. I., & Webster, S. (2016). The rise of negative partisanship and the nationalization of US elections in the 21st century. *Electoral Studies, 41*, 12–22.

Adler, E. S., & Wilkerson, J. D. (2013). *Congress and the politics of problem solving*. Cambridge University Press.

Alexander, B. (2021). *A Social theory of congress: Legislative norms in the twenty-first century*. Lexington Books.

Anderson, S. E., DeLeo, R. A., & Taylor, K. (2020). Policy entrepreneurs, legislators, and agenda setting: Information and influence. *Policy Studies Journal, 48*, 587–611.

Anzia, S. F., & Jackman, M. C. (2013). Legislative organization and the second face of power: Evidence from US state legislatures. *Journal of Politics, 75*(1), 210–224.

Arpan, L. M., & Pompper, D. (2003). Stormy weather: Testing "stealing thunder" as a crisis communication strategy to improve communication flow between organizations and journalists. *Public Relations Review, 29*(3), 291–308.

Ballard, A., DeTamble, R., Dorsey, S., Heseltine, M., & Johnson, M. (2022a). Incivility in congressional tweets. *American Politics Research, 50*(6), 769–780.

Ballard, A. O., DeTamble, R., Dorsey, S., Heseltine, M., & Johnson, M. (2022b). Dynamics of polarizing rhetoric in congressional tweets. *Legislative Studies Quarterly, 48*, 105–144.

Barber, M., & Schmidt, S. (2019). Electoral competition and legislator effectiveness. *American Politics Research, 47*(4), 683–708.

Barberá, P., Casas, A., Nagler, J., Egan, P. J., Bonneau, R., Jost, J. T., & Tucker, J. A. (2019). Who leads? Who follows? Measuring issue attention and agenda setting by legislators and the mass public using social media data. *American Political Science Review, 113*(4), 883–901.

Baumgartner, F. R., & Jones, B. D. (2010). *Agendas and instability in American politics*. University of Chicago Press.

Baumgartner, F. R., & Jones, B. D. (2015). *The Politics of information: Problem definition and the course of public policy in America*. University of Chicago Press.

Bennett, W. L., & Iyengar, S. (2008). A new era of minimal effects? The changing foundations of political communication. *Journal of Communication, 58*(4), 707–731.

Berger, J., & Milkman, K. L. (2013). Emotion and virality: What makes online content go viral? *NIM Marketing Intelligence Review, 5*(1), 18–23.

Bianco, W. T. (1997). Reliable source or ususal suspects? Cue-taking, information transmission, and legislative committees. *Journal of Politics, 59*(3), 913–924.

Bimber, B. (1991). Information as a factor in congressional politics. *Legislative Studies Quarterly, 16*(4), 585–605.

Birkland, T. A. (2006). *Lessons of disaster: Policy change after catastrophic events*. Georgetown University Press.

Bleich, E., & Pekkanen, R. (2013). How to report interview data. In L. Mosley (Ed.), *Interview research in political science* (pp. 84–106). Cornell University Press. http://www.jstor.org/stable/10.7591/j.ctt1xx5wg.9

Boin, A., 't Hart, P., & McConnell, A. (2009). Crisis exploitation: Political and policy impacts of framing contests. *Journal of European Public Policy, 16*(1), 81–106.

Boin, A., McConnell, A., & 't Hart, P. (Eds.). (2008). *Governing after crisis: The politics of investigation, accountability and learning*. Cambridge University Press.

Box-Steffensmeier, J. M., Cunha, R. C., Varbanov, R. A., Hoh, Y. S., Knisley, M. L., & Holmes, M. A. (2015). Survival analysis of faculty retention and promotion in the social sciences by gender. *PloS One, 10*(11), e0143093.

Brader, T. (2006). *Campaigning for hearts and minds: How emotional appeals in political ads work.* University of Chicago Press.

Brant, H. K. (2024, September). Polarization and the ties that bind: Congressional staff turnover. *Congress & the Presidency, 51*(3), 324–357.

Brody, R. (1991). *Assessing the president: The media, elite opinion, and public support.* Stanford University Press.

Brudnick, I. A. (2024, June 27). *Congressional salaries and allowances: In brief.* CRS Report No. RL30064. Congressional Research Service. https://www.congress.gov/crs-product/RL30064

Brudnick, I. A. (2020, November 5). *Senators' Official Personnel and Office Expense Account (SOPOEA): History and usage.* CRS Report R44399. Congressional Research Service. https://www.congress.gov/crs-product/R44399

Burgat, C., & Russell, A. (in press). Mutual intolerance: Declining civility in official office communications. In B. Alexander (Ed.), *The idea of Congress: Congressional norms in an age of conflict.*

Cheng, Y. (2018). How social media is changing crisis communication strategies: Evidence from the updated literature. *Journal of Contingencies and Crisis Management, 26*, 58–68.

Cheng, Y. (2020). The social-mediated crisis communication research: Revisiting dialogue between organizations and publics in crises of China. *Public Relations Review, 46*(1).

Coleman, J. (2020). *UK community radio production responses to COVID-19.*

Connor, C., & Russell, A. (2024). Rapid response and uncertain agendas: Senators' response to Dobbs. *Policy Studies Journal, 52*(4), 751–775.

Cook, G. (1989). *Discourse.* Oxford University Press.

Coombs, W. T. (2007). Protecting organization reputations during a crisis: The development and application of situational crisis communication theory. *Corporate Reputation Review, 10*, 163–176.

Coombs, W. T. (2011). Political public relations and crisis communication: A public relations perspective. In J. Strömbäck & S. Kiousis (Eds.), *Political public relations* (pp. 223–243). Routledge.

Coombs, W. T. (2014). State of crisis communication: Evidence and the bleeding edge. *Research Journal of the Institute for Public Relations, 1*(1), 1–12.

Coombs, W. T. (2015). The value of communication during a crisis: Insights from strategic communication research. *Business Horizons, 58*(2), 141–148.

Coombs, T., & Holladay, S. (2010). *The handbook of crisis communication.* Blackwell Publishing Ltd.

Coombs, W. T., Frandsen, F., Holladay, S. J., & Johansen, W. (2010). Why a concern for apologia and crisis communication? *Corporate Communications: An International Journal, 15*(4), 337–349.

Coppins, M. (2018, November). The man who broke politics. *The Atlantic.* https://www.theatlantic.com/magazine/archive/2018/11/newt-gingrich-says-youre-welcome/570832/

Cormack, L. (2016). Gender and vote revelation strategy in the United States Congress. *Journal of Gender Studies, 25*(6), 626–640.

Crilley, R., & Gillespie, M. (2019). What to do about social media? Politics, populism and journalism. *Journalism, 20*(1), 173–176.

Crosson, J. (2021). Extreme districts, moderate winners: Same-party challenges, and deterrence in top-two primaries. *Political Science Research and Methods, 9*(3), 532–548.

Crosson, J. M., Lorenz, G. M., Volden,C., & Wiseman,A. E. (2021). How experienced legislative staff contribute to effective lawmaking. In T. M. LaPira, L. Drutman, & K. R. Kosar (Eds.), *Congress overwhelmed: The decline in congressional capacity and prospects for reform.* Online Edn. https://doi.org/10.7208/chicago/9780226702605.003.0013

Curry, J. M. (2015). *Legislating in the dark: Information and power in the House of Representatives.* University of Chicago Press.

Curry, J. M., & Lee, F. E. (2019). *The limits of party: Congress and lawmaking in a polarized era.* University of Chicago Press.

Curry, J. M., & Lee, F. E. (2020). What is regular order worth? Partisan lawmaking and congressional processes. *The Journal of Politics, 82*(2), 627–641.

Denisova, A. (2023). Viral journalism. Strategy, tactics and limitations of the fast spread of content on social media: Case study of the United Kingdom quality publications. *Journalism, 24*(9), 1919–1937.

Dryzek, J. S., Bächtiger, A., Chambers, S., Cohen, J., Druckman, J. N., Felicetti, A., Fishkin, J. S., Farrell, D. M., Fung, A., Gutmann, A., Landemore, H., Mansbridge, J., Marien, S., Neblo, M. A., Niemeyer, S., Setälä, M., Slothuus, R., Suiter, J., Thompson, D., & Warren, M. E. (2019). The crisis of democracy and the science of deliberation. *Science, 363*(6432), 1144–1146.

Eastham, K., Coates, D., & Allodi, F. (1970). The concept of crisis. *Canadian Psychiatric Association Journal, 15*(5), 463–472.

Esterling, K. M. (2007). Buying expertise: Campaign contributions and attention to policy analysis in congressional committees. *American Political Science Review, 101*(1), 93–109.

Evans, H. K., Cordova,V., & Sipole, S. (2014). Twitter style: An analysis of how House candidates used Twitter in their 2012 campaigns. *PS: Political Science and Politics, 47*(2), 454–462.

Evans, H. K., Gervais, B. T., & Russell, A. (2022). Getting good and mad: Exploring the use of anger on Twitter by female candidates in 2020. In S. D. Foreman, M. L. Godwin, & W. C. Wilson (Eds.), *The roads to Congress 2020: Campaigning in the era of Trump and COVID-19* (pp. 53–71). Springer International Publishing.

Fenno, R. F. (1977). US House members in their constituencies: An exploration. *American Political Science Review, 71*(3), 883–917.

Frandsen, F., & Johansen, W. (2022). Strategic communication: A discipline in the making? In J. Falkheimer, & M. Heide (Eds.), *Research handbook on strategic communication* (pp. 14–32). Edward Elgar Publishing.

Furnas, A. C., Crosson, J. M., & Lorenz, G. M. (2021). Pandemic pluralism: Legislator championing of organized interests in response to COVID-19. *Journal of Political Institutions and Political Economy, 2*(1), 23–41.

Gainous, J., Segal, A., & Wagner, K. (2018). Is the equalization/normalization lens dead? Social media campaigning in US congressional elections. *Online Information Review, 42*(5), 718–731.

Gainous, J., & Wagner, K. M. (2013). *Tweeting to power: The social media revolution in American politics.* Oxford University Press.

Gandy, O. H. (1982). *Beyond agenda setting: Information subsidies and public policy.* Ablex.

Gaynor, S. W. (2022). *Follow the leaders: Policy presentation in the US Congress* [Doctoral dissertation]. University of Maryland, College Park.

Gervais, B. T., & Morris, I. L. (2018). *Reactionary republicanism: How the Tea Party in the House paved the way for Trump's victory.* Oxford University Press.

Gilpin, D. (2010). Organizational image construction in a fragmented online media environment. *Journal of Public Relations Research, 22*(3), 265–287.

Green, M. N., & Crouch, J. (2022). *Newt Gingrich: The rise and fall of a party entrepreneur.* University Press of Kansas.

Grimmer, J. (2010). A Bayesian hierarchical topic model for political texts: Measuring expressed agendas in Senate press releases. *Political Analysis, 18*(1), 1–35.

Groeling, T. (2010). *When politicians attack: Party cohesion in the media.* Cambridge University Press.

Gulati, G. J. (2004). Members of Congress and presentation of self on the World Wide Web. *Harvard International Journal of Press/Politics, 9*(1), 22–40.

Hacker, J., & Pierson, P. (2006). Still off topic: A reply to Pitney's rejoinder. *The Forum, 4*(1), 0000102202154088841119.

Hall, R. L. (1998). *Participation in Congress.* Yale University Press.

Hall, R. L., & Deardorff, A. V. (2006). Lobbying as legislative subsidy. *American Political Science Review, 100*(1), 69–84.

Hemphill, L., Russell, A., & Schöpke-Gonzalez, A. M. (2021). What drives US congressional members' policy attention on Twitter? *Policy & Internet, 13*(2), 233–256.

Howard, N. O., & Owens, M. (2022). Organizing staff in the US Senate: The priority of individualism in resource allocation. *Congress & the Presidency, 49*(1), 60–83.

Jamieson, J. P., Hangen, E. J., Lee, H. Y., & Yeager, D. S. (2018). Capitalizing on appraisal processes to improve affective responses to social stress. *Emotion Review, 10*(1), 30–39.

Jenkins-Smith, H. C., & Sabatier, P. A. (1993). The study of public policy processes. *The Nation's Health*, 135–142.

Jin, Y., & Liu, B. F. (2010). The blog-mediated crisis communication model: Recommendations for responding to influential external blogs. *Journal of Public Relations Research, 22*(4), 429–455.

Jones, B. D., & Baumgartner, F. R. (2005). A model of choice for public policy. *Journal of Public Administration Research and Theory, 15*(3), 325–351.

Jones, B. D., Theriault, S. M., & Whyman, M. (2019). *The great broadening: How the vast expansion of the policymaking agenda transformed American politics.* University of Chicago Press.

Kasperson, R. E., Renn, O., Slovic, P., Brown, H. S., Emel, J., Goble, R., Kasperson, J. X., & Ratick, S. (1988). The social amplification of risk: A conceptual framework. *Risk Analysis, 8*(2), 177–187.

Kvale, S. (1996). The 1,000-page question. *Qualitative Inquiry, 2*(3), 275–284. https://doi.org/10.1177/107780049600200302

Keeler, J. T. (1993). Opening the window for reform: Mandates, crises, and extraordinary policy-making. *Comparative Political Studies, 25*(4), 433–486.

Kernell, S. (2006). *Going public: New strategies of presidential leadership.* CQ Press.

Kiewe, A. (1994). *The modern presidency and crisis rhetoric.* Bloomsbury Academic.

Klein, J. (2007). Where should we stand to get the best perspective on collective violence? *Critical Sociology, 33*(5–6), 957–980.

Kousser, T. (2019). Tweet style: Campaigning, governing, and social media in Australia. *Australian Journal of Political Science, 54*(2), 183–201.

LaPira, T. M., Drutman, L., & Kosar, K. R. (Eds.). (2020). *Congress overwhelmed: The decline in congressional capacity and prospects for reform.* University of Chicago Press.

Lasorsa, D. L., Lewis, S. C., & Holton, A. E. (2012). Normalizing Twitter: Journalism practice in an emerging communication space. *Journalism Studies, 13*(1), 19–36.

Lee, F. E. (2008). Dividers, not uniters: Presidential leadership and senate partisanship, 1981–2004. *Journal of Politics, 70*(4), 914–928.

Lee, F. E. (2016). *Insecure majorities: Congress and the perpetual campaign.* University of Chicago Press.

Lipinski, D. (2001). The effect of messages communicated by members of Congress: The impact of publicizing votes. *Legislative Studies Quarterly, 26*(1), 81–100.

Liu, B. F., Austin, L., & Jin, Y. (2011). How publics respond to crisis communication strategies: The interplay of information form and source. *Public Relations Review*, *37*(4), 345–353.

Liu, B. F., & Fraustino, J. D. (2014). Beyond image repair: Suggestions for crisis communication theory development. *Public Relations Review*, *40*(3), 543–546.

Lupia, A. (1992). Busy voters, agenda control, and the power of information. *American Political Science Review*, *86*(2), 390–403.

Macdonald, M., Brown, M. A., Tucker, J. A., & Nagler, J. (2025). To moderate, or not to moderate: Strategic domain sharing by congressional campaigns. *Electoral Studies*, *95*, 102907.

Macias, W., Hilyard, K., & Freimuth, V. (2009). Blog functions as risk and crisis communication during Hurricane Katrina. *Journal of Computer-Mediated Communication*, *15*(1), 1–31.

MacKuen, M., Wolak, J., Keele, L., & Marcus, G. E. (2010). Civic engagements: Resolute partisanship or reflective deliberation. *American Journal of Political Science*, *54*(2), 440–458. https://doi.org/10.1111/j.1540-5907.2010.00440.x

Maltzman, F., & Sigelman, L. (1996). The politics of talk: Unconstrained floor time in the US House of Representatives. *Journal of Politics*, *58*(3), 819–830.

Manheim, J. B. (1991). *All of the people, all the time: Strategic communication and American politics*. M.E. Sharpe.

Manheim, J. B. (1993). The war of images: Strategic communication in the Gulf conflict. In S. Renshon (Ed.), *The political psychology of the Gulf War: Leaders, publics, and the process of conflict* (pp. 155–172). University of Pittsburgh Press.

Mann, T. E., & Ornstein, N. J. (2016). *It's even worse than it looks: How the American constitutional system collided with the new politics of extremism*. Basic Books.

Matthews, M. R. (1960). *U.S. Senators and their world*. University of North Carolina Press.

Mayhew, D. R. (1974). Congressional elections: The case of the vanishing marginals. *Polity*, *6*(3), 295–317.

McCarty, N., Poole, K. T., & Rosenthal, H. (2016). *Polarized America: The dance of ideology and unequal riches*. MIT Press.

McCubbins, M. D., & Schwartz, T. (1984). Congressional oversight overlooked: Police patrols versus fire alarms. *American Journal of Political Science*, *28*(1), 165–179.

McGregor, S. C. (2019). Social media as public opinion: How journalists use social media to represent public opinion. *Journalism*, *20*(8), 1070–1086.

McNair, B. (2016). *Communication and political crisis: Media, politics and governance in a globalized public sphere [Global Crises and the Media, Volume 16]*. Peter Lang Publishing.

Montgomery, J. M., & Nyhan, B. (2017). The effects of congressional staff networks in the US House of Representatives. *Journal of Politics*, *79*(3), 745–761.

Morris, J. S. (2001). Reexamining the politics of talk: Partisan rhetoric in the 104th House. *Legislative Studies Quarterly*, *26*(1), 101–121.

Mortensen, P. B. (2012). It's the central government's fault: A study of elected regional officials' use of blame shifting rhetoric. *Governance*, *25*, 439–461.

Moses, L. (2023). *Interests on the internet: Political elites, interest groups and influence on social media* [Doctoral dissertation, Ohio State University]. http://rave.ohiolink.edu/etdc/view?acc_num=osu1689849626062125

Niven, D., & Zilber, J. (2001). Do women and men in congress cultivate different images? Evidence from congressional web sites. *Political Communication*, *18*(4), 395–405.

NextGov. (2014). https://www.nextgov.com/ideas/2014/09/congress-basically-still-your-grandparents-when-it-comes-internet/95468/

Oga-Baldwin, W. Q. (2024). Validation crisitunity: A response to Al-Hoorie, Hiver, and In'nami (2024). *Studies in Second Language Acquisition*, 1–13.

Peters, R. M., Jr., & Rosenthal, C. S. (2010). *Speaker Nancy Pelosi and the new American politics.* Oxford University Press.

Poole, K. T., & Rosenthal, H. L. (2011). *Ideology and congress* (Vol. 1). Transaction Publishers.

Reynolds, M. E. (2021). *Making Congress a better place to work.* Brookings.

Russell, A. (2018). US senators on Twitter: Asymmetric party rhetoric in 140 characters. *American Politics Research, 46*(4), 695–723.

Russell, A. (2021a). Minority opposition and asymmetric parties? Senators' partisan rhetoric on Twitter. *Political Research Quarterly, 74*(3), 615–627.

Russell, A. (2021b). *Tweeting is leading: How senators communicate and represent in the age of Twitter.* Oxford University Press.

Russell, A., Evans, H. K., & Gervais, B. (2024). Not ready to make nice: Congressional candidates' emotional appeals on twitter. *Social Science Quarterly, 105*, 1848–1856. https://doi.org/10.1111/ssqu.13439

Russell, A., & Howard, N. (2021, November). *Constrained communications? Choices in congressional representation [Paper presentation].* Center for Effective Lawmaking Conference.

Russell, A., & Macdonald, M. (2025). Congressional communications in a digital era. In eds. L. C. Dodd, B. Oppenheimer, R. B. Rubin, & C. L. Evans (Eds.). *Congress reconsidered*, 13th Edition. CQ Press.

Russell, A., Macdonald, M., & Hua, W. (2023). Sit still, talk pretty: Partisan differences among women candidates' campaign appeals. *Journal of Women, Politics & Policy, 44*(3), 354–370.

Salisbury, R. H., & Shepsle, K. A. (1981). US congressman as enterprise. *Legislative Studies Quarterly, 6*, 559–576.

Scher, S. (1963). Conditions for legislative control. *Journal of Politics, 25*(3), 526–551.

Schickler, E. (2005). Institutional development of Congress. In P. J. Quirk, & S. A. Binder, (Eds.), *The Legislative Branch* (pp. 35–62). Oxford University Press.

Schwartz-Shea, P., & Yanow, D. (2013). *Interpretive research design: Concepts and processes.* Routledge.

Seelye, K. Q. (1994). Gingrich first mastered the media and then rose to be king of the Hill. *The New York Times.* https://www.nytimes.com/1994/12/14/us/gingrich-first-mastered-the-media-and-then-rose-to-be-king-of-the-hill.html

Sellers, P. J. (2000). Manipulating the message in the US Congress. *Harvard International Journal of Press-Politics, 5*(1), 22–31.

Shogan, C. J. (2010). Blackberries, tweets, and YouTube: Technology and the future of communicating with Congress. *Political science & politics, 43*(2), 231–233.

Sievert, J., & McKee, S. C. (2019). Nationalization in US Senate and gubernatorial elections. *American Politics Research, 47*(5), 1055–1080.

Sinclair, B. (2006). *Unorthodox lawmaking: New legislative processes in the US Congress.* CQ Press.

Skocpol, T., & Williamson, V. (2016). *The Tea Party and the remaking of Republican conservatism.* Oxford University Press.

Smith, S. S. (2007). *Party influence in congress.* Cambridge University Press.

Smith, S. A., & Russell, A. (2022). Different chambers, divergent rhetoric: Institutional differences and policy representation on social media. *American Politics Research, 50*(6), 792–797.

Soroka, S., & McAdams, S. (2015). News, politics, and negativity. *Political Communication, 32*(1), 1–22.

Stratmann, T. (2000). Congressional voting over legislative careers: Shifting positions and changing constraints. *American Political Science Review, 94*(3), 665–676.

Straus, J. R., & Glassman, M. E. (2016, July). Navigating Congress in the age of partisanship. In *Party and procedure in the United States Congress* (p. 1). Bloomsbury Publishing PLC.

Strömbäck, J., & Kiousis, S. (2013). Political public relations: Old practice, new theory-building. *Public Relations Journal, 7*(4), 1–17.

Strömbäck, J., & Nord, L. W. (2006). Do politicians lead the tango? A study of the relationship between Swedish journalists and their political sources in the context of election campaigns. *European Journal of Communication, 21*(2), 147–164.

Suhay, E., & Erisen, C. (2018). The role of anger in the biased assimilation of political information. *Political Psychology, 39*(4), 793–810.

Theocharis, Y., Barberá, P., Fazekas, Z., & Popa, S. A. (2020). The dynamics of political incivility on Twitter. *Sage Open, 10*(2), 2158244020919447.

Theriault, S. M. (2013). *The Gingrich senators: The roots of partisan warfare in Congress.* Oxford University Press.

Theriault, S. M. (2008). *Party polarization in Congress.* Cambridge University Press.

Theriault, S. M. (2013). *The Gingrich senators: The roots of partisan warfare in Congress.* Oxford University Press.

Tromble, R. (2018). Thanks for (actually) responding! How citizen demand shapes politicians' interactive practices on Twitter. *New Media & Society, 20*(2), 676–697.

"Tweeting Red: Angry Emotional Appeals in Congress." (with Whitney Hua and Maggie Macdonald). Presented at the APSA Conference 2020.

Valentino, N. A., Hutchings, V. L., Banks, A. J., & Davis, A. K. (2008). Is a worried citizen a good citizen? Emotions, political information seeking, and learning via the internet. *Political Psychology, 29*(2), 247–273.

Volden, C., & Wiseman, A. E. (2014). *Legislative effectiveness in the United States congress: The lawmakers.* Cambridge University Press.

Wawro, G. J., & Schickler, E. (2007). *Filibuster: Obstruction and lawmaking in the US Senate* (Vol. 134). Princeton University Press.

Wigley, S., & Fontenot, M. (2010). Crisis managers losing control of the message: A pilot study of the Virginia Tech shooting. *Public Relations Review, 36*(2), 187–189.

Williams, R. (2000). A note on robust variance estimation for cluster-correlated data. *Biometrics, 56*, 645–646.

Windt, T. O., Jr. (1973). The presidency and speeches on international crises: Repeating the rhetorical past. *Speaker and Gavel, 11*, 7.

Yanow, D. (2003). Interpretive empirical political science: What makes this not a subfield of qualitative methods. *Qualitative Methods, 1*(2), 9–13.

Index

For the benefit of digital users, indexed terms that span two pages (e.g., 52–53) may, on occasion, appear on only one of those pages.

Tables, figures, and boxes are indicated by an italic *t*, *f*, or *b*.

A

adaptive messaging, lack of, 30
Adobe Creative Suite, 25
Affordable Care Act, celebration of anniversary of, 122–123
AI. *See* artificial intelligence
AI Working Group, 57
American AI Initiative, 150
anger
  anger-driven digital environments, partisan implications of, 130–132
  anger elections, 126
  angry Twitter content, 125–129
  as reputation-building effort, 25–26
approval processes for content production, 82–85
artificial intelligence (AI)
  digital demand in future of, 150–151
  future directions and, 56–58
  potential uses in House, 144
asymmetric resources, 8–10, 34–35
  See also crisis implications, asymmetric resources and constrained capacity
asymmetries of policies and information, 34
The Atlantic, on Gingrich, 42–43
audiences
  ability to narrow audiences, 121
  target audiences for constituent communications, 141–142

B

best practices for congressional press office organization, 59
Biden, Joe, 5–6, 56, 96–97
bloggers, congressional access to, 117–119
blogs, as communication channel, 49–50
Bloomberg Law, on congressional attention, 19
Boehner, John, 48–50
boundedly rational actors, 87
Brannon, Ike, 86
budgets
  influence on digital priorities, 91, 94, 95–96, 97–98, 152
  as issue for communications staff, 96–97
Bush, George W., 39–40

C

cable news show participation, 16–17, 97–98, 114–115, 123–124
campaign-level digital communications, 142–143
Cantor, Eric, 48–49
catch-up in congressional communication. *See* history of catch-up in congressional communication
Centers for Disease Control and Prevention, 6–7
centralization, asymmetric resources and, 8–10
chaos culture, 26–27
civic relationships, 116–117
civility, role of, 132
clickbait, journalists' experiments with, 119–120
clips, demand for, 53
committee leaders
  influence on senators' presentation of personal brand on Twitter, 111
  relative resource advantages of, 106
  resources for, 65
  See also party and committee leadership
Committee on House Administration, 56–57
communication
  as basic tenet of functioning legislative institutions, 139–140

campaign-level digital communications, 142–143
collaborative, 97
communication asymmetry, maintenance and reinforcement of, 97–98
communication capacity, weaknesses in, 25
communication comprehension, 139–140
communication crises, 26–27, 133
communication culture, impact on congressional capacity, 13
communication directors, roles of, 12
communication hierarchies, 3, 89–90
communication investment, 95
communications directors, 60, 63
communications directors (House), 74*t*
communications directors (Senate), 66–67, 66*t*
communications professionals, roles of, 138–139
communication strategies, sources of, 130
effective, importance of, 149
communication shops. *See* congressional press offices, organizing of
communications staffers
adaptation by, 40–41
age of, 59
characteristics of, 60
longevity in, 98–99
media environment of, 20–21
numbers of, 61
support for early social media, 52
communications staffing, variations in, 64, 65*f*
communication subsidy
definition, 92–95
description of, 3, 23–24, 34–35
of party leaders, 15–16
use of term, 89–90, 92–93
Comparative Agendas Project schema, 101–102
Comparative Print Suite, 57
conflict, 43–44, 119–120, 130–132
See also anger; partisan conflict
confrontations, 43–44
Congress
adaptation to digital information climate, 31–32
antiquity of, 49
characteristics of digital communication in, 88
crisis culture in, 3, 85
crisis of communication in, social media and, 33
daily operations, impact of digital media on, 4–7
digital advancement in, 39–40
digital capacity of, 99–100
digital communication environment of, 25–26, 36, 134–136
digital tools and technology, 13, 151–152
expanded audiences for, 40–41
hyperpartisanship in, 35–36
incentives for going digital in, 130
influences on daily operations of, 132
influences on functional capacity of, 10–11
information flow within, 30
information in, 8–9
institutional rules, 49
largest technology changes, 41–42
negative pictures of, 114–115
partisan divide in, 16–17, 35–36
primary function of, 137–138
rapid response capabilities, lack of, 1
rapid-response communication strategy, 14–15
in rapid-response mode, 6–7
resource and chamber differences in policy communication, 100–104
role of communications within, 25
understanding operations of, 22
unwritten folkways of, 132
use of digital communication and social media, 1–3
See also House of Representatives; Senate
congressional capacity, velocity of communication and, 12–14
congressional communication
communication crisis cycle, 3–4
communication culture, 22
communication hierarchies, 7–8, 89–90
congressional press office, organizing of, 59–86
as a crisis, 22–27
crisis framework for, 19–38
crisis implications, asymmetric resources and constrained capacity, 87–113

congressional communication (*Continued*)
crisis implications, partisan pressures and political incentives for digital, 114–133
as defense mechanism, 5–6
drivers of, 92–93
the future and implications of digital Congress, 134–152
history of catch-up in, 39–58
introduction to, 1–18
prominence of role of, 25
research methodology, 153–158
congressional communication ecosystem, Twitter as platform for, 30–31
Congressional Data Coalition, 99–100
Congressional Hackathon, 48–49, 56–57, 150–151
congressional leadership communications, 78–80
congressional offices
components of, 137–138
funding of, 34–35
See also budgets; congressional press offices, organizing of
congressional policymaking, complexity of, 8, 115
congressional press offices, organizing of, 59–86
communications staff, uses of, 76–77
content production processes, 82–85
crises, organization communications around, 85–86
Cruz (Ted) and, 71–75
Fetterman (John) and, 69–71
House, range of alternatives for communication teams, 74–75
House communications staff, 73–74
introduction to, 59–62
leadership communications, 78–80
Lucas (Frank) and, 75–76
office layouts, 62–63
organizational charts, 63
overview of, 15–16
Reed (Jack) and, 68–69
reporter relationships, 80–82
Senate communications staff, 65–68
staffing, 62–64
typologies of congressional communications, 64–68
Congressional Research Service, 37, 51
congressional staffs
on communications climate, 4–5
investing in, 148–149
primary focus of, 63–64
responsibilities of, 26
Connor, Adam, 51–52
Conservative Opportunity Society, 42–43
constituent communication, 140–143
constituent population, influence on senators' budgets, 108
constrained capacity. *See* crisis implications, asymmetric resources and constrained capacity
content production processes, 82–85
"Contract for America" (Gingrich), 40–41
Coolidge, Calvin, 41–42, 47
coronavirus crisis, 1–2
crises
all hands on deck to response to, 9
characteristics of, 6–7
crisis culture, 3, 148–150
crisis cycle, 14–15
crisis exploitation, 35–36
crisis information, spread of, 31–32
description of, 28–31
digital-driven, as the norm, 19–20
impact of, 9–10, 12, 28
nature of, 30–31
as opportunities, 85–86
organization communications around, 85–86
as political weapons, 35–36
as social constructs, 30–31
social media–driven crises, 30–31
sources of, 28–29
stages of, 29
Twitter-perpetuated crises, effects of, 8–9
crisis of communication
cycle of, 88, 120–121
foundation for, 53–54
fuel for, 59
as identity crisis, 137–140
implications of, 33–36
in political settings, 28–29
summary of, 136
crisis framework for congressional communication, 19–38
asymmetric resources and priorities, 34–35
conclusions on, 37–38

congressional communication as a crisis, 22–27
crises, description of, 28–31
crisis communication, implications of, 33–36
information overload, digital adaptation to, 31–33
introduction to, 19–22
overview of, 14–15
partisan conflict, perpetuation of, 35–36
principles of, 22–23, 25*f*
statement of, 22–23
crisis implications, asymmetric resources and constrained capacity, 87–113
communication subsidy, definition in Congress, 92–95
conclusions on, 112–113
introduction to, 87–89
model and results on, 107–112
overview of, 16
resource and chamber differences in policy communication, 100–104
resource differences in partisan politics on Twitter, 105–107
resource-driven organization and management, 95–100
resources, importance for digital, 89–92
resources, role in shaping digital outputs, 100–107
crisis implications, partisan pressures and political incentives for digital, 114–133
conclusions on, 132–133
conflict- and anger-driven digital environments, partisan implications of, 130–132
digital partisan divisions, 124–125
going viral, news media incentives for, 119–122
introduction to, 114–116
minority-driven messaging, 124–125
overview of, 16–17
Twitter, angry content on, 125–129
Twitter, different possible outcomes of civic relationships on, 116–119
Twitter, institutional incentives for, 122–124
crisitunities, 19–20
Cruz, Ted, 24*f*, 71–75, 90–91, 136–137
C-SPAN, 37–39, 42–44
cult of personality, Gingrich's, 44–45
culture, of House *versus* Senate, 80

D

Dean, Howard, 46
Deconflict (calendar tool), 143–144
Democrats
"Build Back Better" legislation, 29–30
Trump as target of anger on Twitter, 128–129
deputy communications directors (Senate), role description, 66*t*
digital
bipartisan push for, 117–119
Congress's reliance on, 95
digital assistants (Senate), role description, 66*t*
digital communications, 9–10, 47–48, 130
digital content, 23–24, 55, 83
digital demand, in artificial intelligence future, 150–151
digital directors, roles of, 12
digital directors (House), role description, 74*t*
digital directors (Senate), role description, 66*t*
digital engagement, impact of incentives for, 23–24
digital era, Twitter in, 50–54
digital integration, reasons for push toward, 50–51
digital management, description of, 144–145
digital managers (Senate), role description, 66*t*
digital media, 14, 17–18, 22–23
digital partisan divisions, 124–125
digital policies, amid platform uncertainty, 144–148
digital political engagement, changing nature of, 37–38
digital politicking, description of, 130
digital reform, opposition to, 143
digital tools, 9–10, 91, 143
early constraints on, 117
factors supporting, 112
partisan pressures and political incentives for, 114–133
roles of, 15–16, 96–97

digital (*Continued*)
shift from whether to use digital to how best to use digital, 54–56
staffers for, 50
digital Congress. *See* the future and implications of digital Congress
distance of constituency to DC, influence on senators' budgets, 108, 109*t*, 111*f*, 111–112
Dobbs case leak, 20–21, 114, 115*f*
Drudge Report, 50

E
earned media, 80–82, 140–141
elected officials, reputation maintenance, 5–6
See also members of Congress
email
internet, and new media in Congress, 45–50
senators' use of, 52–53
environments, social media–driven, 119–120
event-driven communication, 28

F
Facebook, 34–35, 51–52, 55
Fauci, Anthony, 1
Federal Emergency Management Agency, 28
Fenno, R.F., 15–16
Fetterman, John, 65*f*, 69–71
Franking Commission, 117–119
franking rules, 49, 114, 117, 141–143
fundraising, through digital means, 51–52
the future and implications of digital Congress, 134–152
conclusions on, 150–151
constituent communication, inability to serve as solution, 140–143
digital demand in artificial intelligence future, 150–151
digital policies amid platform uncertainty, 144–148
future directions and artificial intelligence, 56–58
House, building internal sources of digital support in, 143–144
introduction to, 134–137
limited solutions to crisis culture, 148–150
overview of, 17

G
Gephardt, Dick, 138
Gingrich, Newt, 15, 39–46
going viral, 119–122
Google, 34–35, 51–52
Graham, Lindsey, 52–53
Grassley, Chuck, 62–63
Greene, Marjorie Taylor, 74–75, 123
Groeling, T., 128–129

H
Hawley, Josh, 62–63, 114, 119–120, 120*f*
HDS (House Digital Service) team, 143–144, 145*f*
Hemphill, L., 101–102
Heritage Foundation, 48–49
high-arousal emotions, 124
Hill offices, as fiefdoms, 62
history of catch-up in congressional communication
digital era, Twitter in, 50–54
future directions and artificial intelligence, 56–58
internet, email and new media in Congress, 45–50
introduction to, 39–41
overview of, 15
satellite TV, 41–45
social media, risks of poor implementation of, 54–56
House Democratic Policy and Communications Committee, 122–123
House of Representatives
building internal sources of digital support in, 143–144
communications staff, 8, 73–74, 76–77
communication teams, range of alternatives for, 74–75
email pilot program, 45–46
expenditure reports, word "digital" in, 27
House Democrats, Easter 2022 graphic, 93–94, 94*f*
House Digital Service (HDS) team, 143–144, 145*f*
Lucas's communication team, 75–76
media competition for, 123

Member's Representational Allowance, 73, 97–98
numbers of tweets sent, 13
Office of Emergency Planning, Preparedness, and Operations, 87–88
press offices, congressional leadership communications, 78–80
press offices, staffing of, 73–74, 74*t*
press offices, type 1, 75–76
press offices, type 2, 76–77
reputation building, lawmakers' presentation and digital output for, 102, 103*f*
Sergeant of Arms Emergency Management Division, 87–88
Speaker's office, communication staff, 95–96
Twitter activity in the 115th Congress, 101–103, 102*t*
typologies of congressional communications, 64–68
Hoyer, Steny, 48–49, 56–57, 78, 98–99, 123
Huffington Post, online media reporters from, 50
Hutchinson, Cassidy, 32
hyperpartisanship, 35–36

I
identity crises, 137–140
industry emissions, Whitehouse on, 5–6, 7*f*
information
in Congress, 8–9
crisis information, spread of, 31–32
filtering of, 97–98, 148
inequities in, impact on reputation building, 92
influences over supply of, 89
information exchange, asymmetries in, 25
information game, tweeting to stay ahead of, 10–12
information overload, 10–11, 20–21, 31–33, 44
information sharing, 47–48, 121
power of, 10–11, 31–32
resource asymmetries in, 91
Instagram, 54–55
interest actors, 40
internet
email and new media, 45–50
Stevens on, 46–47
Issa, Darrel, 46–47

J
Jeffries, Hakeem, 56–57
Johnson, Ron, 99
journalists
expectations of, 26–27
media environment of, 20–21
participation in policy process, 121–122
preferences of, 119–120
relationships with congressional press offices, 80–82
roles of, 8–9, 11–12

K
Kaine, Tim, 90–91
Kennedy, Edward (Ted, Teddy), 47, 117, 118*f*
Krishnamoorthi, Raja, 123

L
Larson, John, 32–33, 124
lawmakers. *See* Congress; House of Representatives; members of Congress; Senate
lawmaking, disconnect between communication expertise and, 44
leaders and leadership
centralization of, 44–45
new technology, acceptance of, 47
as sources of adaptation, 87
See also party and committee leadership; party leaders
legislation, death of, 29–30, 36
Legislative Branch Appropriations Acts, 15–16
legislative enterprises, 92–93
legislative subsidy, use of term, 93
Lieu, Ted, 24*f*
limited solutions to crisis culture, 148–150
Lira, Matt, 150–151
livestreamed events, 33
local/state press secretaries (Senate), role description, 66*t*
Lucas, Frank, 75–76

M
machine learning (ML), 150
Madison, James, 10–11
Maloney, Carolyn, 128–129, 129*f*

Manchin, Joe, 29–30, 60–61, 80
mass media, shift toward, 41–42
Matthews, M. R., 101
McCarthy, Kevin, 56–57
McCollum, Betty, 129*f*
McConnell, Mitch, 1–2, 98–99
McHenry, Patrick, 46–47
McNair, Brian, 26–27
media
  AI-powered media-monitoring tools, 57
  changing nature of, impact on congressional rules, 117
  mass media, shift toward, 41–42
  new media, 39–40, 43–44, 49
  paid media, 140–141
  role in amplifying negativity and conflict, 130–131
  roles in disasters, 6–7
  See also social media
members of Congress
  communication by, 116–117
  essential goals of, 10, 137, 152
  role of communication in success or failure of, 34–35
  as single-minded reelection seekers, 6
  Twitter, use of, 102–104, 104*t*, 128–129
  use of digital tools by, 88–89
  See also House of Representatives; Senate
Member's Representational Allowance, 73, 91, 97–98, 148–149
minority-driven messaging, 124–125
minority party lawmakers, communication of partisan priorities, 124–125
ML (machine learning), 150
multichannel platforming, 145
multilingual communication, 57
Murphy, Chris, 92–93
Musk, Elon, acquisition of Twitter, 60–61, 134–135, 144–145, 151–152

N

National Artificial Intelligence Initiative Act (2020), 150
national policy debates, 101
natural language processing algorithms, 57
negativity, incentivization of, 132
  See also anger; conflict
new media, 39–40, 43–44, 49
news
  evolution on Twitter, 22–23
  news cycle, 10–11, 52–53
  news frenzy, as new normal, 44–45
new technology, struggle with adoption of, 149–150
The New Yorker, on congressional crises, 19
Noem, Kristi, 129*f*
norms
  communication norms, 25, 30
  congressional rules, structures, and norms, 34
  digital norms for information sharing, 121
  traditional press norms, 50–51
  Trump's normalization of Twitter, 40

O

Obama, Barack, 51–52, 130
Ocasio-Cortez, Alexandria, 3, 24*f*, 39, 60–61, 89–90, 136–137
Office of Emergency Planning, Preparedness, and Operations (House), 87–88
O'Neill, Tip, 43–44, 121–122
online harassment, 131
online self-presentation, House *versus* Senate differences in, 100–101
operational crises, 28
Ossoff, Jon, 62–63

P

paid media, 140–141
partisan conflict
  implications of, 116
  pervasiveness of, 35–36
  as reputation-building effort, 25–26
  Twitter and, 114–115
partisan pressures. *See* crisis implications, partisan pressures and political incentives for digital
partisanship
  angry tweets as conduit for, 125–126
  approach to digital and, 119
  causes of, 121
  Gingrich and, 43–44
  hyperpartisanship, 35–36
  partisan implications of conflict- and anger-driven digital environments, 130–132
  partisan leadership, 50–51, 115
  partisan tweets, 105–107, 108–109, 109*t*

party and committee leadership
asymmetric advantages of, 89–90
communication influence of, 34–35
communications teams of, 78–80
leadership of digital advancement, 40–41
resource advantages of, 88
role in digital politics and communications shifts, 39–40
party-driven digital engagement, 116
party leaders
asymmetrical information advantage, 15–16
centralization of party office–appropriated spending, 105–106
communication, investment in, 138
influence of extra resources for, 112
pressure for viral content, 122–124
tweets by, 108–109, 109*t*
Pell, Claiborne, 40
Pelosi, Nancy
communications staffers, 76
internal digital communication, support for, 47–48
new media, use of, 39–40
new technology, use of, 47
press team, 138
Trump's tweets, response to, 5*f*
YouTube, use of, 46
perceptions, as source of crises, 28–29
platform uncertainty, digital policies amid, 144–148
Pocan, Mark, 76–77, 77*f*
polarization, pervasiveness of, 35–36
See also partisanship
policy and policymaking
policy communication, resource and chamber differences in, 100–104
policy information in tweets, 105
policymaking, challenges to, 15–17
policymaking institutions, 37
policy process, Twitter's impact on, 16–17
Politico
on "Build Back Better" legislation, 29–30
on congressional crises, 19
as news source, 22–23
politics
political climate, hyperpartisan nature of, 19
political communication, conflict-driven nature of, 130–131
political conflict, incentivization of, 60
political gamesmanship, nature of, 42–43
political incentives for digital. *See* crisis implications, partisan pressures and political incentives for digital
political leaders, visibility of, 41
political power, centralization of, 9
political success, key factors in, 152
political weapons, crises as, 35–36
See also partisanship
Porter, Katie, 41, 42*f*, 99
postcrisis analysis, 30
power
centralization of, 9
existing power structures, impact of, 112–113
of information, 10–11
power asymmetries in Congress's digital environment, 136–137
Twitter's power, 116
press assistants (House), role description, 74*t*
press assistants (Senate), role description, 66*t*
press credentialing, 117–119
press offices, Senate *versus* House resources for, 101
See also communications staffers; congressional press offices, organizing of
press releases, email and growth in numbers of, 45–46
press secretaries
duties of, 49
in House, role description, 74*t*
in Senate, role description, 66–67, 66*t*
press secretaries/legislative staff (House), role description, 74*t*
press shops, daily routines of, 15–16
principals and staff, disconnect between, 139–140
Progressive Caucus, 97
public audiences, fragmentation of, 55
Public Relations Society of America, 148

R

radio, shift toward, 41–42
rapid response, realities of, and communication crisis, 4–8
Reed, Jack, 68–69

Reid, Harry, 15, 47
reporters. *See* journalists
Republican Party, use of new technology, 48–49
reputation-building
  complexities of, 124
  in a digital media environment, 22
  discourse of, components of, 130
  lawmakers' presentation and digital output for, 102, 103*f*
  online, 3
  resources and, 112
  tools for, 39
research methodology, 153–158
  interviews, 96
  interviews, description of, 61
  interviews, uses of, 13–14
  mixed-methods approach, 14
resources
  asymmetric resources, 8–10, 34–35
  chamber differences in policy communication and, 100–104
  differences in, in partisan politics on Twitter, 105–107
  importance for digital, 21–22, 89–92
  problematic allocations of, 149
  resource advantages, 88–89
  resource-driven organization and management, 95–100
  resource imbalances, impact of, 95–96, 107
  resource-related digital, conclusions on, 112–113
  role in shaping digital outputs, 100–107
retweets, 52–53
rhetoric
  angry rhetoric, 126–128, 127*f*
  bombastic, rise of, 132
  emotive rhetoric, 126
  ideology-driven, 130–131, 142
  negative and angry, 132–133
  as source of crises, 28–29
  Trump's, on Twitter, 130
  Twitter's impact on, 16–17
Roll Call
  on *Dobbs* decision, 72
  on Johnson's staffing pivot, 99
  on post-Twitter environment, 135
  Supreme Court leak, coverage of, 119–120, 120*f*
  on Twitter, 134–135
  use of McConnell's Tweets, 1–2
Romney, Mitt, 121, 122*f*
rules
  congressional, impact of, 91
  media's changing nature, impact on, 117
Russell, A., 101–102n.6, 127–128
Ryan, Paul, 48–49

S

Salisbury, R. H., 91
Sanders, Bernie, 62–63, 97–98, 136–137
satellite TV, 41–45
Scalise, Steve, 48–49
Schatz, Brian, 3, 65, 92–93
Schumer, Chuck, 39–40, 98–99
scooplets, 39–40
Scott, Rick, 114
Select Committee to Investigate the January 6th Attack, 32
self-presentation, in a digital media environment, 22
Senate
  AI Forum, 56–57
  communications staff, 8, 65–67
  Cruz's creative department, 71–75
  digital content, approval process for, 83–85
  Fetterman's press office, 69–71
  party leaders, predicted tweet content for, 110*f*, 110
  press office roles, 65–66, 66*t*
  press offices, range of alternatives for, 67–68
  press offices, type 1, 68–69
  press offices, type 2, 69–71
  press offices, type 3, 71–75
  Reed's press office, 68–69
  reputation building, lawmakers' presentation and digital output for, 102, 103*f*
  Senate Democratic Media Center, 39–40, 79, 97–99
  Senate Radio/TV Gallery, 117–119
  Senators' Official Personnel and Office Expense Account (SOPOEA), 106–107
  Twitter activity in the 115th Congress, 101–103, 102*t*
  typologies of congressional communications, 64–68

"Unwritten Rules of Covering Congress," 81
senators
analysis of tweets by content type, 108–109, 109*t*
budgets of, factors affecting, 108
email, use of, 52–53
facilitation of national reputation of, 101
sensationalism, incentivization of, 132
Sergeant of Arms Emergency Management Division (House), 87–88
Sharp, Adam, 51–52
Shepsle, K. A., 91
Sherman, Jake, 136
"Silent Cal" persona (Coolidge), 41–42
Simpson, Homer, 19–20
Simpson, O. J., 44
The Simpsons, 85
situational assessments, lack of, 30
social media
audience specifics by platform, 55–56
Cantor's support for, 48–49
congressional reliance on, 21–22
consequences of, 3
high-arousal emotions on, 124
impact of, 11–12, 17–18, 26–27, 53–54
negative aspects of, 32–33
norms of, 54–55
risks of poor implementation of, 54–56
social media managers, 84
sources of impact of, 37–38
speed of transition to, 51–52
training in use of, 94
See also tweets; Twitter
"Social Networking and Constituent Communications" (Congressional Research Service), 37
Social Stats, 143–144
SOPOEA (Senators' Official Personnel and Office Expense Account), 106–107
speechwriters (Senate), role description, 66*t*
staff and principals, disconnect between, 139–140
staffing, balance between policy and communications staffing, 99
See also communications staffers
state size, influence on senators' budgets, 108
Stevens, Ted, 46–47
Supreme Court, leak on *Dobbs* decision, 20–21, 114, 115*f*
Szpindor, Catherine, 143–144

T
talking points, 93–94
Talking Points Memo, online media reporters from, 50
target audiences, for constituent communications, 141–142
technology, impact of, 41–42
See also media
tele-town halls, 140–141
television, Gingrich and, 43–44
TikTok, 54–55, 139–140
TikTok influencers, 49
traditional press norms, 50–51
Trump, Donald
impeachment of, impact on communication, 93–94
as Tweeter in chief, 114–115
tweets on four progressive minority congresswomen, 4, 5*f*
Twitter, normalization of, 40
Twitter, rhetoric on, 130
Twitter as preferred policy tool of, 60–61
TV. *See* satellite TV
tweets
analyses of, 100–112
angry, as conduit for partisanship, 125–126
angry, by male and female candidates, 127–128, 128*f*
with angry content over time, 126, 127*f*
from House members, rise in numbers over time, 126, 127*f*
impact on Congress, 124
numbers of, sent by members of Congress, 13
policy rhetoric in, 17
probability of tweet content by state distance and population, 110–111, 111*f*
retweets, 52–53
statistics on tweets per member of Congress and individual and institutional factors, 102–104, 104*t*
valence tweets, 105, 107

Twitter
activity in the 115th Congress, 101–103, 102*t*
angry content on, 125–129
civic relationships on, different possible outcomes of, 116–119
as complicating factor in disaster or crisis, 6–7
in digital era, 50–54
evolution of news on, 22–23
impact of, 60–61, 120–121
implications of rise of, 133–135
importance in Congress, 15
influence of, 99–100, 114–115
institutional incentives for, 122–124
limitations of, 26–27
McConnell's use of, 1–2, 2*f*
as megaphone, 54–55
as news source, 22–23, 23*f*, 24*f*
normalization of, 20–21, 125
partisan attacks on, 116
partisan politics on, resource differences in, 105–107
as path to name recognition, 140
as platform, shifts in, 135
as political weapon, 124
primary audience for, 37
roles of, 2–3, 11, 148
Sharp at, 51–52
shift to primary resource, 54
Trump's rhetoric on, 130
Twitter-driven communication climate, impact of, 36
Twitter-driven media environment, role in Congress's communication crisis cycle, 3–4
Twitter-driven political ecosystem, impact of, 26–27
Twitter-perpetuated crises, effects of, 8–9

U

uncertainty
digital uncertainty, questions concerning, 144–145, 146*t*
in strategic political choices, 144–145
unwritten folkways, of Congress, 132
"Unwritten Rules of Covering Congress" (Senate staffer), 81
USA Today
operational changes to, 46
rise in importance, 39

V

valence tweets, 105, 107
Van Hollen, Chris, 70, 114
velocity of communication, 12–14
viral communication, 119
viral content, 122–123
virtual connections, 12
Volden, C., 108
voter mobilization, 126

W

Warren, Elizabeth, 114
The Washington Post, on Sherman, 136
Whitehouse, Sheldon, 5–6, 7*f*
Wiseman, A. E., 108
Wyden, Ron, 29–30

X

X. *See* Twitter

Y

YouTube, 33, 39